D0839623

# Resurrection

DONALD D. WARNER

**Outskirts Press, Inc.**
**Denver, Colorado**

# Foreword

As a child, I often enjoyed looking through the wrong end of a telescope; everything seemed so tiny and far away. As one matures and learns how to adjust the lens, this time looking through the correct end of the instrument, all that was distant seems to be closer and clearer. As one learns to rotate the lens, the abstract becomes real; that which is misshapen takes on a new dimension, new meaning. And, in a strange way, it seems as if one could reach out a hand and touch that which before seemed so far away.

Donald Warner has adjusted his lens and fitted his telescope of memory in a way that draws us all closer, to a life, a mind, a soul which has evolved and matured through poverty, racism, war and death. Warner takes us on a journey to a side of American life which for many existed only in shadows, in forgotten hollows on the "outskirts" of town. He has taken us into the tragedy of police brutality and taught us of discrimination before we coined the phrase "racial profiling".

Warner shared his heroines (for most are female in this culture of disenfranchised men), the greatest star being Mozelle, his wise and tolerant mother who continues, even now, to watch over this loving son who uses his memory, his "events", his "being to become" as a didactic for all of us to understand that "resurrection" is not the hand of someone else; but it is the act of self-recognition and acceptance of the presence of God and spirit within us that allows us to see our faults, to reject them and to resurrect ourselves to a new life.

Warner's kaleidoscope journey from the lowly fields of Crestmont outside of Philadelphia through a persistent and obsessed desire for more education to the apartheid world of social division of the 1950s, to Korean villages in war and the discovery of love of family sets a context for a man who walked with Dr. King; who became obsessed with raising the hopes and the aspirations of young African American males admonishing them to choose life and opportunity rather than violence and gangs. This is an educator who rose to the head of one of the most respected school superintendents in the nation; this is a man who shaped hundreds of young lives through cajoling, example and discipline.

And this is a man who, after all of this, pursued a new "resurrection" as a man of the cloth, embracing his faith as the ultimate tool for promoting self awareness and salvation.

Any autobiography suffers the dangers of false perspective, tainted egoism and self-congratulation. Donald Warner evades all these pitfalls. His life is a series of essays, each one imparting lessons and values that provide those of us who thought we knew the man, the keys to the richness of his friendship, his vision and his courage.

*Resurrection* offers every reader a pathway to self understanding. Every reader will find pieces and parts of himself within its classic journey. For Warner, the journey continues, the perspective gained, the images clearer. For all of us, through the telescope of his mind and words, Donald Warner has brought us closer to touching who we are.

Peter F. Burnham, Ph.D.
President, Brookdale Community College
Lincroft, New Jersey

# Dedication

This book is dedicated to Beth, Nicolas and Thomas Warner, and our courageous role model, loving wife and mother, Mercedes R. Warner, whose direction is always towards positive images of success in a world in need of a new resurrection.

I acknowledge with gratitude the encouragement and efforts of Peter F. Burnham, Steve Nacco, Jean Karl, Pamela Childers, Janice Anderson, Mary Johnson, Jesse Garrison, Lisa Savage, Debbie Orrigo, and Vernel Walker, plus the love and support of my grandchildren, Alexandria, Gabriella, and Sophia, who in the midst of fate, time, occasion, chance and change, will know love, happiness and eternal joy.

# Table of Contents

# Introduction

There exists in the history of humankind deep, dark, downy things which impact our destinies and determine and define complexities of character, attitude, personality and morality. Many of our external ineptitudes, once conditioned by family and friends, find great solace in a socio-political, economic milieu which supports the disintegration of the indefinable soul; thus much of our journey throughout life is rooted in trial and error. In the midst of this playful yet deadly badinage, we fall prey to negative results which require our full energies. Once unable to rise above our inadequacies and frustrations, we tend to fall into the dark abyss of failure, and are in need of multiple resurrections before we can lift ourselves above the earth into an ethereal framework of new structures and new destines that define, finally, who we are.

Resurrection can not be limited to the Christian

belief of the after life associated with a future destiny of glory with the Triune God. Instead, life must be redefined in its present state, and resurrected out of the hells of its existence on a daily basis. Human kind always exists, both individually and collectively, within the framework and spectrum of being and becoming. Who I am now is not who I am three seconds from now, or who I am becoming three years from today. Therefore, multiple resurrections or new beginnings are both necessary and prevalent in a society replete with chance and change.

# Chapter One
## CRESTMONT

### THE FIRST DAY

How often I recall Cousin Nickie and Cousin Jeanne humorously stating, "This is the first day for the rest of your life." How many first days, I thought, could I possibly endure? Jeanne and Nickie were of the same ages as my older sisters Dorothy and Audrey. As a younger impressionable listening partner to their conversations, I wondered how it was possible to have a "first day" after birth. After all, isn't birth considered your first day? However, those delightful beginnings as a child in the midst of near desperation growing up in Crestmont, Pennsylvania, caused me to rethink my beginnings and to re-experience the warm, passionate, intellectual, wit and wisdom of the many stable

1

women and occasional men who captured my attention, and served as positive role models and driving forces in my attempts to resurrect a life doomed to failure, especially given the early negative socio-economic conditions under which our family existed during the period of time historically labeled the Great Depression.

As a child, I never gave much thought to the plight of our family and/or the entire community and its environs. It was merely our way of life. In my mind, no other greater world existed beyond the outskirts of Crestmont. Neither television, modern communications or advanced technology existed, so how was I to know that a different world with a global economy persisted beyond the party line telephone hanging loosely on the wall, and the occasional radio listening we were afforded once a week when "Deddy" Bob, my father, tuned in to the ominous broadcast news from Gabriel Heater with his dooms day messages about World War II.

What led me to stumble upon a newness in life, a resurrection of sorts of my total being, to the point where I could begin again, feeding as it were in greener pastures, following a new, yet unidentifiable, charismatic shepherd, who would lead me away from my slaughtered existence in the time worn shacks and instability of the hometown? Little did I realize that the new awakening, the resurrection, the new beginning I sought rested within, waiting to be recognized and called forward by a series of unanticipated events fashioned by forces external to my understandings, but cushioned by the love and direction of my mother Mozelle Emily Warner, her sisters and my Aunts Beulah, Willa Belle, my nurturing sisters Dorothy, Audrey and Charlotte, who along with big brother Bobby and younger brother Norman prodded, pushed and cajoled until my utter helplessness gave way to joy unrealized.

Securing that "joy" was not mine alone, but became the pure province of the involvement of community persons whose values and moral turpitude sailed beyond the limited horizons of a people partially mesmerized by an unending cycle of poverty, exemplified in the lack of opportunity for unskilled African American men to be real men in the sense of obtaining employment and consequent self worth, enabling them to elevate themselves and become true heads of their families. Thus, strong neighborhood women, such as Mrs. Dorothy Armstead, Mrs. Artie Jackson Brown, Mrs. Mary Strickland, Mrs. Helen Bennett Johnson, Mrs. Dorothy Case, Ms. Marietta Jones, and Mrs. Mabel Williams provided nurturing and a framework for excellence invading my space and directing my every move. The framework and structure taught by the women and accompanied by the wisdom and knowledge of Mr. Dennis, independent contractor, and Dr. Harold Woolfolk, pharmacist, strengthened my resolve to the point where neither the mine fields of Korea, the dung heaps of "The Bottom", the violent gangs of Philadelphia, the rhetoric of

Elijah Poole, the continuances of educational apartheid in city and suburbs alike, could stop the eventual resurrection of a new and becoming self taught individual, fueled by the passionate persuasions of Dr. Martin Luther King, Jr., Rev. Milliard Harris, the evolution of Civil Rights, and a intensified depth of religious fervor.

As God is my witness, through it all, because of it all, I have matured to love unflinchingly, to endure, to survive in the knowledge that the potential for self-resurrection rests in each individual. It is dynamically fashioned and shaped by the divine intervention of the presence of the God of grace in us all.

## THE BOTTOM

It is early morning, and I lie awake in bed in our five bedroom, two story home remembering the mid nineteen thirties when our impoverished family of eight children rested in bed, sleeping two up and two down on bed bug ridden mattresses that reeked of kerosene my mother rubbed in the crevices of the mattresses to kill the insects which plagued our existence day and night. There were two bedrooms, one reserved for Mozelle, my mother and "Deddy" Bob my father. The other room housed the three girls, plus a makeshift hallway housing a bed where the three boys slept two up and one down. Two of our brothers died of unknown reasons, or at least unmentionable reasons, long before I could remember their names. Thus, we were reduced to six children, three boys, and three girls early in life.

Our rented property was perched at the top of a small incline below the railroad tracks on a less than one quarter acre lot in an unincorporated town called Crestmont. Crestmont was divided into two sections. The local people called our section, where the Warner's, Pinckney's, Deans and Dinkins' family lived, "The Bottom." The other section, a mile and a half toward the North where the Johnson's, Harvey's, and Robbin's family lived, was dubbed "The Top." Many of the African Americans there could afford to pay the small lifetime mortgages on their homes. This is where Horace Green, the only Black Republican I have ever known lived, along with the Johnson family. Mrs. Helen Bennett Johnson was my fifth grade teacher at Park Elementary School, located in what was commonly called Willow Grove Heights. There existed in our town a disquieting attitude about those who lived at "The Top" side of town, as compared to those who merely existed in "The Bottom".

Interestingly, two strong odors permeated the homes of "The Bottom." One was the smell of large heads of wild skunk cabbage that grew beneath our bedroom window, and the other was the stench of human manure that Mr. Dinkins dumped into large undeveloped fields about a ten minute walk from our house. Mr. Dinkins owned two or three cesspool trucks that he used to collect human feces from the underground septic tanks of nearby wealthy residents of Abington Township. Once the trucks were filled to capacity, Mr. Dinkins drove to the bottom lands in Crestmont and spread the dung over the acres of land he owned at the south end, on property that separated Crestmont from the brick ovens adjacent to Roslyn, Pennsylvania. Roslyn was another totally white town that stood on the southern border line of Crestmont, where the townswomen worked as domestics, taking in washing and ironing and cleaning the homes of our well to do neighbors who could afford domestic help. Mozelle served as a domestic, primarily for one woman named Mrs. Wagner. It was Mrs. Wagner who donated used clothing to the family. The boys passed down their knickers (trousers) from one to the next. Fortunately, I received the hand me down clothing after my oldest brother Bobby grew too large for them. By the time Norman, my younger brother, received them, the knickers usually had holes in both pockets, which meant that marbles, one of our boyhood games, had to be carried around the knees, as the frayed pockets could no longer contain them.

In our backyard directly below the railroad tracks, next to the house, was an artesian well that my father dug and shored up each year. The well provided water for the house, as indoor plumbing was not a part of our life until many years later after I married and moved to our first apartment in nearby Philadelphia.

Just as Mr. Dinkins poured and mixed large bags of lime in his fields of dung, we too poured lime into the two seated outhouse that was sometimes frequented by large rodents. We were especially fearful at night when only a candle helped to light the way, or one lightly brushed his hand across the wooden platform to guess at where the toilet seat was located. During the lengthy summer days, the large willow tree that blanketed the back year would grow long meandering roots. These roots would find their way into the liquid chambers of the out house, and cause it to be imbalanced until dug up, dried and cut into branches to be burned in our Ben Franklin cooking stove.

The artesian well and I became very familiar friends, as on several occasions my father would lower me into the well on a rope to determine the water level, and at times to use a small shovel to dig deeper into the well while he pulled buckets of mud up to the top of the well. The mud was dumped into our garden to serve as rich fertilizer for the vegetables – tomatoes, collard greens, sweet potatoes, green pole beans, lettuce and other vegetables grown in the back yard. Once vegetables were picked and harvested, my father and brothers flagged down the slow moving freight trains, and we traded vegetables for large chunks of bituminous coal that we broke into pieces and burned in the pot bellied stove in our living room area. Unlike today's wood stoves, the pot bellied stoves only heated a distance of about two feet, as there were no fans designed to propel the warmth into other areas of the house.

The only fans we owned were the small cardboard fans taken from First Baptist Church, donated by Mr. Gibson, the local funeral director, whose hearse broke down at my oldest brother Bobby's funeral.

My oldest brother, Bobby was my hero. He took me with him every place he went. He was a large two hundred pound black man, very muscular, handsome and unafraid of white people. Neither was he frightened of Mr. Jiles, the black policeman who patrolled Crestmont, nor afraid to walk through the adjourning white neighborhood where we were prohibited from walking after dark. No community person ever outright told us, but during the 1930's and 1940's we knew not to walk the streets of Abington Township after dark. However, fearless Bobby always managed to defy the odds.

How clearly I remember the day Bobby was arrested in Atlantic City, New Jersey for shooting craps with a group of young men outside one of the casinos. I'll never know how Mozelle, our mother, found out. Perhaps it was from our cousin Tat Lindsay, Bobby's boyhood pal, who traveled with him on most adventures. However, I was twelve years of age when Mozelle tied a few dollars in a large blue railroad handkerchief, and directed me to go to Atlantic City to bail Bobby out of jail. It was the same blue railroad handkerchief that we attached strings to and threw up into the sky as a parachute. This time the mission was different, and I was frightened out of my wits. The trip required a two mile walk to the number 55 bus stop on route 611, where I boarded transportation and rode to Olney Avenue in Philadelphia to board the underground subway to center city. Next, I purchased a greyhound bus ticket to Atlantic City, and had to find the local police station and give the person at the desk the large blue railroad handkerchief with the note and money resting beneath the knot that momma had tied twice over.

The first two legs of the trip were relatively comfortable until I reached the subway and had to ask individual strangers which subway stop led to center city, where I might exit and board a greyhound bus. I shuffled my way though the turnstile and on to the subway train that lunged forward, rocking back and forth to a point where I almost dropped the blue handkerchief. I immediately stuck the handkerchief into the front pocket of my knickers. Fortunately, my mother knew the exact cost of each conveyance, and had the money separated in small specific envelopes that I opened and presented to the various transportation clerks. Finally, I walked around city hall, made my way several blocks to the greyhound bus terminal, and requested a one way ticket to Atlantic City. I sat, as directed by Mozelle, next to a window on the left side of the bus and shifted the blue handkerchief to my left pocket away from the silent man who sat snoring in the seat next to mine. After a 30 to 40 minutes ride that felt like a lifetime, I arrived in Atlantic City, disembarked and asked a rather stout policeman how to find the police station. Once there, I walked through the large, heavy doors, gazed upwards at the robust Irish policeman seated at the intake desk, and gave him the note and the large blue railroad handkerchief containing the money. He quickly directed me to a wooden bench at the right side of the large room, and told me to sit and not move while he whispered to another policeman, who thirty to forty minutes later returned with my brother, Bobby. He was still my hero, and never once discussed why he had been suddenly incarcerated. I gave him the final envelope that Mom had prepared, and he purchased tickets home to Philadelphia and subsequently back to Crestmont, where Mozelle greeted him lovingly and without question. She hugged me tightly, and requested that I rush to bed to rest after a long day's journey to strange environs.

With my hero back home, Mozelle was plainly pleased until a year later when Bobby appeared before a local judge with two of his friends. They were all given the option of incarceration or enlistment into the U.S. Army. And so my hero with whom I had stood in front of the wealthy homes in Abington Township, where we were given a few pennies on Halloween to dance and sing, disappeared for a few years near the latter part of

World War II, only to finally be discharged and free to challenge the awaiting arms of death.

One might surmise that Bobby had received several resurrections and/or opportunities to start anew, and yet his conflicting life style was exemplified by his defiant march up the concrete stairs of the Glenside Train Station. He was trailed by me as he held my hand in a place where only white travelers dared to tread. We boarded the train at a train station previously never used by African Americans. This is what he loved. He was strong, independent, and full of himself. Again there was the unwritten code and mystique held by the people of Crestmont, that the Glenside train station was out of bounds for African American travelers who needed to board trains. Crestmont Station, where we resided on less that half acre rented plots never to be called our own, was our designated station.

And so the strong, vibrant, independent, full of himself Bobby found his final trumpeter, when one Saturday night he disembarked from the local #55 Bus four stops prior to the designated Crestmont stop, and proceeded to take a short cut through Abington Township past the homes where the domestics from Crestmont labored during the day light hours. As he climbed Rubican Avenue traversing to the top, an armed policeman stopped and shouted: "Halt, stand where you are!" Bobby responded by running into the shadows behind the houses of the wealthy residents. Porch lights, spot lights suddenly awakened the night, while the policeman sounded his patrol car siren chasing Bobby down the street, finally emptying his loaded pistol into Bobby's back. He was pronounced dead and accused of breaking and entering homes in the wealthy section of Abington Township, where blacks worked as domestics and never had the courage to challenge the darkness.

This was Mozelle's oldest son, and we were too impoverished to even think about investigating Bobby's death. It was the funeral director, Mr. Gibson, who described the bullets lodged in various portions of Bobby's back. The police accused him of breaking and entering some unidentified property in an area on the wrong side of town where African Americans were never seen except in the heat of the day, under the blazing sun, while they cleaned large houses of dust and grime and scrubbed toilets with kerosene disinfectants too strong for gentle hands.

As we started the long process of shoveling dirt atop Bobby's coffin, I remembered that nothing seemed to work right for my gallant hero. Even after the funeral Mr. Gibson's hearse broke down outside First Baptist Church. It was well into the evening when the last shovel caressed the dirt, and spilled its load onto the grave housing the remains of my hero.

The death of brother Bobby caused me to rethink who I was, to resurrect as it were a new image, one that could exist without his energetic presence in a town where women served as domestics and men seldom found work, except when government programs such as the Worker's Progress Administration (WPA) were prevalent, or when farm trucks cruised our neighborhood looking for day laborers to weed long rows of vegetables, pick tomatoes and corn, bail hay, weed carrots, and milk cows.

My father, "Deddy Bob", also named Robert, seldom if ever found work except once when he worked as a firemen shoveling coal into the huge coal burning boilers at the Glenside Laundry. This job was short lived. Most of the time he and the other men in town could be found "out back" in wooden shacks that they built as a place to drink liquor. Uncle Oscar, who worked as an independent plasterer for a construction company, devoted the entire second floor of his garage to a gathering place for men who wished to caress the grape, and imbibe large quantities of homemade wine and store bought liquors. "Deddy" raised a few chickens for food and eggs. By the end of winter most of the chickens had been eaten by his six children, and vegetables from the garden were canned in large masonry jars filled with garden beans, blackberry jam, and cucumbers from the garden. When our chickens were all eaten we were hard put for food, except for the few pennies Mozelle collected from washing and ironing for Mrs. Wagner and others. Food was often supplemented by the large chunks of government cheese that Audrey, my sister, and I carried home after standing for hours in long welfare lines waiting for our handout.

Speaking of chicken, one early Saturday morning I watched Deddy Bob sprinkle a trail of corn from the neighbor's back yard into our yard. Slowly, two fat hens pecked their way across the adjacent property and into our yard where Deddy captured them, rung their necks and boiled them in hot scalding water. Next we plucked the feathers from the fresh stolen kill, and filled our stomachs with a sumptuous meal of chickens and dumplings. Thus, times after the Great Depression were very difficult, causing many men in town to become untreated alcoholics, while living with their families on land never to be called their own.

Through some unknown miracle, we were able to move out of the bottom to another rented house closer to the middle of town, but not in the area known as "The Top." This new home, new for us but very old, possessed a heater built into the ground in a two story house without a cellar. Each day after the rains came, the heater flooded, and we were without heat. We survived with Mozelle's black Benjamin Franklin iron kitchen stove that burnt wood and coal that we picked daily from the leavings of the large freight trains, whose engineers threw the ashes overboard on to the tracks. We walked the tracks most of the summer, and into the winter carrying buckets to pick the dark black coals to burn in our Ben Franklin stove.

However, at least we did not have to contend with the old artesian well, and this time we were blessed with a two seated out house that was considered luxurious for its day. However, water was still a problem and the boy's job was to carry buckets upon buckets of water each day, about a quarter of a mile, from the spring on our neighbor Mr. Vaughn's property below the railroad tracks. Especially painful was carrying buckets of water on Saturday nights for purposes of the Saturday night bath ritual, where large metal tubs were filled with boiling hot water. First the girls bathed, followed by the boys. The water was usually changed after the third person bathed. Nevertheless, we were fortunate in that Mr. Vaughn raised pigs and at slaughter time he provided the neighbors with meat, enough to last a few weeks during the cold winter months. One of the residual benefits for children was the pig bladders we blew air into and used as balloons that we batted around the yard for hours. Between government supplies, Mr. Vaughn's handout, the vegetable garden and Mozelle's domestic work, we managed to survive on a consistent menu of beans and rice almost daily.

Oil for kerosene lamps and the oil stove we used to supplement our lack of heat was provided by Mrs. Benson, who sold oil on a credit basis. She stored oil in large metal containers located in a damp basement room. Once a month, Mozelle sent me to pay the oil bill. Her credit was good; all you had to do was to tell Mrs. Benson your last name and she marked it in a black ledger. The oil drums had a long hand pump on them that she used to pump oil into your hand carried oil container.

As a boy we were charged with several outdoor duties and responsibilities. Carrying water from the spring in Mr. Vaughn's backyard was just one of many duties. In the early spring season, digging the large garden shovel by shovel was an arduous task, along with yearly white washing all the rocks along the property, plus the picket fence and tree trunks. Ours was not an elaborate yard; however, work was plentiful on a daily basis, especially given the very large weeping willow tree that encompassed the entire backyard and hovered over the roof of the house. Thus daily cleaning branches from the house roof, the yard, plus pulling up roots that directed themselves towards the liquid substance in the out house became common everyday chores. Also, once or twice a week we walked the railroad tracks picking up coal leavings from freight trains that engineers threw out from their steam locomotives.

All however was not work, for when time allowed during the summer, Al, Tony, Jules and I would walk the railroad tracks waiting for a slow freight train that we could board, and hitch a ride to Heating's Swimming Hole, a good fifteen to twenty miles distance to the north and east above Hatboro. As we walked the track, we would playfully climb the inclines on the sides of the tracks and jump down from the incline onto the track. Usually, one could spot the freight train from a distance and warn the others of its approach. Hitching a ride on a freight train was not a simple task. First you had to make certain to distance yourself outside the view of the train engineer. Then you had to run along side the train pulling at the large doors until you could locate an empty box car. Hopefully no tramp or vagrant would be found riding inside the box car. When luck was on your side the sliding box car doors would be left open, and all one had to do was to "push up" into the car, and then reach out to help your friends running beside the train. Once aboard the train it was important to watch for the next exchange, and then find a soft spot on the ground to jump. The exchange was usually in Hatboro; then we had to hop a second freight traveling towards the swim hole. Once in the area of the swimming hole, we jumped off, rolled down the embankment and walked a few miles into the woods where we swam naked until dark and then started home again. In many instances we walked the railroad tracks the entire distance, especially on the way home.

Although from my point of view the girls never had as much work, they helped Mozelle with washing clothes, hanging large white bed sheets on the clothes line and then ironing and placing them folded into large straw woven baskets. Clothing was collected primarily on Saturdays by patrons from Abington Township and Roslyn. However, the long summer days left more than adequate time to frolic and play. As boys, we had our own little gang of friends. Joe Dinkins, Jack Harvey, Tony Williams, Jules Adams were just a few of my close friends. We built tree houses and bunkers together in the adjoining woods where we camped in the early evenings, but often had to rush home when the municipal siren sounded. This was commonly known as the five o'clock whistle. When the siren sounded, one rushed home to dinner where the entire family gathered each day. To be late meant no dinner, and if by chance you were allowed to eat you were the last person to be served, which meant that only a few half scraps would be available to you. In addition, you were sent to bed early as punishment.

Once at the dinner table, one was not allowed to engage in conversation unless and until an adult interacted with you via questioning. The entire meal ritual was formalized into question-response conversations. To leave the table, one had to raise a hand and request permission, which was often not granted. I learned early to control all bathroom privileges to take place either prior to meals or immediately thereafter. After dinner you immediately completed school homework assignments, or were privileged to listen to the ominous radio newscaster Gabriel Heater telling of the horrible conditions in the world and the United States' inability to deal forthright with its foreign powers, primarily Germany and Japan. Once a month you might receive permission to sit in the living room which held a large sacred chair reserved for Deddy Bob, and an old wind up victrola that Mozelle's boss lady Mrs. Wagner had given us. If Deddy was at home and sober one had to sit in complete silence and not speak unless addressed.

Later when my older sisters began to date and court young men, I was assigned the task of waiting at the top of the stairs until the victrola wound down. Then I dashed downstairs to rewind the victrola, and hastily retreat to my station atop the stairs.

Victrolas and radios weren't the only music in my earlier life, for most of the music I enjoyed was rendered on Sunday morning at First Baptist Church. Crestmont could brag of three major churches, First Baptist, the African Methodist Church and what we delightedly called the Holy Rollers. First Baptist and the Methodist church both held rather traditional services under their respective denominations; however, the Holy Rollers, as we affectionately called them, were Pentecostal in their worship services. Unlike First Baptist, where Deacon Barnes was the only vibrant long time fixture, Pastor Shake Harper conducted very animated services. On Sunday evenings my pals and I usually visited and sat near the rear of the small edifice trying not to be noticed. The people there spoke in tongues, participated in mesmerizing dance rituals, and loud shoutings of "Praise the Lord, Hallelujah and Glory to His Name." They were accompanied by a young pianist friend of ours named Betty, who played, very fluently, articulated music "by ear" with little or no perceivable knowledge of being able to read musical notes. Her piano playing was perfected with every possible jazz beat and nuance known to man. The music was beautifully keyed to whatever song a person might decide to sing. All Betty had to do was hear the first note. From one vocal note, she would develop a complete set of chords to provide background music for the singer and the song. She was not educated in music, but possessed her own near genius musical style. It was in the midst of shouted "Hallelujahs" that she graced us with her musical genius, backed by the cadences of a drummer whose drum beats were louder than the shouts and as rhythmic as percussionist Max Roach synchronizing the organ playing of Wild Bill Davis at an Atlantic City, N.J. night club.

However, it was at First Baptist where I learned to sing tenor with the choir taught by Mrs. Beller, who insisted upon four part harmony and strict adherence to written notes from the Baptist Hymnal. Unlike, Betty, the organist also read music with a slow direct Episcopalian music style. However, other musical opportunities presented themselves, and I became a singing mascot for the Unity Male Chorus. The male chorus was formed of adult male members from Crestmont, Doylestown, Hatboro and other near by Pennsylvania communities inclusive of selective streets such as Davisville Road and Division Street where African Americans settled adjacent to white communities, where they too served as domestics. Even the notorious Diamond Street in Philadelphia now domiciled by African American citizens was once totally white with black servants living on Norris Street, a small one way street located directly behind Diamond Street.

**Unity Male Chorus**

The Unity Male Chorus traveled to various locations as far away as Virginia, Delaware, Merchantville, N.J. and other non-descript country places where several churches existed. The men provided for my every existence, and taught me the ways of Christian living from a male perspective.

One of the more interesting trips occurred in Mr. Cook's automobile as we traveled to and from Richmond, Virginia. It was taken for granted that we couldn't eat in the various restaurants along the road; therefore, we packed large quantities of food and drink for the trip, and took bathroom privileges where we could, which meant sometimes on the side of the road, or at the back door when one of the black cooks allowed us to sneak into the kitchen chambers to use the toilets. What made this long enduring trip so memorable was not the church meeting or the stops along the road. It was the fact that Mr. Cook invited his wife and their small miniature dog that she carried on her lap. The dog was short haired and very much a "yapper". She barked at everything that moved as we drove through Philadelphia, to Delaware, Maryland and finally into Virginia. The barking was mild compared to the quiet noxious odors emitted from the dog's bowels. Mrs. Cook seemed never to be fazed by the odors. She herself was a rather large woman, and at first I was confused as to the author of the odors. As a mere passenger it would have been rude of me to complain about the dog, plus I was squeezed into the front seat between Mr. Cook, the driver, and Mrs. Cook and her dog. Mrs. Cook had access to the window, but never once opened it to give the other five passengers needed air. Instead she complained about the freezing temperatures outside, while we politely nearly suffocated inside, enduring the stench of a dog whose digestive system needed relief.

Such was my limited musical training, but the star, celebrity, master vocalist at First Baptist Church was Mrs. Artie Brown Davis Jackson. Mrs. Jackson was the only contralto in town, and she sang what we commonly referred to as tenor bass. It was rumored that at age 62, she had outlived, worn out and survived at least three domineering husbands, thus the long tedious name. However, Artie Brown Davis Jackson was always meticulously attired, a fashion model of the day. She was sometimes dressed in a long, lemon ripe, hour glass silk dress with her dark, brown, carefully combed hair tightly bunched beneath a bright, yellow, broad framed chapeau. When she came strutting down the aisle leading the choir to the choir stand, all heads in the congregation turned to acknowledge her presence, hand clapping, foot patting, shouting hallelujah as she sang tenor bass to "Leaning on the Everlasting Arms", straight out of the *Gospel Pearls.* [1]

During the time before television, the internet, mobile telephones and computers, the village church was the major influence of hope and new ideas in town. It was the socio-economic, political harbinger of new ideas. It is here that we molded friendships and bonded in a sense of community where everyone was considered family. People who were not your birth relatives were addressed as cousin, aunt, uncle, grandmother, grandfather, dad and mom. Such was the case when Nate, the community "wine-o" died. Everyone knew Nate. Children were cautioned to stay out of his way and not to spend time conversing. Nate was the son of Pastor Shake Harper, sanctimonious preacher for the church group we called the Holy Rollers. Intoxicated everyday, Nate begged pennies, nickels and dimes from whoever would spare some change. Nate was extremely polite saying "yes, ma'am" and "thank you, sir" to every person from whom he begged "chippy change". However, one bright, sunny day Nate, as was explained by his friend, Tat Lindsay, "up and died". No longer could he be a community fixture begging in the streets of Crestmont. Interestingly, Nate, the wine-o was disclaimed by his preacher father, who refused to attend the funeral. Yet Nate's funeral was one of the largest ever attended in town. Nate in his drunken stupor, in his need to claim the grape King of Kings touched more hearts, changed more lives than all the fanatical babbling of his righteous and profiteering preacher father. Who knows, maybe forgiveness and repentance was Nate's final request before succumbing to liver failure. Perhaps he'll be one of the great surprises at the final resurrection?

## Wisdom and Spider Webs

Fortunately, Abington Township schools were among the best in the nation, even with its segregated elementary school that serviced Crestmont, a community housing the majority of the township's black population. Our mailing address was listed as Willow Grove; however, we attended Abington Township Schools in Montgomery County as opposed to schools where Willow Grove proper students were obliged to attend. We were blessed with an elaborate educational system. Park Elementary School, where I attended, was totally segregated with the exception of one Italian family, the Pelegi's. Mike Pelegi was assigned my grade, but not in my class. Mike was assigned to a special needs class and was separated from the rest of us; however, Mike and I became close friends and served newspapers together. I was absolutely thrilled to be able to attend Park Elementary. During the warm months, I carried my shoes tied around my shoulders to the classroom door where I put them on so as not to appear different. As the years mushroomed and we were given physical education and soccer, I was pleased to have a pair of heavy duty brogans with metal cleats on the heels and toes. They were great for kicking the soccer ball.

My older sister Audrey escorted me on the first day of school to meet Mrs. Johnson, my first grade teacher. It was here that I heard my real name for the first time, because my nickname "Pete" was what everyone called me, but my birth certificate name was Donald. I quickly learned to spell and pronounce my name, because Mrs. Johnson carried a ruler and did not fail to slap your hands for mistakes in the classroom. Secretly, I feared she might one day slap me on the head as my father always cut all our hair off on a bi-monthly basis. Therefore whenever my hand was slapped, I flinched and ducked a little so as to protect my head. Nevertheless, school was fairly smooth sailing until grade four when Mrs. Cunningham was teaching prepositions and asked the class specifically, "What do I mean by my but?"

Immediately I laughed loudly, for in my imagination I added a second letter "t" to the word making it "butt." However, once news of the incident reached my father, I was spanked unmercifully and my "butt" really ached to the point where setting was temporarily difficult. However, I survived until I reached grade 5 and a second Mrs. Johnson, Mrs. Helen Bennett Johnson, became my teacher. She was a strict constructionist, who frightened me, because she lived in Crestmont and attended First Baptist Church. She sang soprano on the choir with Mrs. Artie Brown Davis Jackson, the tenor bass. Never will I forget the Sunday morning, 11:00AM service, when I made the decision to join church and accept Jesus as my personal savior. During this time in our history one was required to sit on the mourner's bench, and be questioned by several deacons and the preacher until you confessed your sins and pledged allegiance to the Triune God. This was no simple matter, as sometimes it took close to an hour for certain individuals "to see the light." What frightened me the most was the fact that every time I made a statement and/or looked up from the mourner's bench, my eyes immediately contacted and were confronted by Mrs. Helen Bennett Johnson of whom I was deftly afraid. Nevertheless, much to my surprise, she approached me in class the next day, hugged me and congratulated me for joining the church.

With the exception of one day every quarter,

school was like the Disney World Magic Kingdom. I loved learning and couldn't get enough homework. Consequently each report card period, I received all A+'s on my report card. I mention this only because once my friends learned of my grades on the way home, they would challenge me to a fight or call me the teacher's pet. In order not to fight, as I was very skinny and frail, I would avoid the gang of friendly's and run home alone every report card day. Had I protected myself from their fists, my father would have spanked me anyway for being involved in a fight. Therefore, I avoided conversation with other students on report card day, until the following afternoon when report cards were a thing of the past. Nevertheless, Mozelle took great pride in my elementary school achievements, hugging, congratulating and encouraging me. It's difficult to explain how Mozelle managed to equally love all six children, and yet have each individual child feel special.

Promotion from Park Elementary was long awaited and well deserved. I anxiously awaited entry from our small segregated school system, whose demographic included only students from Crestmont, to a large integrated junior high school experience with students from the greater Abington Township municipality. I entered Abington Jr. High School as a proud, achieving, academically able student with a report card marked with excellent grades. However, I soon found out that my educational experience at Park Elementary was inferior, and I could only earn C pluses and D's as grades. The educational expectations were significantly different. One had to write legibly, compute in basic math class and excel in industrial shop areas. In fact, my writing skills were horrible; therefore, each day I sat behind a white student named Joy and copied her writing style until I had perfected the utilization of curves and straight lines to form legible words. By the end of the semester I had mastered a perfect writing style.

Mastery, however, was not the case in Mr. Slegles industrial arts class. There was not one single project in wood that I could complete without help from my classmates. Each class was slow, drudgery filled with the anxiety of possible failure. Two of my friends, Jack and Abby planed, sanded, painted and shellacked my projects while the teacher was busy helping other students. Industrial art classes were especially important for black boys at the time, because our school counselors directed us to trade schools, never once thinking we could develop academic skills to allow entry to college or that students from Crestmont would ever be able to afford a college education. However, one day Mr. Slegles caught me in the process of having Jack plane a straight edge on a piece of wood designed for the hanging shelf I was building. He arrogantly accused me of cheating, and I loudly retorted, "You are a liar, Mr. Slegles". It was the year 1944 and one did not challenge a teacher, nor could one call the teacher a liar loudly in front of all the other class members. Immediately, I was sent to see Mr. Brady the principal, who never asked why I was sent to his office. Instead he abruptly pulled me into his office, picked up a large wooden paddle and approached me with what he perceived to be appropriate punishment for my misbehavior. He requested that I bend over and drop my trousers to receive proper correction. Instead, I bolted out of his office, jumped the office counter where the secretary worked and ran most of the way home through Abington Township, down the large hill at Rothly Avenue, where we roller skated in the fall and sledded during the winter, and arrived home in a huff and puff to explain to my mother what had just occurred. Naturally, what Mr. Brady failed to do, my father did. The next day my sister Audrey escorted me back to junior high school where it was explained that I had been punished at home. I apologized twice, once to the principal, Mr. Brady, and once to Mr. Slegles, the shop teacher, loudly enough for the entire class to hear. Fortunately, I did not have to undergo the humiliation of a spanking by the school principal.

By the time I reached senior high school, I was more attuned to the academic expectations, and my grades improved significantly. As expected from all students, I participated in extra curricular activities and sports. The most spectacular and humiliating extra curricular activity was the school musical where we learned songs such as "Stout Hearted Men," but for one stage number we were requested to paint our faces black and pretend we were minstrels from the old days of the deep south.[2] We held hands, swayed to the music and sang the lyrics of Stephen Foster's "Swannee River." [3] I had a personal choice to make, but did not choose to excuse myself from the production. However, that particular high school drama production was not as humiliating as one particular session in Mrs. Jensen's high school English class. As in many of my classrooms, I was the only African American student and when Mrs. Jensen was teaching poetry to the class, she presented a short discussion of Paul Lawrence Dunbar, the only recognized black poet mentioned in the textbook. The poem of warm, meaningful cadences was written using Negro dialect. Mrs. Jenson evidently assumed that because I was a Negro, or colored, or black or African American that I could read the perfected dialectical nuances of "When Melindy Sings." Actually my mother, Mozelle, who was fully educated in Newport News, Virginia could recite Paul Lawrence Dunbar, "The Raven" and Lincoln's "Gettysburg Address" from memory, and often did in front of the children.[4] I had never attempted speaking in Negro dialect, and when insensitive Mrs. Jensen called my name to read the poem my tongue turned inside my mouth, the saliva dried, and haltingly I tripped through: "Gwan an quit dat noise, Miss Lucy. Put dat music book away. What's de use to keep on trying? Effin you practice twell you're gray…" [5]

Painfully, I completed the first quatrain when my eyes in trepidation began to water. I reached into my rear pocket, pulled out a large, blue railroad handkerchief and began to wipe the sweat from my brow while brushing away the tear drops. Bursting forward to the front of the class, I asked to be excused from the classroom, rushed through the classroom door into the corridor where I sat cursing the day when Mrs. Jensen, the white English teacher, confused my skin color with a culture so sophisticated that only the learned linguistics of my mother could read and recite its history.

Thank goodness English was the final period of the day. I rushed out to the soccer field to play soccer with Mr. Gant's soccer club. Unfortunately I was unable to make the team and switched to the cross country team, where I ran for four seasons always coming in with the final ten runners, but never finishing last.

As mentioned earlier all students were expected to compete in sports. My choice was cross country and track. I spent 4 days at football practice, but soon learned that 129 pounds even with full equipment was not enough to make the team. My great break came in summer track where I ran the 120 low hurdles, and participated as a stand in on the 440 distance medley relay team. Much to my surprise, I was asked to run the second leg of the 440 relays at the Penn Relays held in Philadelphia, Pennsylvania. We didn't win; however, it highlighted my short sports career. I have never missed a Penn Relay celebration since high school, with the exception of the three years I spent in the United States Marine Corps.

As you may have guessed, the choice of a high school career to pursue was very difficult. With six children in the family, a father who was in today's terms on alcoholic, and a loving mother whose only income was obtained during domestic work, the likelihood of my attending a college or university was quite slim. Every counselor assigned to me at both the junior and senior high school advised me to take courses leading to a trade; however, Mr. Roberts my short hand teacher convinced me to aim for a career as a male secretary. By now my academic skills were near excellent; therefore, just in case there was a chance for college, I enrolled in a commercial academic course of study. This allowed me to take necessary academic courses in science, history and mathematics and still prepare for the world of work as a secretary. In Mr. Roberts' classroom, I was the only male student and Gregg shorthand was almost as fascinating as my French class with Mr. Gant. As usual I applied myself to my studies with great enthusiasm and only found it necessary to "cut", or absent myself from school illegally once. This was on the occasion when Nat King Cole, singer and one of my music heroes, was performing in Philadelphia at the Shubert Theatre.

My buddy, Al Robbins and I planned the day well in advance. We took the school bus to Abington High School, then walked to Welsh Road.

We boarded the #55 Bus to Olney Avenue and onward to center city Philadelphia, where we walked to the Shubert Theatre. However prior to boarding the bus we walked, to Elkins Park and played pool until it was time to travel to Philadelphia.

What a marvelous afternoon! We managed to secure seats in the middle balcony. When Nat King Cole walked across the stage, his conked hair glistened. He was taller and his skin tone was much darker than I had supposed. Then the first note of "Unforgettable" was sung in dulcet tunes never to be heard again, not even by his daughter Natalie, whose beautiful voice pales in comparison. Our eyes glistered and our hearts pounded as we listened from the balcony forgetting all our concerns, especially the fact that we were illegally absent from school. What a glorious memorable experience for two seniors .

Thank goodness I had an after school job working for Mrs. Weaver, my Social Studies teacher who lived in a large two story stone house directly behind the high school. She and another woman lived together and were able to purchase their home on teacher salaries. They reminded me of two very old stoic women of the 18th century, but they were actually only about 45 years of age. I cut their grass, swept the pavement and cleaned various sections of the house. Because of them, I was able to obtain a second after school part time position with their next door neighbor, Gueseppi Agostino.

Giuseppe Agostino was a retired, Italian tenor. His forte was classical music, and after a few weeks in his employment we agreed that he would give me vocal lessons in exchange for small tasks around the yard, similar to my job next door at the Weaver's. What a delight! On Saturday mornings I could be heard practicing the musical scale and singing tunes from classical music that I never knew existed. Consequently with my improved voice I was engaged to sing at several weddings, especially favored was "Because, you come to me with naught save love…"

During the latter part of the junior year in 1949 my brother Bobby invited me to join him as a "cleaner of rats" for a local furrier, Mr. Litchenstein, whose farm warehouse was near the Hatboro/Doylestown, Pennsylvania area, not too far from our old swimming hole. The area was quite rural at the time and not the suburban entity it is today, 2007. Our part time responsibility during the winter months, and full time commitment during the summer was to clean and hang killed animals on stretch racks to dry, so that they could be taken to the furrier to be fashioned into wearing apparel, such as mink coats and jackets. The collected animals included mink, muskrat, squirrel, opossum etc.—any trapped animal boasting fur was eligible for skinning. I was somewhat familiar with the actual trapping process, because Deddy Bob, my father, trapped and killed muskrat and opossum at the creek and in our back yard. He usually made stew and muskrat pies with the animals, and served them with his special brand of homemade biscuits that were hard and resembled hockey pucks. This was a part of our specialty of delicious meals beyond the daily routine of beans and rice.

Scraping the fat and skin from the rats was filthy, dirty business. The animals usually carried a noxious odor, and the process included cutting off their tails with a machete like tool so that they would not stink. Then we scraped away the fat down to the skin, and hung them in the ceiling to dry. It was long, hard, tedious work; however, on occasion we were asked to accompany the boss to Eastern Shore, Maryland to collect "rats". We drove rapidly, always on the watch for state troopers. We became hungry on the route and wished to stop for food from time to time. I soon learned and experienced what my mother from Newport News, Virginia had experienced all her life. When we stopped to eat, it was clear from the boss that my brother and I could not enter the diner or restaurant to eat; instead, we quickly learned to go to the rear door, knock and ask the cook for food. We did this several times on the trip, but never were we given choices or a menu from which to choose a meal. We ate whatever was given us. Thus, I received my first full initiation into the real American culture where African Americans were not to be served at lunch counters or in restaurants. This very different from our road trips with the Unity Male Chorus, as we always packed food baskets and ate at the side of the road or the local churches fed us sumptuous meals. Eastern Shore had its own southern mystique. Always we were invited into attics through back doors or to outdoor sheds in back yards, where trapped dead furs were hung to be dried. We collected the rats, piled them into the truck and moved to the next destination. This was usually an all day procedure, and we returned home near evening, placed the rats on large flat tables for skinning or hung them from rafters to await scraping and skinning in preparation for the furrier.

Graduation from high school arrived before I was prepared to leave. Actually, I skipped the Senior Prom, primarily because the young girl I was madly in love with graduated the year before, and there were no interesting dates available, nor had I particularly relished the previous senior prom. At that prom I was at my best in a dark black rented tuxedo, pleated shirt and shiny black shoes that were too small. Although I had been somewhat of a wall flowers most of my life, the actual prom went well and I was able to pretend myself a dancer, especially when they played what we usually determined to be a "slow drag". My date Peggy was a gorgeous, beautifully shaped brunette from Maryland, who lived with her aunt in Crestmont at "The Top" section of town. However, after the prom when we were riding about thirty miles from home base accompanied by another couple, Peggy and I had a very serious disagreement over another senior she had dated who pretended to be a friend of mine. Consequently, I asked the driver to stop the car so that I could exit. What a horrible mistake. I walked and didn't arrive home until 6:30A.M., tired and disgusted, never to actually meet with Peggy again. After graduation she returned to Maryland, and that was our last and final encounter.

There stood I after graduation ceremonies with commercial academic training, no job, no money, and no place to call my own. When asked to write my goals and objectives for the future in the Abington Class of 1950 yearbook, I simply stated: "I just want to be somebody". I had never really been employed beyond the grass cutting, house cleaning chores at the Weaver's and the Agostine's, plus working as a farm hand weeding carrots, bailing hay and milking cows for farmers when the trucks came to town to pick up day laborers.

The first opportunity for employment was recommended by Uncle Oscar, an independent contractor who worked as a plaster finisher of walls and interiors. The job was with a contractor installing cement on a very large factory floor. My task was to transport large barrels of cement from the truck, and dump them in an area designated by the person in charge of preparing the floor. Large boards were laid on the dirt floor as a pathway over which we were to wheel the cement. At the time I weighed only 131 pounds, and the cement that I pushed and dumped for six consecutive days was at least three times my weight. Never before had I been so challenged, weary, tired and exhausted at the end of the day, as in the days I carried and pushed cement. After five days the job was completed, and I vowed never to work in the construction trades again.

Two of my friends Perry and Tony told me of a position posted at the local department store in Jenkintown, Pennsylvania, just a short ten minutes ride from Crestmont. I applied for the position as "stock boy" in the shoe department of Strawbridge and Clothier and was employed immediately. Most fascinating about the job was learning the many names of quality shoes. I purchased my first pair of leather British Walkers which gave me a huge sense of pride, especially for a boy whose history included placing newspaper inside shoes to cover the holes in the sole, and carrying one's brogans to school while we trekked approximately two miles in our bare feet. What joy! As an accomplished stock boy I was soon transferred and given the delicate task of stock boy in the lamps and china department. There I learned packaging skills and the delicate intricacies involved in faultless breakage. Faultless breakage is when a piece of china slips out of your hand to the floor, breaks and you claim it was already damaged in the original packaging. No matter how astute I became at delegating blame to others, I still realized that I was at a career dead end, and must soon come to grips with my unresolved destiny. I needed a resurrection of sorts as a catalyst to provide direction to the unknown, and yet  be challenged by the adventures of life.

## Stout Hearted Men

To be perfectly honest, there was also a deep, hidden desire to become a "man" so that I could stand face to face with Mr. Robert Warner, Jr., my father, and challenge and engage him in a fist fight, if necessary, so that I might feel justified for his lack of manliness and abandonment in raising his children and treating Mozelle, my mother, disdainfully and with quiet disrespect.

Robert Warner, or Deddy as we called him, not daddy but Deddy, was one of a group of men living in Crestmont, who were never able to find work, not even yard work. They had little or no sense of allegiance to family, and spent their days and evenings drinking wine and cheap liquor in the shacks they built in the back yards of their houses. Just about every house in Crestmont contained a shed or shack in the backyard, where liquors were hidden and stored for the local men of the community to share and commiserate. There were very few evenings when Deddy didn't come home reeking of liquor or just plain drunk. Very few citizens owned cars, except Mr. Quigly, Wesley's dad; therefore, drunk driving or what we commonly refer to as DUI was not an issue. In stark contrast to the virtues that Mozelle taught inclusive of never stealing, never hitting girls, Deddy would literally "beat the living daylights" out of my older sisters without reason. I possessed a quiet but deep hatred of him for that, and only recently have I forgiven him almost 50 years after his death. In fact Mozelle, who taught us not to steal, robbed the pennies out of his pockets as he slept drunk at night. The confiscated pennies, nickels and dimes provided for the daily ritual of beans and rice that became our staple each night at the dinner table.

One man in town Dunny Dinkins, son of Mr. Dinkins the cesspool man, dressed eloquently in fashionable wool overcoats and shined shoes. Each morning around 6:00A.M., as I peered out the hall bedroom window you could hear his brogan cleats clicking on the roadway as Dunny strutted through the streets of Crestmont. As he paraded each morning, you could hear a shrill piercing sound as Dunny whistled a low, deep- down, dirty blues tune. Most of the time it was the lyrics of: "C.C. Rider, See what you done, done; Lord, Lord, Lord. Done made me love you, now you done found another man…" [6] No one in town could whistle as loudly as Dunny. The only problem accompanying his early morning ritual was that Dunny was parading towards Willow Grove proper, dressed for work; however, every one in town knew that Dunny never had a job. It was his way of avoiding having to work for his father, who judging from the amount of dung and waste dumped in our fields and the size of his house and property, had a successful business.

Dunny's father, Mr. Dinkins was one of the few successful business men in town. Another such person was Mr. Gibson, the funeral director, who eventually made financial and permanent arrangements for most if not all the citizens of Crestmont. He always presented himself in a pressed dark suit and a broad, full, but temporary smile. He was a true death angel disguised as one sent from heaven to do God's work prior to the resurrection. Yet Mr. Gibson in no way garnered the respect and admiration of Dr. Woolfolk, pharmacist and organist for the First Baptist Church choir. "Doc", as we affectionately called him, owned and operated the only drug store in the town. It was located on a major highway or throughway, Eastern Road, which led to neighboring Roslyn to the South and Willow Grove to the North. Thus business from passer bys and travelers was both welcomed and expected. Seldom if ever did our family visit a doctor; therefore, prescriptions weren't normally a part of our household. In most cases, we were sent to Aunt Clara who made cough syrups and black salve from mixtures of road tar, sassafras roots and other herbs that we dug in the near by woods each year. Sassafras tea boiled from roots was very popular as a digestive remedy. Coupled with black salve that was purchased locally at the drug store and other concoctions possibly ordered from Sears Roebuck Catalogs. Aunt Clara, a relative from my fathers side of the family, remained our substitute family doctor until 10th grade when I was required to obtain a sports physical by the school district. My mother was forced to send me to Dr. Pinkney, an African American licensed medical doctor who lived on the upper edge of "The Top" and could pass for white. In fact, I thought he was Caucasian until my mother explained his history to me. However, my local hero was Tee Dee's father, Mr. Dennis, who was a stone mason. He lived in "The Bottom" just beyond the railroad tracks across the street from Deacon Barnes in a large stone and brick mansion that he engineered and built. Never before have I witnessed such workmanship as in the stone walls surrounding the house. At the top of each stone, he planted pieces of broken glass designed to keep intruders away from the property. It was a work of art worthy of placement in the Philadelphia Museum of Art.

Unlike our single bedroom home, Mr. Dennis's house was very large with at least five bedrooms, spacious living quarters and a full finished stone basement with thick glass panels as windows. It was in this basement that we were privileged to have teenage gatherings and parties, to dance with the young ladies in town and to practice the intimate dance in the deep shadows called the "grind." Beyond our local bunk houses built on the property next to Grandpa Vaughn's house, Mr. Dennis' large home was our closest playground.

And so my father, an undeclared alcoholic, along with many of the capable black men in Crestmont, was not much of a role model nor did he communicate or have goals designed to improve our designated life style. We were clearly living in a rut without any perceivable hope for change. Deddy and Mozelle (Momma, as we affectionately called

42

her) were opposites in all things. The question never asked was, "What did you ever see in him?"

Mozelle, Aunt Beulah, Aunt Willa Belle all migrated together from Newport News, Virginia after they graduated from Normal Schools. Interestingly, they were from a family of thirteen children. All were well educated, intelligent, goal oriented members of the community. Grandpa Willis was a supervisor in the Newport News area ship yards and earned a better than decent living. Mozelle was well read, in tune with the literary classics and generally knowledgeable about the world and its environs. All of the sisters I met were. They came North to find employment and husbands. Mozelle, married Deddy, Aunt Willa Belle married Oscar Harris and Aunt Beulah married Willy from Philadelphia. Both Mozelle and Willa Belle lived in Crestmont. Only Willa Belle's husband Oscar was gainfully employed as an independent plasterer and was always in demand by various local contractors. None of the men they married were high school graduates, and Deddy for whatever reason only had a third grade education. The men were not ignorant; however, they were not able to participate in formal educational programs primarily because in the agricultural society of their birth, young men had to work as farm laborers and brick yard helpers in order to help finance the family and meet basic survival needs.

Nevertheless, the women with all their acumen and education were unable to find employment except as domestics. In the early years, Crestmont, primarily filled with African American residents, served the houses of the rich and wealthy in near by Abington Township, Roslyn and Willow Grove. Interestingly, each local wealthy community surrounding Crestmont had its own special streets and sections near their towns where blacks lived who serviced the homes in surrounding areas. Jenkintown had its Division Street; Lamont, had its special streets, along with Elkins Park. These were streets where African Americans were allowed to settle and serve as domestics to the larger community. Thus if one researches the early history in the development of suburban and urban African American communities in the north, one realizes why and how Blacks survived before and after the Great Depression of the 1930's, conditioned by the ever pervasive effects of a people whose history was one of enslavement and economic necessity.

**Korean Bunker** **Daisy's Bar**

**Korea 75 Recoilless Rifle** **U.S. Marines age 17**

# Chapter Two
## Man Of War

It took several years after the death of Deddy "Bob" Warner to learn and realize the impact of history that conditioned all that we were allowed to be and become; however, as a seventeen year old graduate of Abington Senior High School, I simply wanted to become a man and stand toe to toe with my father, challenge him and dare him to strike out at me as he had done with my sisters Dorothy, Audrey and Charlotte. My full intention was to strike back and knock him into the ground.

This was my quest, and the fastest way to meet and fulfill the objective was to enlist in the U.S. Marine Corps and become as their propaganda stated "a man". Therefore after a short time of employment as stock boy at Strawbridge and Clothier, I enlisted in the U.S. Marines.

In 1951 the U.S. Marine Corps was all they professed to be, tough, rugged, designed to humiliate and destroy whoever you thought you were, and recast your personality, character and demeanor into a mechanical killing machine. Yes, a killing machine which started with my first day at Boot Camp in Paris Island, Beaufort, South Carolina. Upon arrival, we were immediately undressed, given a locker, military dungarees, a sleeping cot, a bald hair cut and stripped of all perceived dignity. After a series of inoculations for possible diseases I'd never heard about, we were escorted to our new homes, a small Quonset hut, assigned a cot, top or bottom and a drill instructor who addressed us as "pussies and ladies." We immediately began the first of many series of push ups as a first level of punishment and obedience.

The days following were filled with marching drills, 20 mile hikes, bayonet practice, rifle practice, and rifle cleaning classes. Humiliation and retaliation was twenty four hours a day, seven days a week. The purpose was to weed "the pussies" out of the Corps early. One could not develop friendships, as silence was the order of the day and night. One, two, three, four weeks passed rapidly; then one afternoon I was summoned to the Sgt. Major's office for an unknown reason. I entered the small room, stood at attention until given an order to stand "at ease". The Sgt. read a letter from the American Red Cross informing me that my father Robert Warner, Jr. had died, and that I had

48

permission to return to Crestmont for the funeral. Then he shouted, "Dismissed!" I stood silent and confused, slowly walked out of the Sgt's office and ran back to the barracks. All recruits in training were required to run to all destinations. Slowly I packed a small duffle bag for travel home, filled primarily with a dress khaki uniform, underwear, socks, shaving gear and deodorant. I was issued temporary leave papers, and given limited money to purchase a train ticket to Philadelphia. I caught a bus outside the training gates, and found my way into town and the train station. I did not have a schedule; therefore, once inside the train station I rushed to the ticket window to purchase a train ride home, but was immediately questioned by the ticket clerk. "Do you know how to read, Marine?" "Yes sir", I responded. Without further question I looked up above the window and it read: "White Passengers Only". I had never witnessed such a sign previously; however, I was immediately reminded of what my mother had warned me about life in the South. Therefore, I found the "colored" signage, purchased a ticket and sat in the colored waiting area. Next I boarded the railroad car and was assigned seating reserved for colored people and slept the long drudgery ride home, changing trains in Washington D.C. and onward to Philadelphia, Pennsylvania. Once I arrived home there was little conversation as to how Deddy died, except for the sophisticated term "sclerosis of the liver" meaning that Robert Warner, Jr. had drank himself into oblivion. The actual funeral was swift with little fanfare, as Deddy had never once stepped inside a church, not even for my baptism after joining First Baptist Church.

Personally, I was very angry and felt that I had been cheated out of my opportunity to stand man to man, shoulder to shoulder and perhaps be able to knock Deddy to the ground and on his derriere. I was sad, not because of his death, but because of a lost opportunity. My motivation for joining the U.S. Marine Corps had now vanished.

Upon return to Paris Island after the funeral, I was punished for missing five days and had to carry my full locker box on my shoulder whenever I left the barracks, especially on trips to the dentist where I received the first dental treatment I had ever experienced. Also, there was an incident during drill instruction when the drill instructor called for "order arms", and I positioned my rifle improperly. The drill instructor pushed the rifle butt into my mouth and knocked out my two front teeth. With that, the locker box routine continued as I ran to my dental appointments. Nevertheless graduation from boot camp was fast approaching, and I was more than thrilled to leave the swampland and dangerous quick sand that we crawled across in South Carolina, and head for the sunny climes of Southern California for Advanced Combat Training. However, Advanced Combat Training was delayed a few days, because the large transport plane on which we were traveling developed engine problems over Texas. With one propeller malfunctioning, we were forced to land and lay over until adjustments could be made in our flight plans. After necessary repairs we boarded our flight, landed somewhere in Los Angeles and immediately traveled by transport truck to Camp Pendleton, California.

I was assigned to the First Marine Division and given a serial #1200963. It was during advance combat training that I met a young Caucasian marine named Richard Grant. Richard confided in me that he had lied about his age to enlist into the service. I was 17 years of age, but he was only sixteen. He had light blond hair and was as frail as I was at 131 pounds. Much to my surprise I was assigned to a squad and handed the Browning Automatic Rifle (B.A.R.). Each twelve man combat team had a designated B.A.R. man whose task was to provide intense fire power in combat situations. The B.A.R. man was also given certain privileges. For example, I was never to receive latrine duty. Latrine duty consisted of cleaning the toilets and outhouses. This duty was scorned by most of the Marines as a low life task and assigned primarily to privates in the Marine Corps. I was proud of my B.A.R. assignment and, consequently, was able to escape both cafeteria duty and latrine duty.

However, one morning our squad leader entered the barracks and shouted out "Warner, you've got latrine duty." I stated, "No I don't. I'm the B.A.R. man, and we don't get latrine duty!" "Are you refusing to carry out my order to you, Warner?" insisted the squad leader. I then repeated my earlier response to which he reached over to drag me out by my collar. Once he touched me, I drew my bayonet and threatened to kill him if he came at me again. The squad leader left the barracks and "wrote me up" for a court martial. Meanwhile, I cooled down and used my time to sharpen my bayonet and clean the B.A.R. Two days later, I was summoned to appear before an officer of the Marines, as I had been court martialed. I knew that I would be placed in the BRIG (jail) for disobeying a direct order. The officer who questioned me in the small make shift court room inquired of my background prior to the U.S. Marines, and asked me if I understood that when an order is given by a superior it must be obeyed and that my actions were worthy of a dishonorable discharge. I merely shouted, "Yes, sir!" to every statement he made.

Suddenly out of an unexpected burst of compassion he stated: "You are going to receive a second opportunity to be a good Marine. Therefore, I am assigning you to clean all the Quonset huts (living quarters) at night after training. All liberty privileges are eliminated, plus you will climb the surrounding mountains dressed in fall transport gear on Saturdays and Sundays. Furthermore, you will march at the back of the division in full transport pack for all training exercises."

Frankly, I was thrilled not to be given a prison sentence. Later I learned that there were several of us "bad eggs" who marched at the rear of the platoon, and we were laughingly called "the shit bird platoon."

For the next few months I was degraded, given no liberty on the weekends, cleaned living quarters five nights a week and hiked in the mountains in full transport gear every weekend. Each weekend night, when I reached the top of the mountain, I stood erect, at attention, and cursed God for taking my father's life before I could return home to face him man to man. However, the worst part of my punishment came when we were transported to snow weather training at Camp Pickle Meadows in Northern California. During cold weather training I was assigned to break trail in snow that most of the time was at least waist deep, and many times shoulder high. My task was to use my body to break a path in the snow so that the rest of the platoon could follow. There were many days when tears streamed down my face, yet it was a thousand percent better than being in jail. It was during Advanced Combat Training that my weight changed from 131 pounds to 185 pounds. I was at my greatest weight and strength, and felt like an incredible fighting machine.

After a few weeks Advanced Combat Training ended, and we were standing at a ship dock in San Diego listening to a Marine general give a speech which stated "a little war is better than none at all." I assume his opinion was that war was good for the American economic structure. However, at the time

I stood gazing at the largest troop ship I had ever seen, it was difficult to listen to meaningless speeches. It took most of the day to board the ship that appeared to be 10 to 15 stories high, and as long as a Philadelphia city block. We loaded the ship alphabetically, and because my name began with "W", I was one of the final few to board the ship. After boarding I was assigned a bunk in 13C which was the bottom most compartment of the ship, where hammocks were hung five or six high and I received the bottom hammock. The bottom hammock was clearly on the hard deck of the ship, with the person's body above you hanging down into your stomach, depending upon their weight and physical disposition. For a few nights I climbed outside to the deck of the ship, but once the waters became rough and the 10-14 story high ship was in the middle of the Pacific Ocean, it appeared to be just a match box floating helplessly with nothing in sight except more water.

As mentioned earlier, I was now at my greatest strength and weight; however, I was always hungry and could never find enough food to eat. Therefore at night I would sneak into the officer's mess, and steal food to keep me going during the times between meals. As luck would have it, on one particular evening the Marine guard caught me stealing and placed me under arrest. Fortunately it was the last three days of the nineteen day trip to Japan, and I was placed into the ship brig. However, when we docked in Japan, I was released and given ship board guard duty. My task was to watch the empty ship corridors, and guard possessions while the ship was docked and cargo was being unloaded. We were docked in Kobe, Japan. Every Marine on the ship, my entire division was given a night's liberty in Japan, except me. Because I knew I was going into combat in Korea, my thinking was: "Why should I give a damn, when I may never return from battle alive?" I also noted that they were loading cargo out of the ship onto the pier. The large cranes would drop their hooks into the cargo hole, and unload equipment and other goods and materials to the pier. Seeing this, I climbed down to the cargo hole, hid inside one of the combat vehicles, rode out on to the pier and went on liberty with the rest of the 'jar heads" (Marines). It was a glorious all night adventure of loud conversations, sight seeing, drinking Asahi beer and being stared at by the Japanese who were less than friendly to loud rowdy Marines invading their space.

The next morning we all lined up on the pier, and were assigned a place in a smaller craft heading to Korea. Each marine was given a small straw mat upon which to rest on the short trip to Korea. In the midst of all the commotion, no one ever mentioned my former place as guard on the ship as punishment for stealing food, and I became just another squad member headed to Korea. Landing in Korea, we arrived at Pusan, a bay and harbor in South Korea. For the next three months my platoon was assigned on the bay, where we guarded supply trains and supervised Korean laborers as they loaded the various trains whose destination was to the north to supply our troops. The Koreans never used steam locomotion and/or electrical locomotives to move and exchange freight cars. Instead they simply called together two to three hundred men and pushed the large trains into position. Man power was plentiful and cheap.

We were constantly warned not to eat Korean foods and to stick with our K- rations. The Koreans fertilized their fields with human feces. Mr. Dinkins of my hometown could have become a millionaire here selling dung to the farmers, plus there was ample space to dump the waste from his many cesspool trucks.

There were many free evenings when we all ventured to a flop house called Daisy's Bar to become inebriated and test our skills at wooing local female clientele. However, one could readily see that the females at Daisy's Bar were used and used up. As young and dynamic as I was, I was afraid of contracting some weird disease that might cripple me for life. Therefore, I stuck with talking to my friend Smitty, and reminiscing about remembrances of the young ladies of our high school days.

Our sleeping quarters were located on the bay. Often during the early morning hour, we awakened to see girl babies floating in the bay. Girl babies were considered worthless, and consequently were abandoned and thrown into the bay. Even today I can hear the disgusting music emanating from Daisy's Bar piercing the quiet of the night: "she a n do yo yo!" This empty tune follows me even today.

In 2001 at Princeton Theological Seminary while studying the ministry, I met several Korean friends who knew of this song and explained to me exactly what it stated. Interestingly, the tune to the song that we heard each night at Daisy's Bar has now been given the lyrics of a Presbyterian hymn entitled "Christ, You Are the Fullness", a Korean melody attributed to Dale Grotenhuis (1986). I have even heard rumors that the tune was once a part of the Korean National Anthem.

The first three months at Pusan Bay were soon over, and our division was transferred to the North somewhere near the Panmunjom corridor. The truck ride to the front lines is forever sketched in my mind, because within the confines of the open canvassed truck sat at least twelve Marines in full combat gear. All along the dirt road, I could hear the sound of large gun fire. No one spoke and the only sound was that of the truck meandering and bumping its way to our destination. The longer we rode the closer the noise of gun fire seemed to be. I was totally afraid contemplating what might happen next, yet I knew that this was what our Paris Island boot camp and advanced combat training had prepared us for. Finally the trucks stopped, we unloaded and were assigned bunkers on the front lines in no man's land. Again there was complete silence, and I realized the rifle fire I imagined was merely the metal fenders and bumpers on the truck sounding like rifle fire as we passed over the various bumps and gutters in the road.

Our bunkers were made of wooden beams, sand bags and dirt. They reminded me of the bunks we built back in the woods of Crestmont. The only difference was that this bunker had to withstand mortar shell bombing, and other attacks from the North Koreans or "Gooks" as we impolitely called them. Most of the time the fighting and shelling was at a distance. We had built four man bunkers at the rear of the line of demarcation, and forward of the bunkers long shoulder height trench lines were dug as a means of fending off the enemy, should they attack across the large mile long open space area that we called "no- man's- land". When one was not in the trench line waiting and watching or out on night patrol, it was necessary to try to be the first person back inside the bunker, for the bunker was rigged with two make shift bunk beds, one on top and one on the bottom usually on both sides of the bunker. Unlike the hammocks on the troop ship, this time one fought to sleep on the bottom bunk, because at night one could see and hear large rats crawling on the rafters two to three inches above your head. These rats were larger than any sewer rats I would later witness late at night running into the sewers on South Street in Philadelphia, when I would walk about two miles each night to the underground subway station at Broad and South Streets, after visiting with my pen pal and future wife, Mercedes. Our bunkers had their special nightmares attached to them, but that was nothing compared to the night patrols we were assigned, requiring our squad to reconnoiter certain enemy positions late at night. Night patrol became somewhat of a daily ritual, except the various squads took turns going out on patrol. Because we were stationed in or near the Panmunjom area, we were able to slip back and forth in and out of the safety zone to pass by the enemy, and then slip back into the combat zone to complete our mission. This was during the time between 1951 and 1953 when the political powers had established a peace zone or safe corridor within what was considered the line of demarcation between North and South Korea.

After approximately three months on the front lines, Marines were routinely given a couple weeks rest and recuperation in Japan, better known in military lingo as "R and R", but our unit was merely rotated to an area further behind the lines. At no time was geography or location ever mentioned nor did any of us inquire. We were in Korea, plain and simple, and unable to distinguish one area from another once we left Pusan Bay. However, never once did I complain about the harshness of the weather, the mud, the snow, the intense cold. We were blessed with the best in cold weather gear, especially the large lined "Mickey Mouse" snow boots that only the Marine Corps had. They kept your feet warm in the coldest temperatures. When we met infantry men from other units of the armed services, they were always willing to barter for our boots; however, there was never anything worthy of trading for our special equipment, especially our boots. The only item I ever bargained for was a thirty eight automatic pistol that a Marine sold to me as we replaced them on the front lines. It was a time when our company was moving forward to the front lines, and his company was being relieved and transferred back to the United States. As we stood in the long line awaiting orders, a Marine going home shouted: "Hey, Marine, got any money?" I replied, "Yeh, about thirty U. S. dollars, why?" He flashed the 38 revolver and said, "You are going to need this in your sleeping bag". I said, "But I only have $30.00!" and with that we exchanged my last few dollars for a 38 automatic weapon that I kept on my person for the duration of time in Korea, plus three years as a civilian. Private First Class Marines were not allowed to openly holster side arms, only officers; therefore, I kept it hidden and ready for use the entire time I was in Korea.

It was during those final six months on the front lines that I witnessed war at its ugliest. During the first three months on the front, my young sixteen year old friend Billy and I became very close friends. We shared stories of our short lifetimes. He was from a rather wealthy family, and I, of course, given my family history possessed little, if any, material wealth; yet we bonded like "two peas in a pod". Then one early afternoon as we were fulfilling the requirements of duty, someone shouted loudly, "incoming, incoming!" Usually, you could hear the screaming mortar shells as they loomed high above your head, and often we seriously talked about not hearing the one that sends you to your final resting place. Such was the case with Billy. A large mortar shell exploded close to Billy and even though he was wearing a flack vest, the shrapnel splattered his face and ripped under his arm pits and down into his body killing him. I ran over to him, cradled his head and cried out: "Corpsman, Corpsman!". However, it was too late. Billy gasped and suddenly died. Oddly enough I had no home address for him, nor did we ever mention our last names. They pulled me away from him, lifted him onto a stretcher and that was the last time I ever saw Billy, my sixteen year old friend.

Navy Corpsmen were assigned to every Marine Unit. They served as our front line doctors and nurses, and many times we foolishly joked about them as non-combatants. Some of them were held in disregard by a few of the rugged individual Marines, who questioned their worth. However, the most heroic act I ever witnessed was that of a Navy Corpsman rescuing a Marine stuck in no man's land. As you may be aware the Marines have an unwritten code that no Marine is ever left behind on the battlefield. In this case one of the Marine night patrols had not noticed that a wounded Marine was left stranded at night about two miles out in no man's land. When we heard of the situation, our entire squad was wondering who would be asked to volunteer to go back into no man's land in front of enemy lines to bring back the wounded marine. It was now day light and the sun was beginning to break through the sky, when a Navy Corpsmen cried out "I'll get him!" We never mentioned it, but a few of us were relieved we didn't have to return, but no one expected the Navy Corpsmen to volunteer. The plan was to drop Willie Peter shells in front of the Corpsman as he made his way, zig zagging to and fro in front of the lines. We ran to the trench lines, obtained a pair of binoculars and watched as the first shells dropped. Willie Peter or White Phosphorous shells are like smoke bombs. Once the dropped shells explode, it enables one to advance or retreat without being seen. We watched as the Corpsman left our trench line, ran as far as he could with his medical bag strapped to his body, and then plopped to the ground. He waited for the next barrage of shells, ran again, plopped to the ground and repeated the saga over and over again. It took close to an hour for him to reach the wounded man; however, one hour seemed like an eternity as the mortar shells had to be precisely dropped so as not to harm the wounded Marine or the Navy Corpsman. I watched with tearing eyes as the Corpsman finally reached the wounded Marine, and began to administer first aid. He was in radio communication with the white phosphorous mortar team. Then they slowly arose, resurrected as it were, and began to hobble, then rest, then hobble towards our trench lines. The distance back to our trench lines was the same, but this time more arduous and twice as long. Eventually after what seemed to be hours, the two men stumbled into safe distance, and several of us rushed out of the trenches to carry them both the last few yards into our space of safety. This was the most heroic event I ever witnessed while serving in Korea. Never again will I, or any other Marine in the field that day, disrespect or mention anything unfavorable about those who valiantly serve in our medical profession.

War does strange things to the human psyche. I still remember the general on the pier in San Diego exclaiming to our battalion that "a little war is better than none at all". I never quite understood what he meant by that, because, frankly, at the time I was more concerned with the long wait to board the large floating city called a troop ship. More than anything I knew that I was in phenomenal physical shape. My time in the "shit bird" platoon trailing the other squads cleaning Marine quarters every evening and hiking in the mountainous regions surrounding Camp Pendleton, left me in extraordinary physical shape. In fact my overall weight had changed from 131 pounds when I enlisted to 185 pounds of pure muscle. Mentally, I only had one polished skill and that was knowledge of every conceivable technique designed to kill a man and survive in combat. The persistent thought ringing in my mind was "kill or be killed." Therefore, during those final six months when we were out in front of the lines on patrol, I caressed the browning automatic rifle as through it was a sweet loving woman. I cleaned her (B.A.R.) everyday on a regular schedule, caressed her, polished the wood with oil and proudly understood my role within the squad. On one particular early evening on patrol, we entered a village primarily of huts and farmer's quarters. We only saw one man, who ran vigorously to some outer distance when he saw us approaching out of the brush. We had been trained to suspect that villages held insurgents and that people were not necessary friendly, but are the enemy and were setting booby traps designed to annihilate us as quickly as possible. Therefore, as we walked through the village we opened fire shooting into the huts, especially under the porches. I emptied and reloaded my B.A.R. several times as we ran through the village firing, firing, firing. To this day I'll never know how many innocent civilians we may have killed, or whether the village had been abandoned. However on several occasions during the past ten years, I have asked God to forgive me for the man that I had become during those days in Korea when my total demeanor, attitude and character was that of a brazen killer without remorse.

Forty years later I was inspired to write the follow poem:

## Korea Revisited

*She stood young, radiantly beautiful,*
*regal in stature, broad cheeked,*
*Wearing a perpetual smile.*
*It was a though history had*
*swallowed her past, and had*
*forgiven her iniquities.*
*It was her wedding reception*
*planned by friends of the groom.*
*She was Korean.*
*Four decades ago I was trained*
*to kill her, to turn her villages*
*into dung, to avoid her foods,*
*to deny her culture.*
*Is she one of the babies I saw*
*floating in Pusan Bay, or the*
*daughter descendant of the "gook"*
*I was taught to hate?*
*She appears so warm, so generous,*
*so kind, so humble, so oriental,*
*so previous a stone.*
*A jewel that history would have denied.*
*Now I must love her-bask in her warmth,*
*deny my culture and recognize*
*that man with all his brilliance*
*is but a slave to his own inadequacies.*

How magnificent! In a short period of time on the front lines, I was promoted from Private First Class, a single stripe, to what we termed Buck Sergeant, three stripes. Promotions always came at the risk of others for I was soon transferred to a 75 Recoilless weapon's squad and assigned as an ammunition carrier. The 75 Recoilless Rifle, as I remember it, was a long ten foot or longer hollow tube through which one could insert a very large missile or bomb and fire it into enemy lines. It was originally designed as an armor piercing shell and resembled in shape, not size, the hand carried bazooka. The Army usually mounted its 75 Recoilless rifle on a jeep, but the Marine Corps established Marine squads on foot who carried the rifle on their shoulders. As a Private First Class my first task was that of a "ammo humper", meaning that large shells about 2 ½ foot long were strapped to your back, and you were the human supplier to the recoilless rifle unit perched usually at the top of a hill. The weapon was designed to destroy tanks and heavily armored equipment, but enemy tanks were seldom seen, and we used our recoilless rifle to fire into enemy gun emplacements, trench lines, underground caves and other targets where troops were hidden in holes and caverns dug into the hills. As members of the squad were either wounded or transferred to other responsibilities, other members took on their jobs and eventually I was elevated to gunner with the promotion to Sergeant.

One of the dumbest and most ignorant activities

I witnessed, again in early evening, was a summons from other Marines to follow them out of our trench lives to a special location. As we moved outside the parameters of the trench line, we were requested to draw our bayonets. Once drawn we began to ritualistically probe the earth to the left and right of our footsteps and step into one another's foot tracks, as we had to pass through a large field designated to have buried field mines. About twenty of us were cautiously sticking our bayonets into the earth and moving slowly, but precisely through the mine field. Once in the outside of the mine area, I spotted several Marines shouting "Hurry Up; that's enough; move it!" Much to my surprise stretched out in the middle of the field was a small disheveled woman, unclothed, willingly accepting each Marine one at a time for quick sexual performance. Not only was the scent totally disgusting, but the stench of semen and body odor was unimaginable. The entire scene was filthy and unbearable to watch the helpless woman accept man after man into her inner chambers. She never moved except to utter a cough every now and then, while the men dropped their gear and plowed on for thirty hot seconds before they were pulled off and were replaced by another. Such was another example of the ravages of war mentalities.

After thirteen months our battalion was relieved, and we were given orders to return stateside. The return home required stripping down naked and being deloused prior to boarding the ship. I successfully hid my trusty companion, the 38 automatic, in my duffle bag, and managed to walk through security without being questioned. This time they reversed boarding procedures, and because my last name was near the end of the alphabet, I boarded first. The trip back to Sasebo, Japan by small craft was inconsequential. Once transferred to the troop ship, I managed to stay on deck day and night on the voyage home; thus, avoiding the misery of survival on a troop ship. Also, I had learned my lesson regarding stealing food and managed to pocket enough food at meal times to survive the long nights on board ship. During the evening aboard ship and on the top deck, I usually checked my hair line that was slowly balding to the point where the top was completely bald and I had inherited the exact same look of my father and grandfather on his side of the family. After what appeared to a shorter trip than the previous journey to Japan, we arrived in San Francisco, where I were given a thirty day leave of absence from base with orders to report to a supply depot U.S. Marine Corps base just outside Portsmouth, Virginia.

Once again we were deloused, given a quick medical check, a pay check and released on our own recognizance. Knowing that I might never have a second opportunity to sample the local environs, I decided to stay in San Francisco for at least two weeks prior to returning east to Crestmont and then south to Portsmouth, Virginia. A Marine with whom I was not acquainted rented a hotel room near by, so I checked in, threw my duffle bag on the bed and immediately rushed out to sample the city. Most of the evening I spent standing on the corner observing the various people walking to and fro. Suddenly, an automobile stopped and a rather nondescript man shouted out of his car window: "Hey Marine, want to have some fun?" He proceeded to open the car door, and I decided to hop in. After all it was not a prostitute, besides I was packing my hidden 38 automatic and had no reason to be afraid. He immediately drove to a spacious apartment, and wanted me to relax and rest on the sofa while he fixed a few cocktails.

The apartment was rather plush, decorated to perfection with two bedrooms, a spacious dining area and a living room area complete with large expensive paintings on the walls. As he spoke to me, he appeared to carry himself and walk in a very delicate manner. He moved to the rear of the bar to turn on the recording machine. His voice was rather soft and delicate, reminiscent of Benny the only known transvestite living in Crestmont. Then he asked if I would like to have a dash of bitters in my cocktail. I had no ideas what bitters were; therefore, I refused stating "no thank you". In the midst of preparing cocktails, I noticed that he edged towards the apartment door and quietly secured the three locks in place. At this point I became very, very suspicious and told the gentleman I had to return to the base to meet my friends. He proceeded to block the front door in a somewhat lady like fashion swinging his hips and pointing and waving his finger at me. Immediately, I flashed my 38 automatic, directed him away from the door, unlocked the bolts and made a fast exit from the apartment complex where I hailed a cab and returned to the hotel.

The next day I asked the hotel clerk for directions to Sacramento where my father's sister lived. Her name was Rebecca, Aunt Rebecca. She was a strong willed individual who came to visit us in Crestmont once a year; however, she appeared to be quite snobbish often turning her nose up at our living conditions. She obviously thought it was beneath her to associate with the children of domestics. She hated the lack of transportation, and the fact that she had to ride a bus and then walk to reach our home. Fortunately, for her, Aunt Rebecca had married a "well to do" gentleman who could afford the better things in life. Her home was large and exquisite. Unfortunately her husband had died a few years earlier, and Aunt Rebekka was now left all along with no family except her backward, impoverished relatives in Crestmont. However, she was my aunt and I quickly located her in Sacramento. Much to my surprise the spiffy, well dressed prissy and uppity Aunt Rebekka, was now alone, pallid and arthritic, dangerously ill and appeared to be extremely thin. I greeted her, explained who I was, but she was too weak to remember me. In a short period of time I left Aunt

Rebekka in sunny California where she died all alone.

Returning to San Francisco and my hotel room, I spent the next few days at Fisherman's Wharf and other notable sights, made my way back to Crestmont and then to the Marine base in Portsmouth, Virginia.

Portsmouth, Virginia in 1953 was a small southern town housing one movie, a church on the main street and a night club a mile or more down the road on the main street. It was on Main Street that the United States Marines participated in the annual Fourth of July parade. This year the parade was special, because for the first time an African American was privileged to carry the colors. That privilege was given to me. How proud I felt to carry Old Glory, flanked by the color guard down Main Street in Portsmouth, Virginia. Interestingly, the Marine Corps was one of the first military units to integrate after the president's order doing away with segregated troops. I never knew segregation in the Marines; however, only once did I see an African American officer during my three years in the armed services. Nevertheless, I took great pride in carrying the American flag. What I remember most was the heavy wind blowing that day making it difficult to march with the flag. There were moments when I wished I was one of the rifle guards instead of the flag bearer. Given the intensity of the wind, I often gathered the flag in towards me and allowed it to flap in the wind only when we were standing stationary or at rest. The parade route wasn't too long, about three miles, and we were dismissed to enjoy the city as best we could. As mentioned earlier there were only one or two places in town where African Americans frequented. One was the downtown Movie Theatre where I spent many hours engaged in conversation with the young woman who sold tickets to the theatre. After a period of time, I managed to receive free admission to the movies with watered down promises of greater things to come. However, given my duties on base and her constant working schedule, nothing ever solidified in our relationship.

The other note worthy hang out was the local Elks Club that occasionally provided entertainment late into the morning hours. Why no one ever asked for identification in those days is beyond me. It seemed that a uniform gave us access to most places without questions. By this time I was only nineteen years of age, full of myself and sophisticated enough to court two sisters from the same family at the edge of town. It was at their home that I spent most of my leave time from the base. They lived about a mile from downtown Portsmouth, and I was able to walk the distance almost daily to enjoy conversations with the two sisters, both of whom claimed me as their own. However, I soon learned to visit Newport News located across the bay where my hometown friend Alverno Cason, a sailor, was based. Most of the time he was away on ship traveling the seven seas, but he owned an automobile which I talked him into loaning to me so that transportation was not a problem. His car was the key to my existence in Portsmouth, Virginia.

Nevertheless, prior to my knowledge of Alverno's presence in Newport News, Virginia, we usually walked back to the base or hitched a ride with other Marines who owned automobiles. On one occasion, however, a group of us, black and white, decided to take public transportation back to the supply depot. Upon boarding the bus, we all rushed for empty seats. I grabbed the first seat I saw located directly behind the driver. Much to my surprise the driver said I must change my seat. At first I thought it was reserved for a special customer or maybe a handicapped person, then it finally dawned on me that I was an African American and we were in the south. After realizing my situation, I was ready to move to the rear of the bus when my white buddies who had fought side by side with me in Korea stated, "If he can't ride where he wishes, none of us will ride this bus!" Of course, we had had one or two cocktails and were very tired; therefore, I suggested to my friends that it was not a problem and I would change seats. They instead insisted that: "If he can't ride where he wishes, then we will all walk". I insisted again on changing my seat; however, the group of Marines unloaded and we began a long tiring walk back to the base. After about two and one half hours, we arrived at the gate entrance to the supply depot. It wasn't until the next morning that I realized the heroic moments of the night before. Never will I forget those courageous Marines from all over the U.S.A. who made a definitive statement on behalf of all Americans.

One evening as I left the Naval Base in Newport News, Virginia, where my friend Alverno Cason keep his car, I stopped at a local drinking establishment on Church Street. While sipping ginger brandy, I met a sailor who seemed intelligent and well traveled. I explained to him that in my experiences with in the U.S. Marines, I'd met many, many individuals some with and many without personal goals beyond their eventual discharge from the armed services. I asked him if he knew of any colleges in and around the Philadelphia area. He mentioned Temple University, and I held that school in my mind until I was honorably discharged in the following three months.

# Chapter Three
## THE GRANDEUR OF EDUCATION

**Red Bank Regional classroom**

After arriving home, I located Temple University on the map and plotted transportation so that I might visit and hopefully gain admission. As a student at Abington High School, I was enrolled in a Commercial Academic course of study. At the time, 1954, it was not necessary to take Scholastic Aptitude Tests or Preliminary Scholastic Aptitude Tests for college admissions. The first time I visited the main office on Broad Street, I was told I needed an appointment to meet with an admissions officer in the bursar's office. Although my financial situation was the same as when I graduated high school, this time I was guaranteed the use of the G.I. Bill given to veterans. Therefore, I returned to Temple University three days later, and was advised I must take an entrance examination. This frightened me somewhat, because after high school graduation the only academics I knew were found in comic books. Meanwhile, I scheduled to take the test and did so as arranged. Afterwards, I telephoned the bursar's office several times and was finally given a second interview where I learned that I had academic potential, but must attend a summer preparatory class and remain on academic probation until such time as I proved otherwise. This good news represented another "resurrection."

The next immediate problem became one of finding a job that would allow me to attend school during the day and work at night. My friend Perry Dade informed me of a position available at the Roslyn Inn, a local restaurant in the town next to Crestmont. I could walk to work and then catch the #55 Bus about two miles outside of Roslyn to Philadelphia to attend classes.

I applied for the position with Mr. Lynch, the owner, and was immediately employed on the midnight shift to work until 6:00 a.m. on a daily basis. The restaurant and bar was closed on Sundays, because of so called Blue Laws legislation in Montgomery Township which disallowed the dispensing of alcoholic beverages in restaurants on Sundays. Specifically my job was to stock the bar with beer and liquor, to clean the entire establishment, which included washing floors, dishes, bathrooms, and cleaning tables on the restaurant's main floor. One of the delights of the job was that Bill, the cook, began his job at 6:00 a.m. each day, and I was treated to a free breakfast each morning prior to leaving to catch a bus ride to classes at Temple University. Bill, the cook, was a very special person. Not only did he prepare specialty meals for me such as sword fish steaks for breakfast, but one Saturday evening I accompanied him on a ride to his home in Philadelphia. I should also add that Bill loved to sample the best in top shelf whiskey as he prepared meals at the restaurant. He was an excellent chef; however, on the way home from Roslyn Inn, we were stopped by a policeman, who motioned us over to the side of the road. The policeman approached the driver's side of the automobile and immediately began to question Bill: "What's your name?" Bill, a bit into his liquor, replied, "I'm Wise!" Visibly upset, the policeman told Bill to get out of the car, and "We'll see how wise you are". The policeman again stated: "I said, what's your name, mister?" Bill reiterated, "I'm Wise!" Bill was never given to too many words, but once the policeman examined his license and discovered that the driver's license listed him as William Wise, he allowed us to depart with a warning to repair the right rear tail light. Then Mr. Wise and I continued our trip to Philadelphia.

Transportation to Temple University usually took about two hours, as I had to ride the local # 55 bus, then transfer to the underground subway at Olney Avenue in Philadelphia. As a commuter, I studied during the entire ride. Between the wages earned at the Roslyn Inn and the G.I. Bill, I had almost enough money to pay tuition.

As I commuted back and forth each day, the people in Crestmont constantly provided encouragement by asking how I was doing and checking my progress. At the local beer garden, commonly called Crestmont Country Club, the owner placed an empty coffee can on the bar with my name written on it, and people at the bar dropped nickels, dimes and pennies in the can for four years. Each Saturday morning, I emptied the can and used the money to pay for transportation to and from Philadelphia. Ten dollars during these times was a very large sum of money, and on one occasion I was short funds to pay for my English literature textbook. I knew of no one from whom to borrow the money, nor could I necessarily pay it back. There was, however, one long shot in Mr. Chapman, a local store owner, with whom Mozelle had established weekly credit. He was always very cordial to me as a young boy. The only problem was that Mrs. Chapman, his wife, had a reputation as a "cheap skate" who pinched pennies, and there was no way to slip past her, as she was always in the store running interference for her husband. Nevertheless, I entered the store and milled around waiting for Mrs. Chapman to disappear into a rear closet and asked Mr. Chapman if he could please help me. He quietly, quickly shoved the money into my hand, and I rushed from the store forever keeping the secret of Mr. Chapman's generosity during the time of great need.

These were my first two years of misery, working full time, studying, commuting two hours each way from home to Temple University. The one light in the tunnel was meeting my wife Mercedes.

While on the front lines in Korea, I communicated with many of my boyhood friends. One such friend was Joe Dinkins, grandson of Mr. Dinkins the cesspool truck business owner. I had written to Joe asking him to locate the most beautiful girl on the campus at Cheyney State College, and ask her to write to "a poor lonely Marine stationed on the front lines in Korea". Joe chose Mercedes, and she became my pen-pal while in Korea. We wrote letters back and forth during my stay in Korea. Once I returned to the states, I donned my dress blues for the first time and arranged to visit her at Cheyney State College, where she was studying to become an elementary school teacher. Much to my surprise, Joe had actually chosen a very beautiful, intelligent , shapely young woman with whom to communicate. In street terminology, "She blew my mind". She was all Joe said she was and my task was to woo her and seek her acceptance. In many ways we were direct opposites. Her mother owned a large three story home plus two garages that she rented to other residents. The home was enhanced and decorated with large stained glass windows on the exterior, plus they had indoor plumbing complete with fully tiled bathrooms. Susie, her mother, was self employed as a licensed hair dresser. Now divorced, she had previously married a medical doctor who evidently owned a very promising practice. This was indeed the opposite of my family history. We owned nothing except the clothing on our backs, usually donated by Mrs. Wagner for whom Mozelle did domestic chores. My father seldom worked, and the only promising practice engaged in was imbibing alcohol until he could no longer stand. Oddly enough, as previously stated, it was my father's failure as a man that motivated me to try to "be somebody", just as I had written in the high school yearbook.

Long will I remember the many evenings walking two to three miles down South Street in South Philadelphia going to and from 720 South 21st Street where I found my first love. The walk down South Street at 11:00 p.m. at night past darkened, closed store fronts, was not a lovable task. I avoided strangers and disheveled homeless human beings who crouched in the shadows of darkened doorways, or slept on top of street grates hoping to keep warm from steam escaping through underground pipes. Thank goodness I was never stopped, approached or spoken to, because I still holstered my small 38 automatic around my right ankle. A large part of me was still locked into the physical and mental shaping the U.S. Marines had transformed me into –a silent, angry killing machine. I sorely needed to be changed from my own self image, resurrected, and transformed into a new creature.

One of my great hopes was to be able to stop the long distance commuter travel back and forth to college and obtain housing on campus. Also, my friends Julius and Gerald, both veterans from Philadelphia, constantly made fun of my country shoes that were usually encrusted with mud, because of the short cuts I took walking through the fields traveling from the job at the Roslyn Inn to the # 55 bus stop.

As veterans Julius, Gerald and I took many of our classes together. Julius lived on Washington avenue, about two miles beyond Mercedes' home in South Philadelphia , which served as the dividing line between the black community and the old established Italian enclaves.. On the other hand, Gerald lived in West Philadelphia, where he worked part time for one of the Catholic Parishes and was directly responsible to a Catholic Priest for whom he prepared communion wine, laid out proper vestments and completed required custodial duties.

I accompanied Gerald to his place of employment on several occasions. It was interesting that the priests kept their share of the most exotic wines in their individual cabinets, and Gerald and I enjoyed sampling the various liquors as we set up communion and laid out vestments in preparation for services.

These were difficult days as the G.I. Bill barely paid expenses and commuting left me broke on most occasions. At lunch time Julius, Gerald and I usually frequented a bar on Columbia Avenue, a block away from campus, where we sat in a booth and ordered soup on days we had money. When we were without funds, we just sat in a booth and watched the patrons. One day while sitting there broke, I watched a man approach the bar and take money from his trouser pocket. The money was folded and when lifting it out of his pocket, the man unknowingly dropped the folded bill on the bar room floor. Seeing this, I immediately but casually left my seat, strolled over and stood behind the gentleman and placed my right foot over the folded money. Once the man left the bar, I reached down to tie my shoe and picked up the money. It was a folded $10.00 bill. As a good upstanding Christian that my mother trained me to be, I should have returned the money to the stranger; however, I was starving and returned to the booth where we all laughed and enjoyed soup and crackers provided by a stranger we never saw again. That one $10.00 bill provided soup for us for the remainder of the week.

Posted in Conwell Hall on the bulletin board at Temple University were job vacancies and notices. One such notice was a government advertisement announcing job vacancies for mail sorters at the 30th Street post office . I applied for and was accepted as a mail sorter, but had to work the night shift. The night shift was perfect, because the extra money enabled me to find an apartment atop a garage on campus. I shared the large one room apartment with another student named Jene, who graduated that same year. The one room apartment became my home away from home. Very seldom did I travel back to Crestmont except on occasion to visit the family.

Working full time at the Philadelphia post office at night and attending classes during the day, I was now free to find a way to propose to my pen pal with whom I had been communicating since my early days in Korea. In preparation for such an occasion, I saved my money, visited a jeweler in Jenkintown, Pennsylvania, and purchased a diamond ring on a lay away plan. Finally time was on my side. We had purchased tickets to attend the ice skating show and performance in Philadelphia. During the intermission, I displayed the ring and proposed to my future wife. Unfortunately, I had not followed protocol, as I should have asked permission of her mother Susie prior to proposing; however, after the fact, I explained the situation and Susie appeared to be understanding. Meanwhile Mercedes had graduated from Cheyney State

College, and had secured a teaching position at an elementary school in Philadelphia. I, in turn, maintained my mail sorter's position with the postal services and hoped for the best.

A few months later, July 27, 1957, Mercedes and I were married at her home in South Philadelphia, which meant that my friends, along with Rev. K. W. Pierce, Pastor of First Baptist Church , Crestmont traveled into the city to celebrate our matrimony at 720 South 21$^{st}$ Street. On our wedding day, I recall arriving at her home in plenty of time, and clearly remember waiting and waiting and waiting for my mysterious bride to appear. I understood that it was fashionable for the bride to appear late; however, we were pushing the two hour limit and I began to wonder if Mercedes had changed her mind, especially after viewing my humble beginnings in Crestmont for the first time.

When she first met my family, I was certain to bring her to our home early in the afternoon. Mercedes, of course, was so beautiful, intelligent and gracious that it was difficult for anyone not to admire her, and even be somewhat jealous of me for capturing such a prize. My main concern was that she not use the toilet facilities, because that meant a trip into the back yard and the two seated outhouse. Little did I realize at the time that she had spent numerous summers in Denwitty County, Virginia visiting her relatives who also utilized outhouses.

Finally she appeared at the top of the long stairwell. There must have been 25 steps and a long wooden banister separating us. The wedding party cheered and Rev. Pierce finally pronounced us man and wife. From there we exited her home and enjoyed a wonderful wedding reception at the Grande Court of Calanthe, 905-7 South 20$^{TH}$ Street, a few blocks away from her home. However brief the reception, every one appeared to have a wonderful time and Mercedes and I retreated to our third floor apartment in North Philadelphia on 17$^{th}$ Street. We could have lived on the second floor of her mother's home rent free; however, I was determined to be a man and provide for my wife. With neither one of us really possessing any valuables except our wedding presents and wedding rings, we settled into our single bedroom quarters on the third floor of a three story apartment building.

Meanwhile as an English major during my senior year at Temple University, I studied poetry. I began to read and study the poetry of Gerald Manley Hopkins. Hopkins as I later learned was a Jesuit Priest whose poetry reminded me of why my mother, Mozelle, once insisted that we attend services on a regular basis—three times on Sunday, Wednesday night prayer meeting, Tuesday night choir rehearsal, and early Sunday School classes. I was very impressed with the descriptive nuances rhythms and message of "The Windhover", but the poem that turned my life around , resurrected me, was entitled "God's Grandeur'' This poem is a simply stated fourteen line sonnet which makes a statement, asks a question, and provides clear resolution of the question.

## GOD'S Grandeur

"The world is charged with the grandeur of God.
It will flame out, like the shining from shook foil.
It gathers to a greatness like the ooze of oil crushed.
Why do men then now not reck his rod?
Generations have trod , Have trod, have trod;
And all is seared with trade; bleared with toil;
And wears man's smudge and shares man's smell;
The soil is bear now, nor can feet feel, being shod.
And for all of this , nature is never spent;
There lives the dearest, freshness, deep down things;
And though the last lights off the bleak West went oh,
Morning at the brown brink eastward springs—
Because the Holy Ghost over the bent
World broods with warm breast and with ah! Bright
    wings." [1]

After I read, studied, understood and internalized the meaning of "God's Grandeur", I was able to resolve the inner conflict which haunted me since joining the U.S. Marine Corps in 1951. Having done so, I stood at the corner of Columbia Avenue and Broad Street, and sold my 38 automatic pistol to a passer-by, who signed a bill of sale. I was forever free of a mind set that enslaved me and would have eventually destroyed me. Happily I was resurrected by choosing life over death!

Next, I graduated from Temple University, took the Philadelphia School System test for secondary education teacher and was hired as a substitute teacher at Fitzsimons Junior High School in North Philadelphia.

Serving as a substitute teacher in the "heart of the black belt" in North Philadelphia was difficult at best; however, I desperately needed to work to support my family. Meanwhile, I had applied for a teaching position at Abington High School, but this was at a time when very few, if any, African Americans held a position at the high school level. When I visited there in the year 2000 to be placed in the Abington Senior High School Hall of Fame, I did see one or two professionals of color, who were not members of the custodial staff. During my junior high and senior high school days, African Americans did not exist at the secondary level in instructional positions, and as I remember only Park Elementary School hired and retained black teachers. Nevertheless, at Fitzsimons Junior High School, Mr. Berman, the school principal who patrolled the halls on a daily basis, was pleased with my performance as a substitute teacher. When the teacher for whom I was substituting abruptly left the system, Mr. Berman hired me as a replacement teacher.

The students had literally run the teacher out of the classroom. On my first day full time in the classroom, I announced to the class that I was "here to stay. I needed a job to provide for my family and had no intention of leaving, no matter what". With that announcement, the class understood how serious I was about maintaining my job; especially, given the fact that when I arrived home on 17^{TH} Street, I observed that the lock on the third floor apartment door had been tampered with. Slowly entering the apartment, I noticed all the dresser drawers were opened and were completely emptied as were all the closets. Everything we owned had been stolen by intruders-underwear, socks, stockings, suits, dresses, panties, slips, jewelry, everything! Immediately I summoned the police who filled out a report and left my wife, who had arrived home, and I alone and in misery.

I only had one suit, a pair of socks, a set of underwear to wear all week to work. In fact I wore the same shiny blue suit to Fitzsimons Junior High School everyday for two weeks until pay day. Eventually the police contacted us some three months later and asked us to report to the local police station, where they had retrieved many of our goods from a downtown pawn shop. Unfortunately, our clothing was severely damaged and unable to be worn. Slowly, pay day after pay day we were able to purchase new clothing, but never did we fully recover. I felt totally raped, abused, disgusted and somewhat terrified that some unknown thief had violated our privacy. Subsequently the locks were changed and dead bolts were installed, but we lived nervously knowing that someone was watching our every move in and out of the apartment. Within the matter of a couple months, we found another apartment in southwest Philadelphia. This apartment was a second floor spacious rental two bedroom apartment. In those days contracts were by word of mouth and existed one month at a time.

Much to the surprise of my junior high students, I became a very visible fixture in their community. Everyday during the week I visited one or two homes after school. The students would come home or to their apartments and find me waiting outside on the steps to speak with their parents. I spoke to the parent or guardian, depending on the individual circumstances, about individual expectations and having a place where the student could study each evening. Thus, I gained a positive reputation within the student body, and was welcomed in homes throughout the community. Nevertheless, occasional teaching days were tough. Sometimes when exiting the classroom an angry student would kick out the glass in the door. On another occasion I requested a student to either stop popping gum or I would place him and the gum into the wastepaper basket. The student ignored my warning and continued to intermittingly loudly pop gum disturbing other classmates. I had learned early in my career not to give warnings unless you could follow through on your threat; therefore, I walked over to the student picked him up with great force and shoved him into the large waste paper basket, shoulders first. The next morning a rather large intoxicated male parent was waiting outside my classroom door. He had not signed in at the office, but came directly to my room. I explained to the parent what has transpired, step by step. Without showing fear, I looked the parent straight in the eye and stood man to man. The parent said he now understood, and I promised to not have such a reaction again in the future. We parted friends, and he appeared satisfied with my explanation.

Meanwhile, during my first year at Fitzsimons Junior High School, I obtained a part time position with the Philadelphia Recreation Department, and was assigned to Moylan Recreation Center at 25th and Diamond Streets. "Twenty fifth and D" as we called it was the hub of activity in North Philadelphia. It was here that I taught elementary fencing, judo, and puppetry classes. Judo instruction was very popular with the young men. The judo I taught duplicated skills I had acquired in the U.S. Marines. Fencing I had learned from an associate attending Temple University, and I merely taught basic moves with the foil, epee and saber. Again it was a second opportunity to interact with my daytime students on a different level. Also, Mr. Otis Reese, the full time basketball coach, was a good mentor helping me to accommodate to the new environment. Moylan was the basketball hub of the city. During the season Wilt Chamberlain, Kareen Abdul-Jabbar and others frequented the recreation center and provided great entertainment for the people in attendance, especially during the summer league when many of the professional basketball greats participated on the outdoor basketball court. Also, many local musicians practiced at the recreation center. One such group was the Blue Notes, better known as Harold Melvin and the Blue Notes. One of the earlier members was Teddy Pendergrass, before he became famous as a recording artist. Interestingly, I became friendly with the Blue Notes who on many occasions practiced across the street from the center at a home in the projects where Mrs. Turner and her girls lived. On one occasion, I escorted them to an amateur competition at the Apollo Theatre in New York. The Blue Notes were a very classy group, well dressed for the show. I stood backstage as they sang their all time favorite: "If you don't know me...." During the song they removed their powder blue suit jackets and tossed them into the audience assuming the jackets would be returned. Not so! Whoever caught the jackets left the theatre never to be seen again! The Blue Notes learned a powerful lesson from this event, and thereafter merely dropped their jackets on stage a few feet beyond their grasp.

Police presence was always evident near the recreation center and in the housing projects across the street. For some unknown reason my automobile was stopped several times 10:00 o'clock at night after I checked out of the recreation center. I drove a 1955 Orange Buick and usually parked in the projects, as there were no parking spaces available at the center, except the Director's spot. The police seemed to follow a routine ritual, and I cooperated each time I was told to exit my automobile, spread my legs, place my hands atop the roof of the car. They proceeded to pat me down and then ask me to open the trunk. At least once a month I was stopped and searched, yet no one ever asked for identification. At one point, I told the police in their shiny black boots to take me down town to the police station, as I was a teacher and it looked bad to be searched in the street. Nevertheless the searches continued, sometimes over the course of a month, the same policemen stopped me. Between the police searches and my missing hub caps, I felt thoroughly harassed. Hub caps were usual taken between 5 p.m., when I reported to work, and 8:00 p.m. during dinner break. Usually if I checked my car and found the hub caps missing, I would loudly blow a whistle in the gymnasium, stop activity and announce that I'd like to have my hub caps back on my automobile by closing time at 10:00P.M. In all cases my hub caps were returned. Sometimes it took two nights to return them, but in a matter of time they miraculously appeared.

After my original employment at Fitzsimons was in full swing, I decided to take the examination designed for high school teachers. Therefore, I applied, took the test and at the end of my second year at Fitzsimons Junior High, I was assigned a position teaching remedial and advanced reading skills at John Bartram High School in southwest Philadelphia. This was a welcomed change in an upscale neighborhood, and I looked forward to the high school environment. Similar to my experiences at Abington High School, where there were no African American teachers, I soon noted that very few African Americans were assigned to Philadelphia high schools. At John Bartram a few teachers were African American: Davis Martin, Science, Charles Askew, Industrial Arts, Gwen Hewlett, English Department, Leroy Murray, Counselor, John Gilmore, Science, Ellen Sloan, Business. Our student population was over 3000 in 1960 when I arrived and with the addition of a motivation school and commercial annex our total student enrollment reached 5000. There were several full time hall monitors assigned to our school, plus three or four full time police officers. Yet the high school was strictly disciplined and our academic programs were well respected throughout the system. A large majority of the student population lived in neighborhoods within two miles of the school, however a large contingency was bussed or traveled to school via trolley cars. The school actually existed in a neighborhood where the majority of residents were of Italian descent. In fact most of the neighborhood students attended other schools, primarily Catholic, in areas outside our school boundaries. In the mornings, one could view African American students arriving into the neighborhood by trolley car and Caucasian students on the opposite side of the street waiting to board trolley cars exiting the neighborhood. Public transportation was seldom a problem and "snow days or shut down days" almost never occurred.

Upon entrance into the school, I parked in the area designated reserved for teachers, and entered one of the accessible doors. I was greeted by a security guard who allowed me to sign into the building. Next he called an escort on his walkie-talkie, and I was escorted to the principal's office where I met Mr. Hencken the principal. Mr. Hencken greeted me, summoned the vice principal, Mr. Sullivan who welcomed and informed me I would be assigned to a Miss Verda Cavellero, English Department Chairperson. One of his secretaries directed me to the elevator and the second floor where I met Verda Cavellero, a strict Italian constructionist from South Philadelphia. Verda, as we commonly called her, was a no nonsense person, precisely accurate in her dress and mannerism, city school supervisor. In the fifteen years that I knew her, she never mentioned home, family or acquaintances other than those designated to her charge on the second floor, middle corridor where most of the English classrooms were located. I was somewhat of an anomaly to her as I had been hired as stipulated by state requirements as a teacher of remedial and advanced reading skills. She immediately assigned my homeroom and classroom far away from the second floor in the basement of the school where all the student lockers were located. Much to my surprise my classroom, room #13, was the only classroom in the basement of the school in a dimly lighted corridor leading to the school boiler room and a bevy of custodial and maintenance workers, along with a make shift office for security guards. To say the least I felt somewhat isolated at first, until I realized that every student at the school eventually found his/her way to their lockers in the basement, and had to pass room #13 across from the elevator on their way to their lockers.

In addition to my classroom, I was also charged with the assignment of "locker duty," especially during the hour before and after classes. After a month or so, just about every student in the school knew my name and understood my presence. My classroom eventually became the hub for student gatherings and meetings. During my second year at Bartram, Mr. Cooper, vice principal in charge in student activities, asked me to serve as class advisor. There was a small stipend attached, and I gladly accepted the invitation as it meant recognition and a step upward in what was to become a forty-two year career.

Class advisorship, as most are aware, meant planning, initiating and supervising the various multiplicity of student activities during the junior and senior years inclusive of, but not limited to junior and senior prom, graduation, fund raising, chaperoning, class trips, boat rides and a variety of other activities designed to provide cohesiveness and unity within the student body.

While I enjoyed the class sponsor role,

interacted with students and initiated a successful reading program, Verda Cavellero was critical of almost every report I prepared for submission to her as English Department Head. She insisted on margins on all written papers, and made every effort to place negative comments on my daily lesson plans which were submitted weekly to her office. Consequently, my personnel file was the recipient of negative notes and comments. However, we were in the early 1960's and civil rights became a large issue especially in our schools. In order to insure equality of treatment for African American staff and students, Mr. Charles Askew, Industrial Arts teacher, suggested that all minority teachers in our building organize and petition the principal to change and reorder certain sophisticated practices within the school that promoted inequalities. These inequalities are best documented in an October 22, 1960 newspaper headline found in the *Philadelphia Tribune*. The front page article read in large bold black print. "Riots Close School". J. Brantley Wilder and Art Peters, reporters, wrote the following:

**"Bartram Keg of Racial Dynamite".** The sub heading read*: "800 Students Remain Home Fearing Worst."*

"Bartram High School is like a keg of dynamite with a smoldering fuse attached. Unless something is done fast, it's only a matter of time before an explosion will occur. And the next one might make last week's racial disturbance sound like a pop gun by comparison.

To the casual visitor, Bartram High School would appear to be a typical high school situated in a quiet residential community of Southwest Philadelphia. Located at 66th and Elmwood Avenues, the school, which encompasses one square block in area, is surrounded by neat row houses. Nearby residents are accustomed to hearing the sounds of bells signaling the beginning and ending of classes, and seeing book laden males with bobby soxers on their way to and from school.

Last week, the relative calm which surrounds Bartram High School was shattered by what police called a serious racial disturbance and daily newspapers headlined as a "near riot." Some 800 students, the majority of them white, stayed home from school in the wake of new disturbances and suddenly, peaceful Bartram High School, previously regarded as one of the city's most progressive institutions, was being branded as a hotbed of racial strife. This week as a beefed up contingent of police continued to patrol the school on foot and in squad cars, the city Human Relations Commission, several local civil right's groups and the Bartram Home and School

Association all launched independent investigations aimed at learning what has happened at Bartram.

The answer is that 1966 has happened to Bartram and Bartram wasn't ready. Ask any Negro student at Bartram High School the reason for the disturbances and you'll get the same answer. "We're treated differently", one of the students told the Tribune, and begged the reporter not to use his name. "The teachers treat us differently, the cops treat us differently. Whenever there's a disturbance of any kind at the school, the Negro students are always blamed, and if anyone is punished, it's usually the Negroes."

Gangs of white students screaming "white power" attacked several lone Negro students in the school yard last week, knocking their victims to the ground and kicking and beating them. In other incidents, Negro gangs retaliated by attacking white students as they walked home from school. At least three students were treated for cuts and bruises at Mercy Douglas Hospital.

The clashes between white and black students have heightened racial tensions which already were at the breaking point. Wild rumors have circulated through the white community surrounding the school of stabbings, shootings and rape.

Alarmed white parents have kept their children home and a high Catholic official, the Right Rev, Msgr. Phillip Dowling, Executive Secretary of the Roman Catholic's Commission on Human Relations, has bluntly declared that he does not blame the parents for attempting to protect their children.

The atmosphere of hysteria that grips Bartram High School is reflected by a number of other conditions. Negro students huddle together during recess and do not mingle with their white classmates. Even white students who formerly were friendly with Negroes are reluctant to risk the animosity of their fellow whites by overt signs of affection.

Looming as grim reminders of the growing chasm between white and Negro students are the two main entrances to the school building, one on 66th Street which is used by Negroes, the other on 67th Street which is used by whites. Although the use of doors started out as a coincidence, caused by the fact that most Negro students live East of the school while white students live on the West, the doors have taken on new and grim significance." [2]

Meanwhile, the African American teachers

group kept meeting, drawing up concerns and grievances to present to the principal of the high school. Mr. Hincken, Principal, however, was steeped in old traditions remembering the "good old days," when it was a "do as I say" world and staff members were thrilled to have employment. Charlie Askew, our organization president was very aggressive and grew to the point in negotiations with the administration that he was no longer capable of compromise and branded a militant. However, under Charles Askew's leadership we were able to force a change in school principals. I then became the new organization president, and a new principal Louis D'Antonio took the helm. One of the vice principals, Mr. Wasserman, a staunch Jewish educator resigned. To observe Mr. Wasserman in action as disciplinarian was to learn how injustice originates. He was especially severe in his punishment, dispensing punishment far beyond what was proposed and approved in our discipline code book. Surprisingly, if a student of Jewish persuasion found himself in difficulty, Mr. Wasserman doubled the penalty. It was as though no student of Jewish persuasion was ever allowed to error, and, if one did, the penalty would be very harsh. But he resigned soon after Mr. Henken left the school district.

Bartram High School needed a resurrection when Rebecca Segal, a dynamic woman of Jewish descent working in center city for the Board of Education, initiated a city wide Motivation

Program. The Motivation Program was designed for students with above average potential, but given social, economic, and academic situations were not motivated towards achieving eventual entry into a college or university. The program was well planned, quite elaborate with an outstanding curriculum. I was chosen as a motivation teacher and eventually became the Director of the Motivation Program at John Bartram High School. Within a few months the program was moved to a separate facility in southwest Philadelphia. We were separate, but more than equal in academic pursuit. In addition to a stringent academic program we established a "Dons" program. This program enabled high school students to participate as interns with lawyers, doctors, business and industry professionals and other successful entities throughout Philadelphia. Philadelphia was rich in human resources, and the Motivation Program successfully tapped into various agencies, civic, government and the arts. The end result was that students began to know about the world of work and to understand what academic, social and political credentials were necessary for success in life. In addition, in an effort to expand our horizons, we were privileged to attend Broadway Shows, operas, and art museums. On most occasions artists such as Dionne Warwick were kind enough to invite our students back stage after performances. During this time students were in direct contact with the performer, and could ask rather pointed questions about life as an artist and/or performer. In a matter of two years, the John Bartram High School Motivation Program was duplicated in many high schools throughout Philadelphia. This was coupled by summer school programs at Drexel University.

As successful as the Motivation Program was, there were still hundreds of students in need of remedial help and direction in homework assignment and social skills. To that end, the black teachers found a resource in West Philadelphia, and we started an evening Community School where students could receive tutorial help in all subjects. We volunteered two nights a week in our specific subject matter areas; however, the program did not attract many students primarily because of its location, plus it was literally unsafe for children to pass from community to community because of the influence of active violent gangs.

The gang problem was very prominent, but somewhat underestimated by police authorities. At John Bartram High School two known active gangs quietly controlled the behaviors and actions of its members. One was the group known as the 49th Street Gang who lived out of the immediate area, but was a definite potential powder keg within our school environs. The other gang lived closer to the school, and was known as the Paschal Avenue Group. Their actions were less prominent and their names seldom appeared in the newspapers. Consequently, school officials through a series of meetings informally and formally established an unwritten agreement with gang leaders that the school grounds and buildings were "sacred" turf. Consequently, we were fortunate with never having an actual gang fight in the school building. However, because of potential agitation between the various factions, teachers were assigned trolley car duty to serve as monitors and safety guards while students rode the trolleys before and after school. My trolley duty was a trolley ride from the school building loading at 66th and Elwood Streets. From there it was a long somewhat arduous ride to a couple trolley stops beyond 49th Street. Once there, we simply disembarked, crossed the street and caught the next trolley returning to Bartram.

On several occasions, there were altercations between black and white students outside the school building at the two major trolley stops. In the majority of cases white students, not in attendance at Bartram High, but attending primarily Catholic schools outside the neighborhood were returning home via trolley car, while black students were boarding trolleys homeward on the opposite side of the street. Sometimes name calling became quite prevalent causing eruptions into large group fist fights. The police were usually summoned; however, once the sirens were heard and police car strobe lights could be seen, the fighting usually ceased. White students immediately fled the scene and would run into their various homes surrounding 66th and Elmwood Avenues. Therefore, when the police arrived there were only black students left on the neighborhood streets, and they were consequently arrested and taken into custody. On several occasions, I accompanied the students to Police Headquarters to explain the situation; however, each time I was summarily dismissed and reminded that once the students left school they were no longer under my jurisdiction. This statement by the Police Captain ran counter to school policy and school rules that held school teachers and officials accountable for student actions and behaviors "portal to portal."

Because of another school related matter I soon became somewhat of a permanent fixture at the local police precinct, not only involved in student altercations, but also appearing on behalf of Fred DuPree, one of my Industrial Arts teachers, whose home life began to interfere with his ability to be an effective teacher. Fred, in fact, was an excellent Industrial Arts professional. He was skilled in subject matter and the practical application of his trade. Students were thrilled to be a part of his classroom, yet at home he stayed in difficulty as his wife "rightfully" perceived him to be a "player" (one involved with women outside the bounds of marriage). Therefore on at least four occasions when Fred should have reported to school and his classroom, he was situated in jail, arrested for abusive behaviors involving his wife. Each time I went to the precinct, I counseled him to change his behavior at home as it was impacting his employment. In fact, I had appeared before the local magistrate so many times on Fred's behalf that the last time I appeared as a character witness, the magistrate pounded the gavel atop his desk and exclaimed in no uncertain terms: "Warner the next time I see you in my court room advocating for this man (Fred), I'm going to lock you up in his stead." Needless to say that was my final appearance at the precinct on Fred's behalf, and in a matter of months Fred disappeared from the classroom never to be heard from again.

As the years at John Bartram progressed my friendship with Charles Askew, whom administration had labeled militant, blossomed. After our stint trying to establish a community center in West Philadelphia, we then became activists with the Delaware Valley Fair Housing Council. We were fully engaged in the midst of the civil rights revolution hoping to be resurrected as free men. As members of the Delaware Valley Fair Housing Council we participated in "block busting." Block busting was an activity engaged in primarily on weekends and early evenings during day light savings time, when the evenings were longer. It required the presence of two couples (male/female). The first couple, Negroes as we were called then, pretended to be interested in purchasing a home in a predominately all white neighborhood. We engaged the services of a local real estate agency. After touring the designated home, we then opted to purchase the home. In many, if not most cases, once we opted to purchase, the real estate agent would inform us that the home was no longer available. Next we would send a white couple to the same property with the same agent who would opt to enter into an immediate contract with them. It was at this point that the Delaware Valley Fair Housing Council would enter the picture with its legal team to challenge the real estate agency on the basis of discrimination and unfair, unequal treatment.

Meanwhile, my wife and I had saved enough money to purchase a home away from Philadelphia and into the suburban town of Gulph Mills, Pennsylvania. Gulph Mills was a forty minutes commute from Philadelphia and was located close to King of Prussia. Also, it was only a matter of two miles between our home and Conshohocken, Pennsylvania where my friend Charles Askew had built his home several years earlier. Therefore, Charlie, and I became involved in the surrounding area school systems, attending their Board of Education meetings and advocating for Negro students who were undergoing discrimination in their individual school districts. In one case in Ardmore, Pennsylvania, I accompanied a student to a school session designed to have the student classified as a special education student. I accompanied his mother and represented myself as a trained school psychologist. No one ever questioned my credentials; however, given my extensive interaction with the counseling systems at both the junior and senior high school levels, I was well acquainted with the jargon and buzz words utilized by psychologists. Also, I was quite aware of the disproportionate numbers of minority children placed into special education or special needs class rooms. Many of the placements were based on what appeared to be unruly behavior in a particular classroom. Very seldom did teachers extend themselves into the community and into the individual homes of students to gain a perspective of the social and economic conditions impacting the student's ability to survive in a controlled environment called school. Needless to say, we were successful in preventing Daniel's entry into a special education, special needs class. He was given a second opportunity to turn himself around.

During the late 1950's and early 1960's the above encounters were buttressed by entertainment Mercedes, my wife, and I enjoyed while attending stage shows at the Uptown Theatre in North Philadelphia. The Uptown Theatre was located in the heart of the black belt. At that time, such unknowns as James Brown, Horold Melvin and the Blue Notes, inclusive of Teddy Prendergast would appear prior to hearing entertainers such as Jerry Butler, known affectionately as the Iceman. A group called the Temptations was singing a not too popular favorite "*My Girl.*" A portion of the lyrics stated:

"I've got sunshine on a rainy day.
When it's cold outside,
I've got the month of May.

I guess you say,
What can make me feel that way?
My Girl, talking about my girl." [3]

For those of us who listened during the 1960's, the lyricist was saying no matter how dismal the day, no matter what circumstances may surround me, no matter how poor my conditions of servitude-"I've got sunshine." I've got hope. I've got faith. I can turn the system around in my favor. It was in that spirit that we marched during the 1960's. It was in that spirit that when Police Commissioner Frank Rizzo's henchmen crashed a billy club into the shoulder of my friend Charles Askew as we picketed the Philadelphia Board of Education at 21st and Parkway, that we kept moving forward, never devoid of hope, our eye on the prize, sunshine in our hearts. It was in that spirit that communities North, South, East and West, rose up to demand rights and privileges never before accorded certain human beings in the United States of America.

However, just thirty years later song lyrics changed. The Temptations gave way to Craig Mack, A Tribe called Quest, Smith and Wesson, the Notorious B.I.G., Method Man and Mob Deep. Increasingly, lyrics became more violent, more hard core, reflecting an age of hopelessness, homelessness and helplessness. The lyrics of The Shook Ones reflected a new and different attitude stating:

## *Shook Ones*

"To All The Killings
And 100 dollar billions
For real n….s who ain't got no feelings
The worst violent of the violent crimes
We give life to…
I give you fair warning
Beware of killer kids who don't care…" [4]

On the national scene our young people were watching traditional role models crumble before their eyes, and saying, "What's the use?" O.J. was being sliced and diced in Judge Ito's courtroom. Dr. Henry Foster surgeon general couldn't get past the Senate, Ron Brown, Commerce Secretary, and Quibilah Shabazz, Malcolm X's daughter, may both be subjects of a strong governmental "sting" operation. Meanwhile, Iron Mike Tyson was released to the questionable antics of promoter, Don King. So where is the sunshine that the Temptations alluded to 30 years ago.

William Shakespeare wrote, "The Fault, dear Brutus, lies not in the stars, but in ourselves that we are underlings." [5] An old African proverb reminds: "Do not fear the lion, for he is us and we are all in Daniel's den." [6] Both then and now a true resurrection requires us to stop searching for answers. Instead we must look within ourselves, for we are the answer. Never again can we stand back, watch Johnny sell drugs to Mary and keep our mouths shut. Interfere, tell Johnny it's wrong! Tell Mary it's wrong! This means that we can't be seen walking down our local streets wobbling, drunk, stubbing our toes as we curse the pebbles.

Recently at an auction the auctioneer was trying to sell a dusty old violin. "Do I hear $100.00?", barked the auctioneer. No one bid. "Two hundred?" shouted the auctioneer. No one bid. Then suddenly out of the audience, a ragged, disheveled, grey-haired elderly man approached the auctioneer. He took out one of those old blue large railroad handkerchiefs, spit into it and began to rub the violin. The longer he rubbed the shinier the violin became. Then he picked up the bow, blew the dust from it and placed the violin under his chin and began to play:

"Brightly beams our Father's mercy
From his lighthouse evermore,
But to us he gives the keeping,
Of the lights along the shore.
Let the lower lights be burning,
Send a gleam across the wave.
Some poor fainting, struggling seamen,
You may rescue, you may save". [7]

When the old master placed the violin down, there was not a dry eye in the house. The auctioneer continued; the bids began at $5000.00 and escalated upwards.

Sometimes as we live long enough to have

endured life's experiences and have been resurrected to begin life anew, we forget that we are the Masters with the large, blue handkerchiefs. Our new task then is to encourage some human being in the neighborhood, dust them off, polish them, talk to them one by one. Tell them they have history, tradition and a culture. Tell them about how it used to be. Tell them to be proud of who and what they are. Tell them how to beat the system. Tell them about those who achieve regardless of how impossible the odds. Give them a sense of family. Tell them how to be strong men and strong women. Tell them how love conquers all.

When they inquire where the consistency exists in your life, or where can one run when all else fails? Simply say:

"I've got sunshine on a cloudy day
When it's cold outside,
I've got the month of May…"

# Chapter Four
## ACTIVISTS, GANGS
## AND PUSSY CATS

Several dynamic forces appeared to be prevalent during the 1960's, and all held varying views as to how to best achieve freedom and equality in America. Most visible on the local scene, primarily in Philadelphia, Pennsylvania and Camden, N.J., were Stokley Carmichael, H. Rap Brown, Malcolm X, Cecil B. Moore, Bobby Seales and Eldridge Cleaver, to name a few. Each person brought with him a different focus, some more militant than others. Yet while Stokley Carmichael, chairman of the Student Non-violent Coordinating Committee, was declaring war on Tarzan as he spoke with 700 students at Lincoln University stating, that any Black man who fights in Vietnam is a "black mercenary", Cecil Moore, a black lawyer activist and head of the N.A.A.C.P., was busy on the streets of Philadelphia fighting for the rights of the disadvantaged and under privileged. He, perhaps more than any other local figure, did more to change the government and political power structure in the city than anyone else local or national. He was visible, sometimes arrogant, but always at the forefront of the battle for human rights and the dignity of man. In one notable case, he threatened criminal and civil prosecution of the Philadelphia Transportation Company for their role in holding 44 Negro youngsters for ransom while the company tried to collect $83.00 for broken windows from parents. Without payment all 44 would have been prosecuted. Even though each parent was eventually charged .83 cents, Mr. Moore promised to sue the company for full restitution.

Not only was Mr. Moore vigilant in the pursuit of justice, he also sponsored rather flamboyant party fund raisers at one of the local hotel suites. To attend such an event, as I once did with my friend Charles Askew, was to witness the height of opulence. Nevertheless, it was Mr. Moore who gave four Black teachers the opportunity to become school administrators in the Philadelphia School system. Little did we know that there was a document called the Home Rule Charter in Philadelphia that allowed the district Superintendent of Schools to appoint five percent of his staff, and to appoint them with or without credentials. Given the riots at John Bartram and the constant unrest it was obvious that the school needed an administrative staff whose demographic was consistent with the diversity of the student body. Mr. Cecil B. Moore pleaded that case and circumstance with the powers in authority and Dr. Mark Shed, School Superintendent, appointed me Vice Principal at John Bartram High School. Again I was resurrected from Motivation Director to Vice Principal, and given the responsibility as girls' disciplinarian and administrator responsible for the English Department. In one swoop of the pen I had suddenly become Verda Cavellero's boss. No longer would I be stationed in the basement of the school, but now had become an important figure in the front office. As soon as time allowed, one of the first things I did was to review my personnel file and eradicate any negative statement that Verda had made in my file, especially those that spoke of picayune items such as reports without margins on the document. After that, I became totally engrossed in the business of disciplinarian and counselor for the girls under my watch. As mentioned previously, there were close to 4000 students, half of whom were female. At first I felt somewhat uncomfortable as a man listening to the multiplicity of problems and concerns facing young women of that time; however, I soon developed an excellent referral system to the many social/health/welfare agencies in the community, and that began to work miracles in the lives of the young women. Not only were the girls highly sensitive to their own individual concerns of academic achievement, but there were a plethora of home school community related concerns some of which bordered on abuse, homelessness, distress, pregnancies, boy-girl relationships, gang related problems—name it, the girls experienced it. In fact the social conditions of the day heightened the struggle just to be a normal individual maturing in a society under turmoil.

Once Dr. Shed, school superintendent, had promoted the four of us throughout the city of Philadelphia into administrative positions without credentials, it then became our responsibility to seek advanced education credentials that would lead to administrative credentials. I was already attending Temple University as a part time graduate student pursuing a Master's Degree leading to a special reading certification. Again I needed some sort of awakening, a new resurrection. In the matter of six months to a year, word came down from central office that a program was being offered by Pennsylvania State University for minorities to prepare them for upper mobility in a specialized program, with a caveat that the students would return to their respective positions after earning a doctorate. I applied for admission to Pennsylvania State University or "happy valley" as we affectionately named it. I applied for and was granted sabbatical leave from the Philadelphia school system. I took the necessary examinations and tests and was admitted into the special doctoral program at the university. The program was designed for four Philadelphia teachers who would be mentored by four university professors. On our first meeting I met the three other students, John Williams, Robert Hutchinson, and Daisy Richardson, all teachers from different high schools in Philadelphia. We were coupled with four professors, Patrick Lynch, Frank Lutz, Donald Willower, and Margaret Ramsey. Dr. Lynch became my personal mentor guiding me through all aspects of the program of studies. Every week we met as a group of eight to discuss and design our program of studies. Collectively we decided that the greatest concern in our schools at the time was the increasing gang problem that was prominent throughout Philadelphia. Gang members could have a very serious influence on all school activities, both during the school day and at after school activities. For example, one of the more memorable evenings experienced at John Bartram High School was when one of the local pastors in the southwest Philadelphia area called a meeting between all the known gangs in an effort to establish a peace agreement. It was a worthwhile effort condoned by the school administration, and Pastor Wombly had been a staunch supporter of our school program. On a warm spring evening we met in the school auditorium which seats close to 1000 students. Police authorities had been notified, but agreed to be available in the area in case difficulties arose. It was felt that there presence in the building at the time of the meeting would cause the various gang leaders and their "boys" to be suspicious of our intentions.

Approximately two hundred gang members attended the meeting all situated in individual clusters in various sections of the auditorium. Pastor Wombly called the session to order and stated our purpose for meeting. The meeting was moving along quite well until he asked the various representatives from each gang to approach the stage to present their concerns. As soon as the groups reached the stage, and without comment, a fight broke out and the total auditorium was in chaos. I immediately ran outside to summon police officers, who called for backup. In a matter of minutes the building was flooded with police officers in appropriate riot gear. The police, after about thirty minutes, were able to calm the situation as everyone left the area and headed back to their respective neighborhoods. Thankfully no one was seriously hurt, and that was the last time I ever remember seeing Pastor Wombly in or around the school.

Each of the other three graduate students had a story to tell, one more horrible than the other. It was generally agreed with the four professors that we could each study various aspects of the gang problem in our respective school neighborhoods. I did not have a difficulty making a decision and developing areas to research regarding gangs, for I had discovered several gang leaders at school who controlled the inner workings of the student body. One such person was Norman "Bus Head" Allen. A quick review of his anecdotal school records revealed the following:

Father agreed that the boy needs to be in a controlled situation; he intends to place Norman in a boarding school, and hopes to accomplish this within a week.

He understands that we intend to place Norman in a special needs school pending acceptance by the boarding school.

On September 13 parent reported that two gangs were loitering on 58[th.]

A group of Dare men went to the corner and the boys took off. Mr. Dels identified one that was bleeding as Norman Allen.

On September 14 at 3:00 p.m. a parent reported to the principal, Mrs. Jones, that she was escorting her son home when Norman and his gang attacked them. She returned to Dare and feared for her safety. Mr. Dels was then asked to take her home.

On September 16 received a call from a father that Norman and his gang would not let his son come to school.

September 17, I saw Norman and his gang (Roasts) with a group of boys, running Dare 7th graders from our school building.

On September 18, six parents were in to see me regarding Norman Allen and his gang. They stated Norman and his gang would not let children come to school. Some of the parents were so irate as to want to engage him physically or 'kill him'. It was also reported that some parents were driving their children to school because of Norman and his gang.

April 6---Mr. Demos, teacher, sent Norman out of his class room for punching D. Blanch and loud talking.

March18---Mr. Adams heard a commotion in room # 110. He observed Norman Allen in an altercation with Betsy McCall. Norman had been given repeated warnings about his playing, cutting class and fooling behavior, plus annoying girls, hands on girls and his smart talk. At this point a pink discipline slip was written.

January 29---Mr. Demos stated that Norman walked out during the class period and started running the halls.

Home Conditions: Mrs. Richards called home and spoke to Norman's "Uncle" who assured her that he would give the message to Norman's mother. This never happened. Finally the Home and School Coordinator was sent to the home to give the message of the principal's interview. During the interview with Mr. and Mrs. Allen, it was learned that Norman has no uncle and someone has been impersonating a non existent uncle for about a year. Both parents work and it has been difficult getting either of them to Dare School. Mr. Allen works at John Bartram High School, but this information was not listed in the records before the interview. On several occasions Norman said his uncle would be at Dare. This never happened and Norman was suspended on January 29.

School Adjustment: Throughout elementary school, the teacher's report would include inattention, constant talking and poor work habits as the primary causes for Norman's low grades. On entering Dare in the seventh grade, Norman would cut class which resulted in suspension on two occasions. Cutting classes continued in eighth grade and in addition Norman became involved in neighborhood gang activities inside and outside the school. The involvement continued and Norman became a central figure in the "Roast" gang in ninth grade. It was noted that Norman would instigate gang eruptions inside the school which resulted in serious complications involving students, parents and teachers.

By November 2, Mr. Allen, an employee at John Bartram High School, was successful in convincing the school principal to intercede on his behalf and arranged to transfer Norman from the Ratto disciplinary school to Bartram High School. The recommendation for reclassification from remedial disciplinary (Form S158) forwarded to John Bartram High School, released Norman back to a regular school environment where he was closely supervised by his father. However, Norman repeated ninth grade at the high school, passed three major subjects: English, Math and World History and in June was promoted to grade ten. He was reported absent 52 days out of a possible 182 during the school year and late 13 times.

The anecdotal records listed above are representative of the multiplicity of gang problems rampant throughout the city during the sixties. Even today conflict groups, cliques and gangs tend to disrupt city and suburban systems, change school organizations, destroy lives and invade political structures. The problem of gang violence, with its socio-economic and political ramifications, is so large in scope that inquiries into the increasingly violent activities of gangs leads politician and citizen alike to near frustration and hopelessness.

Researchers tend to agree that lower class cultures support the better structured gang. Racial and ethnic conflict is conducive to ganging. In fact, gangs permeate generation after generation in our society forming at all levels and within all classes and economic structures. Several questions remain: What are the real motives for joining gangs and are ineffective institutions, political, social economic and religious, the reason for ganging? Is the disintegration of the family a major cause for ganging? Why is ganging largely attributable to boys rather than girls? Finally, if the family represents: (1) an agency of social control; (2) a transmitter of culture; (3) an economic institution; (4) a basic kinship unit; (5) a basic unit of social organization and (6) a place where role expectations, concepts of fair play, morality and ethics are learned, then surely this basic unit must have some impact on behaviors that lead youngsters to ganging. How much uncertainty can a family absorb before it becomes totally dysfunctional? Norman "Bus Head" Allen, gang leader, provided interesting clues to the above mentioned questions. Therefore, I followed and observed Bus Head day and night for almost two years to learn as much as I could about gang organization and behavior. During the school day it was relatively easy to observe his behavior, and in the evenings I worked out a schedule whereby I could stay in his home and either participate in some of the family activities or observe him in action on the streets. Most of the time, when in the streets of Philadelphia, I stayed a short distance away so as to not disturb or interfere in any of the gang activities.

After one or two months of observation, I began to acknowledge that gangs find their niches not only in urban areas, but also in suburban and rural areas. No one institution feels the impact and seriousness of gang violence as does the public school system. It is the public school teacher and administrator who find themselves coping daily with the uncertainty of rumors, and rumbles, within the school and surrounding neighborhood. It is the teacher and administrator who must change their organized plans in order to cope with the threatening atmosphere created by known gang members. These same gang members, when confronted by school authorities, request trade offs that would, according to gang code, render school personnel safe and protected by gang style tactics. Informal sanctions are passed from gang member to gang member in an effort to establish those teachers, administrators and other staff personnel who have developed reputations or "rep". These are usually staff members who have shown no visible fear of gang members, or those who have made positive interpersonal relationships with gang members through school functions, recreation centers, or rapping with known corner boys.

Students find themselves in one of three positions: (1) involved as a known gang member; (2) not involved with a formal gang, but friendly with one or two corner boys; and (3) totally not involved. Those members categorized as known gang members usually have pink slips, infraction forms, in administrative and discipline offices. These slips cite infractions, extortions, fighting, threatening teachers and students, continued lateness and willful disobedience. In many instances these students are known offenders identified by witnesses. Nevertheless, parents, teachers and students refuse to press charges with police authorities, either because of fear or because the judicial system does not possess the time, space, resources or know how to properly rehabilitate gang members.

The second position, friendly non-involvement, requires high level survival techniques. John, an informant was such a person. He lived in the Roast Gang's territory, was friendly with Bus Head, but never engaged himself in conflict. Instead John found time, through parental support, for scouting and church services. These students are characterized by daily, routinized, ritualistic behavior i.e. frequently making friendly overtures, lending money, running errands, or gathering information for gang members. Seldom, if ever, are they involved in gang rumbles. Tradeoffs and bartering systems increase the non-involved student's opportunity to move freely through gang territory in the immediate neighborhood. Once outside that neighborhood, the student is identified with the neighborhood from which he originates. This phenomenon accounts for many of the innocent violent deaths and beatings of youngsters who have either moved away from their place of birth, or who visit girlfriends in territories outside the immediate neighborhood. For example, a shooting occurred outside John Bartram High school in September, 1969, which precipitated a gang war between the 49th and Sheryl Avenue gang and the Blues Ferry avenue gang. According to juvenile aid and school authorities, a 49th Street youngster visited a girl friend in the Blues Ferry Avenue territory. The 49th Streeter was viewed as an "outsider" and consequently shot.

The third position of total non-involvement is the one least known. The majority of its participants are probably girls who enjoy separate operational norms in schools. For example the average number of girls infracted at Bartram High on a weekly basis during the school year was 23 as compared to 40 young men suspended on a weekly basis. Also, girls are viewed in school as samplings for male prowess, and as sex objects who enhance ego maintenance.

It should be noted that many of the young men in non-involvement categories may be seen in administrative offices, accompanied by parents, requesting transfers to other schools. Some contend with the stigma of not belonging and withstand occasional beatings, extortion and demeaning situations until graduation takes place. Still others hopelessly drop out of school, join the unemployment ranks and/or intellectually stagnate while standing on the street corners of America. Thus efforts by the school become more and more fragmented. The 1968 violent death of a teacher shot in the back of the head by a school student in a Philadelphia school yard helped focus the total problem of gangs and violence in the schools. A saturation or super agency approach was utilized by the then-Superintendent of Schools, Dr. Mark Shed who in a letter addressed to the Philadelphia Board of Education president stated: that he had " consulted with representatives of the Firemen and Oilers' Local…Philadelphia Federation of Teachers, Cafeteria Workers Local Principal's Association, Nurses Association, Home and School Council, School Administrators alliance, representatives of the Police Courts, student body, correctional institutions, community people and concerned individuals from all walks of life." Nevertheless, the frustrations of the schools were equally burdensome to other institutions, even recreation programs which were viewed by many as the answer to solving gang problems; however, I clearly remember being employed with the city recreation department in both North and South Philadelphia for over seven years and knew that known gang members failed to voluntarily participate in organized activities, but instead behaved by strolling in large groups and utilizing the technique of gate crashing to gain admission to certain activities. Crashing the gate refers to presenting such a large group of youngsters to the ticket collector that most of them slip through , while one gang member engages the collector in an insignificant argument over price or color of the ticket. However, a few gang members would participate in my judo and elementary fencing classes.

On January 31, 1972, *The Morning Star* newspaper reported a recent program instituted by the Mayor, police officers and fire department declaring a moratorium on gang members allowing them to surrender weapons without prosecution. They declared the program to be "very successful" even though only five guns were collected, stating: "We hoped there would be more weapons surrendered. It's moving slowly, but if we get any guns off the streets, it's successful". Thus, politicians, clergymen, and citizens formed committees to hopefully influence gang behavior and institute a new safe streets policy.

Such were the socio-political conditions under which Norman "Bus Head" Allen lived during the sixties. Norman was a gang leader in one of the subdivisions of the Roast Gang. The Roast Gang consisted of eight separate units of which the Mad Walkies was the smallest, consisting of only nine members. The actual Roast Gang composition was as follows:

## Roast Gang Subdivisions

| Name | Membership | Composition |
|---|---|---|
| Mad Walkies | 9 | Young boys |
| The Mob | 50 | Peewees, young boys |
| 54$^{th}$ & Nevada | 50 | Young boys |
| 54$^{th}$ & Kansas | 50 | Young boys |
| 57$^{th}$ & Florida | 60 | Peewees, young boys, Juniors, seniors, old heads |
| 57$^{th}$ & Boston | 100 | Peewees, young boys, juniors |
| 57$^{th}$ & Reno | 150 | Peewees, young boys, juniors |
| 58$^{th}$ & Tampa | 25 | Old heads |

Subdivision names usually indicated the corners on which the members congregated. The ages ranged from twelve years up through the mid twenties to old heads. Old heads function as wine purchasers, and weapons distributors. The number of youngsters belonging to different corners fluctuated and depended upon the cohesiveness and stability of a particular corner.

Norman's block, the 5300 block of Johnson Street, was typical of the many streets in the western section of Philadelphia. Children could be seen playing half ball or touch football, racing in and out of the small spaces left by parked automobiles and dodging the flow of traffic, or ignoring the honking horns from drivers who constantly missed the children by mere inches. Throughout the day, the children never seemed to grow tired or pause for meals. The exception was intermittent trips to the corner store for candy, popcorn, and "popsicles". The general rhythm of the 5300 block was rapid, continuous and never ending. Yet if a passerby slowed his automobile or paused momentarily at the graphitized stop sign, he would see 15 year old, 170 pound Norman "Bus Head" Allen panting at the side of the street, gesturing to passing automobiles, angrily shouting, "Hurry up, dude!". The drivers seemingly disregarded Norman's gesturing and instead accelerated to move hastily past Arnold, a brother, Chinaman, Sergeant –at- Arms, and Hammerhead, gang runner for the Mad Walkies.

Norman and his young friends participated daily in the activities of the block. The activities included bicycling, half ball games, boxing, dancing, and "rapping" to the myriad of human types who passed through the neighborhood at near precise times every day. Though characteristically typical of many streets in the neighborhood, the 5300 block was unique as the only racially integrated block within miles. Most of the homes in the block were owned and controlled by St. Angies Hospital. The homes were rented to student nurses, religious sisters and city agencies (The Mental Health Consortium). A few homes were still occupied by elderly white residents, either widowed or financially unable to move out of the area. The corner store was owned and operated by Mr. and Mrs. Greenberg, a second generation Jewish family, and Cindy, their unmarried daughter. The south end of the block housed a corner bar, Johnson's Paradise, where Norman's father, John Allen stopped for an occasional beer when in the neighborhood. To the left of the Allen's home stood a vacant home used occasionally by Norman's gang for short- lived wine parties.

One could travel one block in any direction and find himself completely enmeshed in ghettoized conditions generally present in deteriorating large urban cities. One block to the east of Johnson Street, the "strip," or 52$^{nd}$ Street was located. The south side of 52$^{nd}$ Street provided its clientele with a drinking establishment on almost every corner, interspersed with small unit denominational churches, black power advocates, small businesses, real estate promoters, and the hustle and bustle of undisclosed knavery and wrong doing. Without 52$^{nd}$ Street nearby, neighbors might be prone to state "Sic transit Gloria mundi". It really didn't matter what was located away from Norman's block, because as a known gang member he could not travel off his block without fearing for his life.

To properly understand Norman as an involved gang leader, one had to understand his family background. To meet Mr. and Mrs. John Allen and family was to meet joy, sorrow, love, hate, reward, punishment, reason, passion, pain, pleasure, friendship, and the reality of human beings caught up in a cycle of dilemmas not entirely of their own design. Mrs. Allen was born in a little country town known as Scott, North Carolina. She and her three sisters were brought north to Philadelphia when she was six years of age. They were raised with a strong religious background. She met her husband in grade 9, and married him after seven years of courtship. Mr. Allen described her as "a patient and just mother, honest and fair, a woman among women, thoughtful and considerate, but no longer loving."

Unlike his wife, Mr. Allen was born in the heart of North Philadelphia where one had to survive by any means necessary. The Scotten Crime Commission described the area stating: "The gang problem at this time (1969) is almost exclusively a problem afflicting the Negro community and, more specifically, the black neighborhoods of Philadelphia. The majority of the killings have taken place in North Philadelphia where social conditions are most unstable." At age two his family relocated to Columbia Avenue, North Philadelphia, where the crime rate was equally high. His mother and father were separated, and he didn't know his father's first name until his mother signed him into the United States Army at age seventeen. However his first job was at age twelve packing

Resurrection

bags in the supermarket. Later in age he was
employed by a furniture company, and managed to
earn good grades in school while avoiding any gang
involvement. Mr. Allen married in 1955 right after
separation from the armed services and landed a
good job as section manager, but quit a few months
later to join the Philadelphia police force where he
served for ten years. Meanwhile Norman was
beginning to show increasing defiance and at age
eleven stopped communicating. Next, Mr. Allen
quit the police force after ten years to pursue
ownership of the only Negro owned bar in
Philadelphia. He blamed both political pressure by
neighborhood business men and the crazy antics of
his business partner for forcing him to sell out. By
now Norman had become deeply entrenched in
gang activities, and Mr. Allen, who claimed women
were attracted to his uniform, settled down with one
of the stylish women who were attracted to him
outside his marriage. Therefore, a few years into his
marriage, Mr. Allen was now raising two families
with children, the legal one, plus a companionship
family. Norman, age 13-14, declined more and
more to participate in family activities to church, or
out of town trips, but would attend wrestling
matches on Saturday nights. Just before transferring
to John Bartram High School, he stopped
participating in all family activities, and became a
loner and more and more entrenched with the gang.
Consequently he had been incarcerated and placed
in a disciplinary school by authorities. Mr. Allen

partially blamed Norman's deviant behavior on the fact that he and the other three children knew about the companionship family, and Mr. Allen's activities with an outside woman, Judy Pride.

One of the daily morning routines for Norman's brothers and sisters was that of playful badinage with Mrs. Aiesa, a retired elderly woman who lived next door. Mrs. Aiesa, senior citizen, was full of pep and constantly expressed displeasure over the loud music that blared from Arnold's (Norman's younger brother) record machine, and the noise of visiting youngsters who perched atop the porch railing that divided the two households.

Mrs. Aliesa: "I'll punch you in the nose young man, if you don't get off that banister."

Walter (Arnold's friend): "You old witch, you can't even hold your hands up!"

The boys continued to practice dance steps, as they had formed a singing group, led by Norman, called the "Soul Ambassadors". Meanwhile Arnold shoved his friend Walter, to which Mrs. Aiesa retorted: "That's unfair; that's not nice; that's not cricket, Arnold". To which Walter replied: "She ain't got any sense".

Mrs.Aiesa: " What kind of English is that? You should say, She doesn't have any."

Norman: " If yawl get those steps

together by Memorial Day, we'll have a session. We'll make some money."

Mrs. Aiesa: "All I have to do is tell your daddy; he'll straighten you out".

Debbie, a younger sister, meanwhile was typing songs for Norman. She returned every few minutes to ask Norman spellings for words. Norman misspelled "such" as "shuch". Debbie called him the "block dummy," and then ran into the house. Norman in turn tested all the voices and told them to sing bass: "Get deep, man, get deep." .Arnold screeched in a first tenor voice, and all the young boys laughed. Nevertheless, the Soul Ambassadors practiced singing and dancing for time periods ranging from two to three hours. Flossie and Debbie, who claimed to be Go-Go girls, waited quietly as the boys prepared for their stage debut on Memorial Day. Unfortunately, the Memorial Day event never came to fruition, but Norman was instrumental in organizing and providing leadership for the group.

Norman also considered himself to be the "Isaac Hayes" or "lover" of the group. He had at least 25 names of girls listed in his school notebook, and believed Isaac Hayes, a musician, to be the lover's role model "because he goes deep to the heart". Fancying himself the lover, Norman spent the money earned, washing cars and scrubbing floors at Doris' Restaurant, on purchasing costume jewelry for several girl friends at the cost of .98 cents to

$5.00, but was willing to sell a ring to Arnold for $15.00. Arnold balked at the price and challenged Norman to fight, to which Norman replied: "put your candy arms down, girl. Can you beat me?" Arnold stated, "Yeh, I'll hit you where those stab wounds are". ( Norman had been hospitalized twice for fights resulting in stab wounds.)

In yet another situation Norman sent his younger sister Flossie to deliver a note to Wilbur, a fellow gang member. The note called for a meeting at 10 a.m. the next morning. When Flossie returned she was quite upset as Wilbur and Little Homicide chased her home shouting: "If you come to the meeting tomorrow we can have a Roast Train". Little Homicide was indicating that members of the Roast Gang would use her as a sex partner for the entire gang. That same evening Norman and Chinaman discussed the happenings of the day:

Chinaman: "Boy you should have been up the way yesterday."

Norman: "I heard you were capping (shooting a pistol). Why were you up the way?"

Flossie: "He was talking to the Mob girls." (The Mob was a subdivision of the Roast Gang)

Chinaman: "Today 54th and Nevada, Rex and Sommer Streets came up and capped at us. We ran."

Norman: "What yawl run for?"

Chinaman: "We're not like you—going to get cut up. Guess what, little Homo has a sister."

Norman: "Which one of the girls in the Laundromat was the sexiest?"

Chinaman: "I don't know."

Norman smashed him hard in the chest: "You lie! You lie!"

Meanwhile Mrs. Allen came out on the porch and scolded Flossie: "You don't know who to go with, Chinaman or Hammerhead. My goodness, look at Mr. Greenberg's window. Sometimes I feel like making Norman and Hammer get a bucket of water and scrub that wall". The wall was graphitized in large white printing with the names "Roast Gang, The Mad Walkies, Bus Head, Hammer, and China". Mrs. Allen directed Arnold to sweep the porch of the empty house next door, while Norman listened to recordings of Pig Meat Markham and Dick Gregory.

## "ABSALOM, MY SON, MY SON" [1]

On Sunday, March 21, 1971, Mr. Allen and I lounged on the front porch. Mr. Allen consistently spoke about the immediate family. He stated that his wife was a very religious woman, and thinks "her luck is good, especially at the race track". Further, "My marriage was too early and that's why I am still feeling my oats." Pointing to his daughters, Flossie and Debbie completing a puzzle together, he mentioned: "This is what I don't enjoy with Norman. There are few things we can discuss, unless it's hi-fi. It might be because Norman identifies me as a cop." Mr. Allen's eyes watered as he spoke: "Sometimes when it's late at night, I go to each and every one's room. Sometimes I just linger in Norman's room trying to figure it out. I even told him he has an allowance." He then yelled up the stairs, "Tell Norman to get off that phone." Two hours had passed and Norman had not come downstairs.

Finally, at 8:00 p.m. Norman returned downstairs and informed Mrs. Allen that Flossie was on the telephone listening to his conversation. He then switched to little three year old Mary calling her "Little Bus Head," and rushed downstairs to the basement to play pool making loud shouts as he played alone.

At 8;25 p.m. the telephone rang, which Mr. Allen answered shouting, "Nobody named Bus Head lives here" and slammed down the telephone. The following day I asked Norman, "Who do you like best, your mother or father?" He responded, " I get along best with my mother. She lets me go outside as long as she knows where I am. She doesn't want me to go around to the Roast Gang area. Every time I go there I got locked up. I worked at my mother's job this morning and made $3.50 plus a meal. She still gave me money to get lunch tokens today."

## NORMAN "BUS HEAD" ALLEN AT SCHOOL

At the request of Mr. Allen, Norman was transferred to John Bartram High School from the Ratto disciplinary school. As to the Ratto School a former principal wrote:

"…when I came to be principal there, one of my youngsters asked, 'Why is it that when they wanted to name a school for a black man, they picked our school?' This statement or question represents the kind of negative perception the students, teachers and community have about our school. Here was a school that was at rock bottom…at Ratto there was no fine tradition to fall back on. The children had been written off. Attendance was around fifty per cent. Some of the teachers said: 'Well good, some of our biggest problems are out in the streets, who needs them?'

The teachers were down on themselves. It was something of a stigma to be a teacher at Ratto. No wonder! The community viewed Ratto as some kind of jail."

At the request of Mr. Allen, hall monitor at John Bartram High School, Norman was transferred to John Bartram High School, a comprehensive high school with a motivation component and a commercial magnet program.

John Bartram was a predominantly black school situated in a predominantly white neighborhood located in southwest Philadelphia. It's growing enrollment of 4100 students required students to attend on dual shifts. One was assigned either the morning shift or the afternoon session. Lunch was not served to students nor were study periods a part of the educational program. The immediate neighborhood sent most of its students to parochial schools. Racial differences, stemming from changing housing patterns in areas that feed John Bartram, hindered neighborhood school community relationships.

On a cold December morning, Juvenile Aid Officers Hartwell and Rollins came to John Bartram High School to check the attendance record of Norman Allen. Norman had been accused of trespassing at Dare Junior High School. Mrs. Jenson, school secretary, checked the records and found that Norman was marked present and in school on the date in question. Immediately after the two police officers left, Norman was summoned to the office. Upon questioning Norman stated that he had neither a school roster(schedule) or a copy, as it was taken at the police station along with pencils, paper, school tokens and fifteen cents after an arrest for "attempt to kill".

Norman was an afternoon student and his 10th grade physical education teacher, Mr. Vidich, reported that Norman is lazy, comes to class unprepared, but will probably pass because of good attendance. Norman had no knowledge of his teacher's comments, instead Bus Head stood in a jagged line with a group of other students and waited for roll call and consequent class assignment. He was dressed in ragged black sneakers and street socks that hung loosely half way down his legs as though the elastic had finally given way to 170 pounds of ill distributed flab and fat. Norman's top shirt was torn in spots and his shorts were wrinkled and dirty. One could compare the size of his head to the rest of his body and imagine how his nick name "Bus Head" came into existence. During roll call, "Bus Head" playfully challenged two young men by punching them.. He insisted on a "fair one". Finally, the baseball assignment was given by the teacher and 30 students dashed outside to the asphalt baseball diamond. After the teacher reprimanded the total group for time wastage, "Bus Head" received his turn at bat. He hit a home run on the third pitch and ran the bases panting and out of breath.

Mr. Hilltore's math class was different. There was no baseball game, but students moved around the room freely. There was little evidence of structure or classroom order. "Bus Head" was leaning against the chalk board talking to the girl seated directly in front of him. Finally the teacher tried to obtain classroom order. He assigned a math problem to "Bus Head". "Bus Head responded using only one half of the teacher's name, shouting:

"Sure, Mr. Hill". He approached the chalk board punching other students on the way. He tried to complete the problem on the board. As Norman worked he commented to the student at the board next to him, "Why can't you write like the rest of us?" Norman took his seat, reared back in his chair, placed his fingers in his mouth, and watched the teacher Mr. Hilltore at the board. While Mr. Hilltore was explaining a second problem, Norman mumbled to himself and then got up out of his seat to change his problem. He went to the rear of the room, picked up an eraser and finally changed the problem at the chalk board. Then he took his seat and began disrupting conversation with a student named Leroy. Hearing the conversation, Mr. Hilltore shouted, "Bus Head, can you explain the problem?" "Bus Head" then explained the problem and stuck his fingers back in his mouth. Meanwhile a student on the opposite side of the class room called out to Norman, "Hey, Bus Head, want to come to the Soul Masonic dance?" "I can", replied Bus Head, "I have a 24 year old age card." Soon the passing bell rang and Bus Head was lost in the maze of hundreds of youngsters who moved through the crowded halls.

Bus Head was the first student to reach his American history class. The teacher, Mr. Salada, was strict, and ran a well disciplined school. Opportunities to converse were few . In fact, Norman had a book in this class.

Bus Head; "Mr. Salada, today is student election and I have to vote.

Mr. Salada: "Bus Head, you never voted in your life."

In English class, Norman was seated at the front of the room {at one of the two teacher's desks) facing the rest of the class.. I learned from the teacher that Norman had requested a seat up front facing the class. The teacher placed a pre-class quiz on the board. Norman was the first to complete the essay entitled "Mothers are------------". Norman wrote; "Mothers are in my way of speech they are sometimes sweet and then they make me mad.. I can't live without one, it's just that I am in a different world from them. I do things that I feel are cool and she is always trying to make me do things that she did when she was young, you know like make dinner, clean the whole house, wash dishes, be in the house at 9:00 p.m., go to bed at 10:00p.m. and I wouldn't do these things if my life depended on it well. I would try it but I wouldn't do it every day I don't mean to be disrespectful but that's not me. I am not down south or back in the late 30's and early 40's this is 72 and things change. I have a sister who can do what she wants me to do. I'm not saying that I won't do it but it's not my thing."

Norman completed grade 10 in June, 1972, failing English and American History1 with a grade of E (60).He did B (80) work in math and auto shop, passed physical education with a minimal D (70), and received a B (80) in art. He must attend summer school to be promoted; however, the Philadelphia School District did not allocate funds for summer school and Norman had to spend another year in Grade 10."Bus Head" was absent 21 days during the school year ; all days were coded 1 (unexcused parental neglect).

## THE ARENA

The Arena was a large amusement center located in the western section of Philadelphia. It's seating capacity was 9000 for wrestling matches. Norman did not want to attend the Arena , primarily because the Rex Street gang, a rival gang, would be there and he was afraid because the name "Mad Walkies " was written on his dungarees. However, Mr. Allen insisted on Norman's attendance as a family activity.

When we arrived at the Arena, Mr. Allen questioned Norman: "Why are you so quiet?" Norman responded ""You know why, because I'm on Rex Street turf. In fact, they're already here." Norman pointed out a young boy from the Rex Street Peewees with a red dyed patch of hair on his head.

The arena was crowded and filled with Puerto Ricans, blacks and whites. Most of the crowd was noisy and shabbily dressed. Police sirens screamed outside, while Mr. Allen and one of his friends discussed a computer game called "Famous Problems in Topography ". I glanced downward and noticed that Norman's trousers had the names Yvonne, Anna and Brenda written on the left leg with a magic marker, and Bus head Allen and Mad Walkies on the right trouser leg. Norman insisted that the name Bus Head was given to him by his mother's brother, Uncle Robert. He mentioned that he saw his uncle in church on Sundays, but hadn't been in attendance for the past three weeks. Further, he joined in 1968 because he liked what the minister "was talking about". In addition he mentioned that he was playing pool earlier with "Duncan, one of my young boys. we made a rule, if you can't beat me, you are not a junior any more. Just before you came I was fighting all the young boys at 57th and Boston Streets". Meanwhile Norman and Arnold, his brother, were engaged in conversation. Arnold stated: "What did God say when he made the first black person?" Norman answered: "What stupid?" To which Arnold replied, "Oops, I burnt one!"

The evening at the arena was punctuated with floor fights from certain members who had paid admission, yet carried their street corner hatreds and animosities to the entertainment hall. As participants from the audience fought and police guards arrested them in the midst of cheering and booing from the crowd, Norman sat quietly occasionally hollering and shouting approval and/or dismay at the various individuals who chose the Arena as their battlefield. However, three major events were scheduled leading up the major event of the evening, the cage match between Pedro Morales and Bull Dog Brauer. As Norman shouted, "Get out of the ring, Bull Dog", police took positions outside the ring to hold back the crowd as they tossed food stuffs and cans into the ring. The crowd was nearly rioting as Norman exclaimed: "The first Puerto Rican wrestling champion in the world!" Interestingly, at the conclusion of the matches Norman and Leroy were sent home with another friend of the family, Leroy and Mr., Allen and a strange woman entered another automobile and drove away to Willingboro, New Jersey. Little did I know at the time that Willingboro would become a major focus for my life.

The next day following the wrestling matches, Norman and I discussed the strange woman from Willingboro, who suddenly appeared at the Arena and was escorted home by Mr. Allen, his father. Norman also revealed his reason for not wishing to attend the matches:

> Norman: "When I got out of the car, I was a little scared because I was in one of the corners we were fighting turf—Rex Street turf. When I got into the arena, I saw some of Rex Street. I tried to hide at first, but then I said forget it! I ain't worried about them. They kept looking up at me and

pointing at me. I watched them as they walked by. As I was leaving they tapped me on the shoulder and said, 'What's happening Roast?' Something like that. I just kept walking out. They couldn't stab me or anything because of the police around me." I then asked, "Who was that strange woman?" Norman responded, "Judy Pride, she usually goes; Arnold he goes most of the time with my father. The other people they liked it too. You know we were laughing and talking, my little brother making a couple jokes and all that".

"Why were you so quiet during the match?", I inquired.

Norman: "I don't like it unless the person I want to win does something good. I got quiet because I don't like to see the people I want to win losing."

"After we left the arena I went to Willingboro with your father. Do you know anything about Willingboro?" I asked. Cocking his head to the right, Norman said: "I know that Judy lives there and has a son named Lucky, a son named Jerry, and a daughter named Bambi. She was with my father. Sometimes her kids go with us, Lucky and them. They are suppose to be my half brothers and sister. I think that is what my father told me. Sometimes they go to the Arena, but I guess he didn't have enough money to bring them. Judy is not suppose to be known by my mother. One time we came back from Willingboro, the kids and us, and my father let them out on the corner of 52$^{nd}$ Street and went and drove us home, went back in the house, changed, and picked them up. I guess my mother knows about him, because my sister is saying she likes Lucky even though they are half brothers and sisters. I guess my mother really knows about them."

The covert role of the father was deeply complex and I tried not to ask Norman highly structured questions that would have resulted in complete silence or fabrication of Norman's perception of the activities centering around the companionship family.

I approached Norman genteelly as I imposed the next question: "You told me some time ago that you got along best with your mother. You have half brothers and sisters in Willingboro.

What is your thinking now about your mother and father?"

Norman: "Well really that is the way it works with me too, because I'm suppose to go with one girl, I got two and three and four girls around the city, Really the way I figure it, nobody can stay with just one person all the time. True love or not, nobody can stick with them…the same person over and over. You might find one or two in every ten, but not everybody. As far as Judy is concerned, well marriage and still having other brothers and sisters that means she has his (Mr. Allen's) children. Well when it comes to marriage, I don't know because I'm not married. I can't say any thing about it and it is too late to stop any thing now because he already has the kids. He has to support them; he can't put them in a room and lock them up."

"Do you think this has anything to do with why you belong to a gang?", I asked.

Norman: " No, the real reason I belong to a gang? No, I don't think that is the real reason. It is just that, well I found out a little more about why I belong to a gang. Because most of the time my mother and father, they think the streets are dangerous and all that. Well, every body that walks out on the street is part of the danger because somebody, say like my father, goes to the bar one night because he is depressed because my mother is mad at him and Judy is mad at him, like they both put him out of the house and he can't come back for a while until he decides if he is going to force them to let him back like that. So he goes to a bar and gets so drunk that he bumps into somebody and the person says 'Excuse me ' or ' jump out in the street, the street isn't big enough for both of us' you know so, like, a drunk gets scared when somebody threatens him like that so he just pulls out a knife or a gun and shoots somebody like that".

"So Norman", I asked, "how did you feel when you knew that I would learn about Judy and your daddy?"

Norman spoke slowly and deliberately, "I thought everybody knew about Judy, because he was telling everybody in the school office we lived in Willingboro, we had a house in Willingboro, and everybody knew I lived in Philadelphia. They asked me when I came over to the school. They asked me if I lived in Willingboro and I told them no, I lived on Johnson Street. They said your father said he had a house in Willingboro. I thought he had told them that."

"If that's the case, who owns the house where Judy lives?" I asked.

Norman answered, " I think my father does. Mother (Mrs. Allen) and him argue about pay checks paying for the house. Mother says he cuts her short and stuff like that".

The companionship family was a serious part of the Allen Family's life. Judy Pride accounted for much of the time when Mr. Allen was not at home in Philadelphia. Because of her youth (age 30) Judy was demanding of nights out at restaurants and local night clubs in New Jersey, especially Longside, which over the years had been a night spot usually frequented by blacks during the summer months. The popular Cotton Club carried young upcoming musicians and vocalists on its payroll. In addition, barbecue pits and a small carnival like atmosphere permeate the area.

On one occasion Mr. Allen, Judy Pride and I left home for "a night on the town". Their first stop was a local inn. Drinks cost .85 to .95 cents a glass. A three piece music combo rendered music. I ordered Scotch and water, Judy, Canadian Club on the rocks with a twist of lemon, and Mr. Allen, Canadian Club and ginger ale. After researching the menu Judy ordered a small sandwich stating: "I have to eat whenever I go out". From there we ventured to Burlington City where the hustle and bustle of weekend activity was quite brisk. Hundreds of Blacks stood outside the Top Cat Club.. Many danced and plucked their fingers to the loud rhythms that emanated from inside the club. The lady at the door asked for a two dollar minimum cover charge admission price. Judy Pride shouted, "There ain't that much money in the whole town!" We left and visited the Republican Club, then the Democratic Club. Mr. Allen and Judy spent most of the night dancing. We returned to Willingboro where Norman, Chinaman and Hammerhead awaited our arrival. Upon entry I noticed young female visitor was at Judy's house. I asked her;

"Are you the young girl Norman always talks about? He's been saying your name over and over again. Finally we meet."

On the way home to Philadelphia Norman blurted out: "Mr. Warner, you sure lamed (embarrassed) me. That was the wrong girl!" To which Chinaman retorted: "No, it wasn't. You had him! (You asked the right question)."

## GANG LEADER

Norman "bus head" Allen was a known gang leader. School records, police records, fellow gang members all attested to this. In direct questioning of Norman as to how he first began ganging his response was: "In eighth grade some Peewees said, 'my boys want to see you!' Everyday they tried to move on me and draft me in the bathroom at school. I joined the Moon Gang from December to June. In ninth grade I joined the Roast Gang. The Moon had too many different parts, so I quit. They kept hitting me in different corners. I kept hitting the wrong person. I didn't let my parents know. I got stabbed three different times—left shoulder, leg, upper arm. One time some girl gave me her brother's clothes and wrapped my arm. About a week later I took off (bandage) and it (the wound) was healed. Then I became a runner, because I could beat everybody left in the gang. They made me a runner of the young boys. We did all our fighting in the morning at Dare."

## Dare Junior High School Gang

| Name | Reason for Name | Location or Occupation |
|---|---|---|
| Two-Two | Always hustling and bumming money, asking for two bits | High School Student |
| Tank | Large in size | Ratto Disciplinary School |
| Chinaman | Slanted eyes | High School Student |
| Hammerhead | Head shaped like a hammer | High School Student |
| Twin | Brother looks like him | "Free" School Student |
| Mugs | Face looks like a mug | Jail |
| River Rat | Corner hopper, stays with the winner | Dope Addict |
| Cube | Hits like a rock | High School Student |
| Skins | Very light skin | Jail |

# GANG ACTIVITY

Out of the nine Mad Walkies listed, two of the gang members provided constant companionship for Norman Allen. One was a youngster called Hammerhead, age 16. He weighed 130 pounds and usually wore neatly pressed, black slacks and a clean white T-shirt. The nickname accurately described the long, angular, hammer-like shape of his head. Hammer and Norman's oldest sister, Flossie, were close friends. Whenever they were together and not observed by Mr. and Mrs. Allen, Flossie and Hammer could be seen playfully jostling one another off and on the porch banister.

Conversations with Hammerhead were indicative of high verbal ability. He was able to accurately relate a story, using good grammatical expression. He was, at all times, mannerly and consistently thanked me for automobile rides from the Allen's block across opposing gang turf to his home in Roast Gang territory. He always insisted that we keep the car doors locked. His explanation for belonging to a gang was that the Moon Gang, a rival gang, constantly stopped him and threatened him asking,"What corner you from, dude?" He said he usually answered "No where. But as soon as I answered, they beat me up. I occasionally walked with Chinaman and Bus Head, but was not from any corner, but eventually joined because I got tired of being beat up for being from no where."

On June 16, 1971, hammerhead was arrested by

the Philadelphia police for trespassing and damaging private property. The property in question was the empty house next door to the Allen's. The house was owned by the hospital, was modestly but completely furnished, and had provided a place for numerous wine parties for different corner boys and their girls.

The next day, Norman gave the following description of the incident leading to Hammerheads arrest: "Yesterday at 5311, well Chinaman climbed through a window and opened the back door for us and you know we had put together some money and we winded up with $5.00 and some cents. We bought a quart of Thunderbird, a quart of Jumping Jack and one half gallon of Tiger Rose wine. My sister Flossie called some of the girls over and they were suppose to be drinking some of the Thunderbird wine you know. They were suppose to be some of the corner girls. You know everybody is trying everything out and this is the first time any of us had drunk anything. And you know we was going to see how it was the first time drinking and then we was going to talk about Chinaman going with one of my sister's girl friends. Chinaman climbed through the window and Hammer and Flossie came through the house next door. Flossie had called her girl friends. Some men were next door to my house putting carpet on the floor and the man told Flossie to come and show him where the furniture go. He wanted me and him to move the furniture. I told Flossie to stay at the empty house.

The man that works at the hospital saw Flossie, then he ran down the street to get the hospital security guard. We went back into the house and got the wine and transported it over to my house and ran out. The man called the police. I saw a good 12 or 14 wagons and cars altogether, all around there and they came in my house without a warrant. That's why I know Hammer wouldn't got locked up, 'cause they came in without a warrant, opened the door, walked upstairs come downstairs, came in the kitchen, made everybody in the kitchen come to the living room, started cursing, pushing people around and the man came into the house and identified Hammer. He said he saw Hammer as one of the boys that was in the house and he identified my sister, Flossie, as one of the girls he saw in the door.. Then they took Hammer outside. The man was identifying other people. I slowly pushed my sister out the door and told her to go down to Molly's house because there were no cops outside, they were inside the house being busy bodies. My sister slipped outside and went around the corner over her girl friend's house until my father came home.

They threw Hammer in the wagon; they forgot all about my sister and then boarded up the house next door. I think they put a lock on the door and boarded up all the windows and every thing. Cedar Avenue, another gang, was in trouble because when they broke in the house first, they wrote their names on the wall, the refrigerator, and the stove. They put

Rex Street's name on the wall because some of Rex Street was with them and some of Sommer Street was with them at the time and maybe some parts of the Moon because I seen some of their names in the house. So after everybody left my father went to pick up my mother and I transported the wine from under my front steps in the back yard into the house in the back closet. Hammer called my house about 9:00 a.m., told my little brother that he was just getting out of jail."

When questioned as to how many houses on the block were not owned by the hospital, Norman said: "Every house on the block except ours. The DiPetro's, the Laurel's, and the Trama's are owned by the hospital." The hospital stood five stories above the two story houses on the block and the residents were all nurses or hospital personnel. Norman's family was the only Black family on the block.

When Hammer returned, he gave me his version of the arrest stating: "Well, when I got to the station they took down my name, my address, date of birth and phone number. Then the Juvenile Aid Officer came and said he would do anything to try and help me get out of there. I didn't know his name all I know was that he was white. So I slept in there, it was pretty cold in there, I didn't have no sweater or nothing so I froze. Then I heard my grandmother and my sister. So I went home".

# FAIR ONES

Fair ones were fights or boxing matches initiated by gang members as a means of settling disputes. It usually meant that the fighting had to be one on one as opposed to gang fighting one person. In gang terminology, this was considered "fair play".

Mr. Brown, the hospital agent, visited with Mr. and Mrs. Allen on June 21, 1971. He pointed out the horrors of jail to the Allen children, and gave the family a tour of the house next door. Mr. Brown claimed $500.00 in damages. Inside the house was graphitized with the names Chinaman, Bus Head, Hammer, Mad Walkies, Roast Gang, 57th Rex, 56th Cedar, 56th Tide. It was 4:45 p.m. and during the conversation with Mr. Brown, an obviously intoxicated young man approached the porch and asked for Bus Head. He was later identified as Larry. Someone had accused him of stabbing Norman. Mr. Allen, however, interceded shouting, "What do you want?" and "Move on!" Then at 6:45 p.m. Hammer met Howard from Rex Street turf in front of the house and an argument ensued. Norman joined Hammer and a boy named Rick joined Howard. They argued face to face:

> Hammer: "Let's move around the corner."
> Howard: "Don't fuck me that way, baby, you know you can't style (fight)."

Mr. Allen came off the porch and pulled Norman and Hammer away from the two Rex Street corner boys. All was quiet until about 8:30 p.m. Mr. Allen was asleep on the porch when a taxicab stopped in front of the house. Larry appeared for the second time that day. He stepped out of the cab and immediately challenged Bus Head to a fair one. He and bus Head argued loudly. Mr. Greenberg, owner of the corner store, saw the two arguing and separated Norman and Larry. The police arrived. Larry left. The police trailed Larry and stopped to speak with him. Hammer in a loud voice stated: "He didn't scare me one bit." Mr. Allen interrupted: "You can't survive an ambush". Meanwhile the police returned and talked to Bus Head. They told him to "Put a hurting" on Larry the next time and then to call them—"Car # 1418". "What hurts me", said Mr. Allen, "is that if this gang can't get to Norman, they will take it out on the little kids. Norman can't see this." Mr. Allen then pulled a 38 snub nose Smith and Wesson revolver out of his right rear pocket saying, "I guess I won't need this." Hammer then gestured to me to give him a ride home as he was on probation and had to be home by 9:00 p.m.

## Rumble # 2

It was 6:40 p.m. a couple days later when Norman and Chinaman received permission to hitch a ride with me to 57th and Dudlow Streets. They exited. A small boy (Peewee size) ran towards Norman. Police sirens blasted and red police cars saturated the area from all directions. Large crowds of adult spectators gathered. The Peewee told Norman that Rex Street and Sommer Street were gathering at 57th Street. Teefco of the Mad Walkies was at 57th Street with Big Chinaman, Poofy, and the girls. Dupree from Sommer Street approached Norman shouting " Oh, yawl going to swoop (fight)?" "We gang warring, ain't we?" said Norman. Meanwhile Chinaman walked behind Dupree. Startled Dupree said, "You trying to swoop me (attack from the rear)?" Norman stated, "Leave Dupree alone, China", to which Dupree answered: "We came down to give out fair ones". Norman angrily shouted: "What made you decide to give out fair ones after the long gang war ( 2 years)?" Dupree then reported that Big monk of the Roast Gang had passed the word to come down and give out fair ones. It should be noted that Big Monk had called the gang war, but disappeared from the scene as soon as action began. However, Dupree ran to get the rest of his corner boys. Suddenly Plucky from Sommer Street appeared riding his bicycle and shouting to Norman and Chinaman, "I want both of you pussies!" Gino, of Rex Street said, "No, wait until we give out fair ones". The police sat and quietly watched. Chinaman ran through an Alley down to 57th and Harknett street. I followed Norman to Chinaman's house located in the low income housing projects. Almost immediately the streets filled with approximately 200 corner boys from Rex and Sommer Streets. Norman and Chinaman ran to Dudlow Street, and told the Roast corner boys that Sommer Street was "a million thick". The Roast Gang went into Homicide's house and came out armed with long kitchen knives and metal pipes. Norman posted gang members on each corner to watch, while Norman and Teefco took charge giving orders. Every gang stood on its corner. There was no action and then the Roast gang chased Sommer and Rex Street members. Police sirens sounded. The corner became quiet once again

## THE SEA SHORE

Arnold, Norman, June Bug, Chinaman, Eggie and I arrived in Atlantic City, New Jersey at the sea shore around 1:30 p.m. Hammer did not attend because of a pending court hearing. June Bug was new to our group and only visited the Allen's on occasion. He had managed not to belong to a gang. Mr. Allen claimed: "June Bug's more afraid of his father than any gang."

The most consistent pattern of behavior for the boys during the day was that the boys were asked to leave and/or were kicked out of every shop visited on the Boardwalk. Arnold carried Norman's swim suit under his shirt. It appeared as though the group had stolen something. The manager of the first souvenir shop walked toward us pointing his finger, but saw six of us and changed his mind. However, in the second store a sales person followed the boys around the store. Norman exclaimed, "Damn, you can't go anywhere without somebody checking you out!"

The little lady who ran the Oriental Gift Shop stated: "It's all for girls. Why don't you go outside in the fresh air and come back again."

At the Amusement Pier, Norman searched for "the baddest ride", purchased ice cream for everyone, and split a pretzel among the six of them.

After three and one half hours of walking the boardwalk, the boys sought out the beach. Temperature for the day was a high of 78 degrees. No one wished to change to go into the water, so the boys rolled up their trouser legs and chased the waves until everyone was wet and cold. Tired from the long day, the boys slept most of the way back to Philadelphia arriving home at 6:00 p.m. where Flossie was waiting to inform Norman that two visitors from rival gangs had visited--Larry and Ricky of Rex Street.

## HOSPITAL BLUES

During the two years spent with Norman, he was stabbed twice. The first incident occurred on the way home from Bartram High School. It was the last week of school, and Norman was standing near the rear of a public transportation bus when two young men questioned him: "Where you from, dude?" Norman responded his usual, "Nowhere". According to the Juvenile Aid Officer, when Norman lifted his arms above his head to grab the safety strap, one of the two men stabbed him in the chest area. The two young men then jumped off the bus and ran. Norman held his hand over the stab area until he arrived at St. Angers Hospital for treatment.

The second incident occurred early in July and was announced by Debbie, who reported that Norman was stabbed, but won't tell who stabbed him. Flossie volunteered to take me to room # 575 in the hospital. Two policemen sat outside the room. They searched the bag I was carrying before granting permission to visit Norman. Hospital room #575 housed five cases: (1) a gang member from Rex Street; (2) Norman Bus Head Allen, gang member from the Roast Gang; (3) a gang member from Bleeder Avenue; (4) an amputee; and (5) an adult citizen. The three gang members were from rival turfs, but joked with one another about gang warring. Norman described the actual fight that occurred: "It was at the end of 57$^{th}$ Street, but on the corner of 57$^{th}$. When they came up, we walked up. Tank asked Dupree for a fair one. Little Dave and Baldy started fighting. Rex Street started getting thicker and so we started backing up and they said don't back up like that. So we kept backing up. They said if you keep backing up like that we're going to charge you. So Junior started running. I was in the middle of the crowd of Sommer Street. They started running and I started running and they caught me and started stabbing me and started swooping on me too. Then they started running. The Roast came up with sticks, then I went up 57th and Dudlow and got a drink of water. They started cleaning the blood off to stop the blood from running. Then my father drove down Dudlow Street and took me to the hospital. Howard Joyson from Rex Street was the one that stabbed me.

The news of Norman's stabbing was well known in the neighborhood. Various members of the family and the community reacted:

Mr. Greenberg: most of the family is very nice, except Norman. He's a trouble maker.

Mr. Allen: I'm not going to the hospital to see Norman. I'll break his neck when he gets out.

Mrs. Allen: As long as he's my son, I'll go to see him.

Mr. Allen: I know you are going to take him whatever he wants.

Mrs. Allen: You'd better be home when I return. You'd better not take any trips across the bridge both (Willingboro, and the companionship family).

## THE HERO

On July 28, Norman was released from the hospital. He was back on the block reestablishing himself with all who watched. A young boy walked past the house. Norman shouted: "Hey boy, what you doing walking on my street?" The young boy threw his hands up in the air and said, "Go away hospital case." Meanwhile the man next door came out to wash his car. Norman again shouted loudly, "That man doesn't have to wash his car; he just wants to see what we're doing. Hey, Mr. Warner, got some new joiners—girls—got to go through the choo, choo train. Do you know what a train is, Mr. Warner." I responded, "That term has been around a long time. When is the big date?" "August 1st at Homicide's house", answered Norman. Norman then talked his mother into allowing me to drive him to the hardware store. He later admitted that he just wanted to see his corner boys. As we drove you could see large groups of boys gathering on different corners. Twenty five youngsters were at 59$^{th}$ and Pine, Osage Gang territory. Seven were at 59$^{th}$ and Harknett, Moon Turf, and four at 8$^{th}$ and Market, Roast territory.

On the way, we met Chinaman and Solo. They examined Norman's wounds. Norman acted the hero, smiled and recounted the rumble. He reported a larger group of boys at 59$^{th}$ and Harknett headed their way. Solo, Roast Gang member, displayed a large 45 caliber pistol tucked away under his shirt.

It pressed against his stomach. Solo said: "We're ready Jack". We drove another block and met Foo and Rock. Norman described Foo as the runner for the entire corner. "The runner is the supervisor. He tells you to do this or that", explained Norman. Norman reported that the Roast Gang had three guns. "Solo carries the 45; Chinaman , a zip; and Rocky loves a 38."

## Weapons for Sale

Norman: "We are trying to collect money so we could buy a shot gun for $25.00, a twelve gauge sawed-off shot gun. And we are trying to save our money for that."

Mr. Warner: "If your gang saves money to purchase a shot gun, how much will it cost?"

Norman: "Cedar Avenue (rival gang) was charging us $25.00."

Mr. Warner: "Where are they going to get a shot gun?"

Norman: "They already have one. I've seen the shot gun; they got it. They said $25.00 for it being that we're pulling (joining units) with them. The boy's house that we kept the shot gun in was raided. They (police) were looking for a stolen T.V. They had a search warrant for a stolen T.V.

and saw the pistols. They didn't have a warrant to search for the guns, but they still could take it because it was all Army surplus equipment. They said they were going to check it out to see if it belonged to the boy. The boy ran away. He's staying with my other corner boy Teefoo. We are trying to get some more stuff, because all we have now is a 38 and five 38 shells. Right now we got about $20.00; we still need $5.00 to get the pistol and everybody's hustling for it."

Mr. Warner: "Who keeps your arsenal for you?"

Norman: "Our money?"

Mr. Warner: "Not your money, weapons. For example, if you get a shot gun, where would you keep it? How would you be able to keep a shot gun in the house?"

Norman: "Anybody can take a shot gun home. Right now the boy that's holding all our weapons is Mr. Homicide. The 38 is over there now with the bullets. The shot gun is going to stay over his house. At first the 30-30 was over my house, but my mother made us clean up the house so I had to get it out of the house before we started cleaning up. So when she went to work that day, I let Teefco and Duncan take the 30-30 down the way ( to their homes). They took it to Fred's house and Fred gave it to Quinton and Little Do."

Mr. Warner: "How do your corner boys get so many weapons?"

Norman: "My corner boys in the Army and all that. They send us pieces in the mail. They take them apart and send piece by piece through the mail and all we do is put them together, but I've been there when a couple pieces have come through the mail to Mr. Homicide. We steal from the Moon. We talk about come on we going to push up to fight Sommer Street. I tell you what—since you afraid to go up—lay in the back give me the pistol and I'll go up and shoot. Then the man will come—the policeman—and everybody will break up and split up. Then I'll go home with the pistol and don't come around the way for a day or two and tell my corner boys what I did. Kept the pistol then I'll come around two days later and tell them I had just got out of jail—my mother just got me out. Then we got ourselves an extra pistol just like that."

Mr. Warner: "Who would you tell you just got out of jail?"

Norman: "I would call my corner boys on the phone and they'd get the word around Bus Head got busted (jailed) with the pistol. And then the Moon would get the word that I'd come out of jail two days later and then we got ourselves another pistol."

# NORMAN'S IMPRESSIONS
# OF THE MAD WALKIES

Norman: "All the boys that be with me all the time they made a new part for us and called it the Mad Walkies part of the corner because most of us we hang together. Every gang war that comes up we are always up in front throwing the sticks and leading off the gang war. They call me, Chinaman, Hammer, Two Two, Dutch, Teefco, Duncan, and Cook (his new name is Suicide) the Mad Walkies.

Monday about 7 oclock 55th and Sommer came down Larch Street. Seven of us were standing on the corner. Sommer Street came about a good 20 thick at first, chased us down halfway to Stillman Street calling us a whole bunch of names about our gang war and do we want to call it off, And then Walkie Two Two called out, 'No, we are not calling it off'. And stuff like that. We picked up sticks ; we were fighting in the middle of the street, and started throwing bricks and stuff. We all ran and grabbed pipes off the strip.. Some boy named Gino from the next street he said the Coast can't rumble, you know. They do say that in curse words. Then my corner boys they call them Major Walkies up there just to show off. Then I walked up there and picked up a pipe and I started slinging at Rick, 55<sup>th</sup> and Sommer. He threw our pipes down. We were just trying to show off in front of the girls because you know they came up our way. So we had on leather jackets, short cut leather jackets. We wear short leather jackets and railroad hats—Lee railroad hats. We threw them off in the middle of the street. And someone said 'They're crazy, they're going crazy, they're snapping' and all that. So we started chasing with our bare fists and ran up Arch Street and then around the corner come a whole bunch more about 40 more. They started standing in the middle of the street. Then the Juvenile Aid came, all of them came. We ran, we split up and met back up on 54<sup>th</sup> and Hampson Street, everybody during that time I was in the street sounding my name. Someone threw a pipe and I turned around and ducked and the pipe hit me in the back of my head and my head was bleeding away. Then Dupree from Sommer Street busted a bottle and came charging at me and I had my hand up open swinging and I blocked one of his. He came real fast and cut my eye a little bit. My eye was bleeding a little bit. I went to one of my girl's houses. They took care of my eye.

That night we went to the State store. I put on my Lee hat and put my collar up a little higher and they put a little dirt on me. I had on a yellow silk shirt and they dirtied that up and I pretended I'd just come in off of work. I walked in the State Store and bought two halves of Tiger Rose for our corner."

## THE RUNNER'S FATHER

Mr. Warner: "Why were you watching the gang fight when you told me earlier that you were the runner, the main man. Why didn't you let somebody else do that?"

Norman: "Because everybody else was in the lot drinking on 58$^{th}$ and Gilbert. Ham and me and Chinaman are the only ones who don't drink. So I told them I would stand on Gilbert Street and watch which way Sommer Street was coming and call them."

Mr. Warner: "Do your corner boys respect you if they know you don't drink? You're not doing the same thing your corner boys are doing, so why should they respect you?"

Norman: "Really, because I have more heart (courage) than they do. They say they get high so they can tell a girl off if the girl doesn't cooperate with them. I told them I wasn't getting high because if I get drunk and be going ziggety zag down the street and Sommer Street comes I can't run and won't know what I'm doing. They'll catch me and I'll be a dead man. My reputations too big to be playing with wine and marijuana and get all doped up and Sommer Street put a sneak attack on us like they did before."

Mr. Warner: "You say your rep is big, but at the same time you said your corner boys said that maybe they're going to have to do something about your daddy."

Norman: "If I'm not there I have nothing to do with it. They said they're going to move on him, because of the time he caught them in my house. He beat me up with his fists. They were standing on the porch. They started to move on him. They asked me that next night and I said no. One of the most liked corner boys is me. Every time something happens around here they come and tell me. At first they were going to move on him. But Mr. Homicide said they were going to shoot him the next time he came on 58th Street. I told them no. He knows the Roast don't dig on him and he's probably put me some place I don't want to be (jail). He knows the Roast don't like him. He tries to keep me in the house. The only time I can get out is after school or last week (public transportation strike). He thinks I might get into trouble in the street. They know that everybody out in the street is trouble."

## Rapping, Rapping, Rapping

Because both parents worked during the day, the Allen home became a gathering place for friends and gang members.. A typical "rap" session included such topics as gangs and sex. A typical rap session was as follows:

Norman: "Here comes Crazy T (Corner Avenue Gang); we were play gang warring them."

Crazy-T: "I quit. They tried to get me in the face. I quit them all."

Norman: "You didn't quit?"

Crazy-T: "All but one, Pine Street. I have to have some protection, but no more front lines. I said, I'll be right back. One more thing made me quit. I was running behind a dude from the Syndicate. He got shot. All I heard was my feet running. I looked back—dude was laid out on Hampson Street."

Mr. Warner: "Who from Rex Street got you Norman?"

Norman: "Gino.They (police) said if I press charges on Gino, we're going to jail because Chinaman said we were gang warring."

Crazy-T: "Sticks are nothing."

Norman: "Ain't nobody using them anymore. I see you come down here to play gang warring."

Crazy-T: "That's just something to keep the blood up."

Norman: "But you're still a chewy ( spray painter) aren't you Tee"

Crazy-T: "Only reason I want to give it up. I ain't got no pay for it. It's that money I got to get into. You better learn until you get folded up in a box (killed)."

Norman: "Still somebody's going to be slick and get you. They know you're from somewhere."

(Al Ski arrives at the house.)

Norman: "You get hurt again?"

Al Ski: "I'm just coming from the hospital. Ain't nothing happening (points to his shoulder) . I came to see you at St. Angers Hospital. They wouldn't let me in. They treat you so rough. I got three bullets in me. I most have got about fifteen needles a day."

Norman: "When I had a tube in me, the doctor came in pulling the tube saying,' Does this hurt?' I said, "Wait a minute, take your hands off the pipe first. I went in for a chest x-ray—didn't get my chest up. This big heavy nurse stomped on my feet, Boom. My chest went up. I took a deep breath."

Crazy-T: "What got you in the arm?" (examining Norman's arm)

Norman: "Oh, it's all right. It's kind of

174

sloppy though" (referring to stitches).

Al Ski: "I saw Red Dog from the Empire at the Day Treatment Center". (juvenile detention center).

Crazy-T: "They keep a steady broken arm limp like position of the arm when walking or strolling."

Al ski: "You should see them coming in from North Philly. Norman:

" What gang runs the whole treatment center?"

Al Ski: "I don't know."

Norman: "Who's the thickest (largest membership)?"

Three girls walk past the house. Crazy-T leaves following the girls

Norman: "They're all Flossie types (very thin legs)."

Crazy-T: (returned) "Those dudes from the Empire catch more toilet seats. They tried to drown a dude in the toilet."

Norman: "I want Rex Street. They tried to get Arnold in the alley. They made him take off all his clothes."

Crazy-T: "I don't dig all that sex stuff, Bus Head, you could be a fighter, if you could box."

Al Ski: (Referring to Norman's wounds) "You caught a bad break, Bus."

Ding: "You caught a good one—look "(points to Norman's rear end).

Crazy-T and Al Ski shout at one another and began boxing.

Crazy-T:" I'm too fast!"

Al Ski: "Let's go to the body."

Crazy-T: "I can't stand for no big n.... like you.'

Prior to the last gang war, Chinaman had been a constant companion of Norman. When Chinaman appeared at the Allen's with his dog, Norman exclaimed: "Chinaman, you're a punk!" Norman constantly accused Chinaman of running out on the Mad Walkies whenever a fight started. Chinaman was finally put out of the gang and only allowed to return at the suggestion of Arnold , Norman's brother.

Norman: "You (Chinaman) always lag behind and then when the action starts, you're a run out. That's why you don't belong to the Mad Walkies anymore. Remember when Osage questioned me. I looked around and you had your face in your hands. I looked again and you were running across the bridge."

Hammer: "I'm ashamed of you leaving the corner in front of Sneeze, especially Sneeze.'

Norman: "He's a run out! I kicked him out."

Arnold: "Why, you're always picking on China. Give him a box so he can rejoin.

Yeh, and box me too!"

Norman and Chinaman boxed. Norman was clearly the aggressor.

Norman: "Why do you always swing and miss?"

Chinaman continued to take the barrage of heavy blows. Next Hammer joined the boxing match, saying: "You want it in the head or body?" Thus one by one, Chinaman received a heavy barrage of blows from Norman, Hammer Head, and even Arnold. At one point even little Mary, age three, counted the blows: "Six, seven, eight, nine, ten". They exchanged blows off and on for nearly ninety minutes until Norman finally announced, "I'm tired". This same method was used to draft other youngsters into the Mad Walkies.

Thus two solid years of life passed as I lived and interacted with the Roast Gang and its subdivision under the leadership of Norman "Bus Head" Allen. Volumes can still be written concerning the Allen Family, its interaction with the streets and the complexities of a companionship family hosted by Mr. Allen in his confusion about the moral compass associated with being a man. Yet, both families and all siblings managed to survive the high degree of everyday uncertainty while living primarily in the heart of an urban ghetto. The energized environment of the city of Philadelphia provided the realistic backdrop for the family to deal with and cope with the in-depth heightened uncertainty that invaded their every action.

The Allen's lived at the edge of an urban ghetto. They were a Black family involved in a struggle for existence that required both parents to work, and to leave a major part of their children's education to the "academies of the streets". The streets in turn flourished with active, violent gang activity, female dominated households and increased crime rates. Yet in spite of all the external forces that impinged upon the Allen household, they managed to keep the family together, They had developed a tolerance for ambiguity and uncertainty.

Norman was a known gang member. The family was uncertain as to the full consequences of the son's gang activity. Would Norman be arrested again or killed outright on the streets. Could he come home unharmed each night? Would he be hospitalized for a third time in a single year? Each family member reacted in their own way, causing an uncertain emotional warmth to radiate around Norman and his gang activities. Norman, in turn, found satisfying relationships within the structure of the Roast Gang's subdivision, The Mad Walkies. However, his status as gang leader was always uncertain as he had to beat every member of the gang to maintain his position. Yet, unlike Norman's immediate family and companionship family roles, the structure within the gang was clear. Norman was the leader of his gang; status and respect was afforded him at every level.

They supported one another even in fights. Norman in turn could be as aggressive as he liked without an authority figure (Mr. Allen) interfering. The gang then was a social system entirely to itself and separated from the ambivalent patterns that existed in the immediate family. Little or no need existed to explain his behavior in the gang. As leader Norman was in charge of accepting or rejecting members. Interestingly, the subtleties of interpersonal relationships existing within the gang did not require the same heightened intellectual capacity for problem solving and goal achievement as in the immediate family. The means of achieving within the gang was clearly stated. The means of achieving within the immediate family was complicated and rendered unconquerable by such givens as age, financial status, and length of time with the family. [2]

# Chapter Five
## THE TRUE REVOLUTION

**Vietnam Protest March**

The 1960's were characterized by several interesting events: barefoot Bikila, an Ethiopian won the gold medal in a major marathon race; Wilma Rudolph, winner of three gold medals was diagnosed with scarlet fever; J.F. Kennedy and Richard Nixon held the first televised presidential debate; Chubby Checker, entertainer, did the twist; Roger Maris broke Babe Ruth's batting record; Yuri Gagarin, Russian astronaut, orbited the earth, followed by John Glenn, an American one year later; Wilt the Stilt Chamberlain established an all time basketball record; Marilyn Monroe, movie star, died; Jackie Robinson was inducted into the baseball Hall of Fame; V. Tereshkova became the first woman to orbit the earth; Ronald McDonald was created; the Washington March featuring Rev. Dr. Martin Luther King attracted over 200,000 participants; President John F. Kennedy was assassinated; Beatlemania hit New York, Casius Clay( Muhammad Ali) defeated Sonny Liston for the world heavy weight boxing championship; The Civil Rights Bill was passed; the U.S. Government declared " smoking is harmful"; President Lyndon Johnson won the election; The cartoon character Peanuts became popular and Twiggy, an English fashion model arrived on the scene; Vietnam protest marches occurred; The east coast experienced a blackout; Batman became a television fixture; A woman entered the Boston Marathon; The creator of Mickey Mouse died as did Trigger the Lone Ranger's horse; The Apollo rocket caught on fire killing three astronauts; The first Super Bowl was initiated; The first human organ transplant took place; Violence erupted at the Democratic National Convention and Richard Nixon won the Presidential election; Jackie Kennedy married Aristotle Onassis; The first black woman was elected to congress; A couple engaged for 67 years finally married; Woodstock rocked; Apollo II landed on the moon and soldiers were drafted for participation in the Vietnam War. Meanwhile musical tunes such as *Raindrops Keep Falling on My Head, Born to Be Wild, Hello Dolly, Come Together, Leaving On A Jet Plane* became popular tunes in America.

None of the events mentioned above however masked the advent of Freedom Riders, sit-ins at lunch counters in Greensboro, North Carolina, sometimes violent resistance to the desegregation of schools, the deaths of civil rights workers M. Schwerner, A. Goodman, John Cheney, the bombing of homes of civil rights workers, setting 24 Black churches on fire, the Los Angeles riot, riots in Cleveland, Ohio, and Chicago, Illinois and the consequent long hot summers of wondering and rioting in the midst of national outcries of "Black Power". Nevertheless, Charles Askew and I stayed busily involved with the Delaware Fair Housing Council, volunteering at the West Philadelphia Community School, and picketing Girard College, an all boy's school at the time, that refused admission to black students. We also participated in the Washington March and later Vietnam Protest marches.

The Washington March was of special interest to me, because I had had the pleasure of personally meeting the Rev. Dr. Martin Luther King,Jr. at the Salem Baptist Church in Jenkintown, Pennsylvania. Jenkintown is located approximately 35 miles north

183

of center city Philadelphia in what is considered the suburbs. It was in this town that I worked at the Strawbridge and Clothier Department store immediately following high school graduation. While living in Philadelphia and Gulph Mills I maintained my attendance and membership at Salem Baptist Church, where I sang on the senior choir and served as editor of the Salem Messenger. The pastor, Rev. Dr. Robert Johnson Smith was very progressive , plus unlike most Baptist preachers I knew, he could deliver a powerful sermon in fifteen minutes and engage the congregation in the necessary gospel to impact their lives on a daily basis. Several guest speakers had been privileged to address our congregation including Rev. M. L. King's father "Daddy King" as he was affectionately known, Maynard Jackson, Mayor of Atlanta, Georgia and several other important personages of the day. Fortunately, I had been requested to introduce several of the guest speakers and Dr. King was one of them. Dr. King joined us following the riots in Cleveland where he had recently spoken. I was an early fan of his, because his speaking talents were unsurpassed, and he advocated change through non-violent means. There were very clear divisions between the statements, educational direction and overall thrust of Malcolm X and Dr. King. Dr. King advocated integration of society though non-violence, while Malcolm X approved of integration, but not without social and economic equality. Malcolm X also advocated our right to self defense by any means possible, as the American Constitution guaranties the right to bear arms. Dr. King's posited: "We must not stop with the cultivation of a tough mind. The gospel demands a tender heart". [1] Malcolm X, a disciple of Elijah Muhammad (Elijah Poole), closely aligned himself with the beliefs and tenets of the Nation of Islam and developed a two pronged attack on the problems of the masses: (1) strive for economic independence, and (2) strive to recover an acceptable black identity focusing on a "Do for self" rallying cry, hard work, frugality, avoidance of debt and self improvement. Within the Nation there had been established over 100 Temples, plus bank ownership, farms, trailer trucks and a printing press. They actively recruited in prisons and on ghetto streets. Especially prevalent at the time was Elijah Muhammad's book *Message to the Black Man in America* which clearly advocated that the white man is a devil by nature.

When Dr. King spoke to the Salem Baptist Church congregation, several other persons and organizations were prevalent and their views were widely known. For example, the Black Panthers received quite a bit of publicity, especially Eldridge Cleaver's book, *Soul on Ice*, and the forth coming battle cry expostulating that if you are not a part of the solution then you are a part of the problem. Meanwhile the Student Nonviolent Coordinating Committee (S.N.C.C.), the Congress of Racial Equality (C.O.R.E.), the National Association for the Advancement of Colored People (N.A.A.C.P.) and James Farmer's American Democratic party all influenced public perceptions of the civil rights movement while H. Rap Brown carried his "rap" to smaller audiences in Camden, New Jersey. Always the Philadelphia Civil Disobedience squad photographed us as we attended the various rallies. The one exception was when the National Democratic Party participated in the democratic convention in Atlantic City, New Jersey. Charlie Askew and I joined the pickets and sat in on the board walk in Atlantic City while the convention members voted to allow Mississippi full membership and privileges into the Democratic National Party. This was my first view of the quiet reserved James Farmer, who was rumored to be a part of the brains behind the civil rights movement closely associated with Dr, King. And so when Dr. King spoke, he was for those of us in the North another preacher man with a message to be heard, and perhaps dismissed until the importance of the now historical Washington March commanded our senses. More importantly, much to my surprise, I was invited to dinner after church with Dr. King and others at the home of the Stanleys in the Germantown section of Philadelphia. As we sat for dinner in the dining room area, I remember clearly the humor expressed by Dr. King, who smiled and sometimes laughed at the many tough situations he had experienced since his entry into the battle for freedom, after his acceptance as Pastor at the Dexter

Avenue Baptist Church. How I wish now that I had taken the time to question and probe his brilliant mind. Little did I realize that I was in the midst of history in the making.

Four to five months after Dr. King spoke at Salem Baptist Church, the Washington March was organized. Communities, churches and other organizations throughout the United States were establishing means of transportation to Washington, D.C.; however, my home town buddy Albert Robbins and I decided to drive the four hour distance to the capitol. We also decided to travel during the night and early morning hours, because reports were rampant in the local press about youth who were throwing bricks at black motorists from the bridges under which one had to drive. This was before the advent of high safety railings and fences that now adorn our bridges. Therefore, we took turns driving and actually arrived at the area near the Washington Monument just as the sun was beginning to appear. It was a very lonely place and no one else was in sight, not even the uniformed park rangers that we were later to observe. Knowing that water would be scarce, we had packed a large bag of grapes to sustain us during the day, as with grapes we would have both fluids and substance. We hoped we would be fortunate not to have to go to the bathroom during the rally. In fact we had eaten as much as our bodies could withstand at the last rest stop, where we ate our prepared sandwiches and used the bushes at the side of the road to relieve ourselves. Fortunately for us no other travelers were around to observe our behavior.            Once we arrived at the Monument, we climbed up the hill to the base of the monument and stood overlooking the grassy knoll. At approximately 8:00 a.m. the first bus arrived and unloaded, then small figures began to approach the grassy knoll. Slowly, the people arrived suddenly coming from all directions, north, east, south and west searching out a place to randomly stand awaiting directions. By eleven o'clock the grass had all but disappeared and was now filled with human beings of all colors and persuasions. Then around noon, we noticed a platform and several microphones had been placed in an area distanced from where we stood watching the throng of human beings engaging themselves in conversations, meeting and greeting various strangers. Suddenly the March organizers began to speak to give the masses of people directions for the day. A. Philip Randolph spoke reminding us of our past history. He also reflected upon the Pullman Porter unions and his work on their behalf. Other entertainers were present, Charlton Heston the movie star who had played the role of Moses in the movies. Lena Horne sang as did Harry Belafonte, Peter, Paul and Mary and others too numerous to remember. Finally, we were given direction to assemble for the march where we were to join hands and march about twenty abreast from the Washington Monument to the Lincoln Memorial. Al Robbins and I joined the march, and I locked arms with a young man who was a Jewish student from a Synagogue in Ohio. We marched hand in hand singing, "We Shall Overcome," and "O Freedom". [2]

As we marched arm in arm linked together in love, I glanced upwards to the top of the buildings we passed, and noticed armed men with rifles at the ready. I assume they were present to quell any perceivable disturbance, but none existed. After one or two short miles we arrived at the reflecting lake at the base of the Lincoln Memorial. There we broke ranks and gathered around the rectangular shaped reflecting pool. One could see the speakers platform from below, so Al and I climbed the steps of the Lincoln Memorial until we were positioned directly across and one level below where Dr. King was to render his now famous *"I Have a Dream"* speech. After several introductions and upbeat rallying cries, the Rev. Dr. Martin Luther King appeared flanked by several people from his organization, plus uniformed park guards. The roar of the 200,000 marchers became evident for this was our defining moment. Dr. King eloquently began his forceful, soul rendering *"I Have A Dream"* speech. As I had followed his travels throughout the United States, some of words were familiar as portions had been spoken in Chicago and at our church in Jenkintown, but then the crescendo and rhythmic patterns began to change. It was as though a word dancer had suddenly appeared, and I dubbed him "Bojangles of the tongue". He was

189

masterfully eloquent, and as he spoke you could hear the echo and reechoing of the crowd, applauding and cheering around and across the reflecting lake. I observed people perched in the trees applauding and shouting as Dr, King so ably spoke of Look Out Mountain in Tennessee, the hilltops of New Hampshire, the mountains of New York, the Alleghenies of Pennsylvania, the Rockies of Colorado, the mountain peaks of California, the hills and molehills of Mississippi and other geographical locations across the United States where we must "let freedom ring" and "speed up the day to freedom". It was a moment of resurrection similar to the biblical explanation of the Pentecost event when all were in one accord speaking in different tongues understood by all.

Reflecting back to 1963, one might question, "Who was this man?" Who was this man who organized a year long boycott, and successfully achieved the integration of buses in Montgomery, Alabama (1955) after Rosa Parks, a 42 year old seamstress refused to give up her seat to a white passenger on a city bus? Who was this man who inspired non-violent protests ending segregation, motivating hundreds of thousands-black, white, young and old to participate in lunch counter sit-ins, freedom marches and freedom rides to achieve equal treatment for all people in hospitals, restaurants, libraries and schools? Who was this man who prompted the largest civil rights demonstration in history as an estimated

250,000 marchers of all races, and religions assembled at the nation's capital requesting civil rights, jobs and freedom for all? (1963) Who was this man who was awarded the Nobel Peace Prize (1964) for creating positive social change through nonviolent means, thus a symbol for world peace? Who was this man who campaigned to help poor people, to draw attention to the need for decent housing, health care and education? Who was this man whose life was snuffed out by an assassin's bullet (April 4, 1968), shortly before he was to lead a planned protest march with the Memphis, Tennessee sanitation workers?

Some say he was just an ordinary man, and even today history records his activities under the general topic of civil rights leader. It is true that when James Earl Ray, the assassin, fired the 30.06 bullet that shattered the right side of his jaw, hit the top of his trachea and moved downward severing the spinal chord and causing instantaneous death, that Dr. king was just an ordinary man. He bled and died like ordinary men do. It is true that when the doctors at St. Joseph's Hospital in Memphis, Tennessee removed the Nobel Peace Prize watch from his wrist, made the classical v-shaped incision across his upper body, and peeled back the skin from his body to remove and examine his inner parts, that Dr. king was just an ordinary man. Even prior to this when the sheriffs of the south and the police chiefs of the north lined the streets with police dogs and fire hoses, it is true that Martin Luther King displayed moments of fear and apprehension . It is true that like ordinary men and women, he deeply loved his family, was fearful of pain, became tired and weary traveling from state to state, from Atlanta to Detroit, to Philadelphia, to Tennessee and back to Birmingham. From that stand point, he was just an ordinary man. However, from the moment J. F. Blake, the bus driver in Montgomery, Alabama, told the then 42 year old seamstress Rosa Parks to change her seat on a crowded city bus—from the moment Rosa Parks said "No", this ordinary preacher man became extraordinary, attracting world wide attention to the inhuman dignities suffered by blacks in America. From that moment forward, the world would be forever changed.

Perhaps one of Dr. King's greatest speeches centered on what he called "the drum major instinct" or the individual desire in man to be out front, to lead the parade, to be important, to be in a position to achieve distinction. [3] He viewed this as a dominant instinct in humankind. He said that out of the drum major instinct racial problems arise, accompanied by notions of superiority. Out of the drum major instinct the struggle between nations to gain and obtain supremacy over others arises. Dr. King believed that the greatest among us is not he who achieves recognition and attention, but he who serves his fellow man. He wished to be remembered as a drum major for justice, peace, and righteousness. "If I can help somebody, then my living will not be in vain".

In another little known event Dr. King described an incident in New York city where while autographing his first book, a woman approached the table and questioned, "Are you Martin Luther King, Jr.?" He answered "Yes" and immediately felt a beating in his chest. He had been stabbed, and was rushed to a Harlem hospital. X-rays indicated that the tip of the blade barely missed the main heart artery, the aorta. The New York Times printed an article stating that if he had sneezed, he would have died. While convalescing and reviewing his mail and telegrams from all over the world, Dr. King opened a letter written by a student from the White Plains High School. It read:

"Dear Dr. King,

I am a ninth grade student at White Plains High school. While it should not matter, I would like to mention that I'm a white girl. I read in the paper of your misfortune and of your suffering. I read that if you had sneezed you would have died. I'm simply writing you to say that I am so happy you did not sneeze."

Dr. King reportedly stated, "I too am happy I didn't sneeze, because if I had sneezed, I wouldn't have been around in 1960 when students all over the south started sitting in at lunch counters. If I had sneezed, I would not have participated in the ride for freedom (1961) ending segregation in interstate travel. If I had sneezed, I wouldn't have seen Negroes in Albany, Georgia straighten their backs up. Whenever men and women straighten their backs up, they are going somewhere, because a man can't ride your back unless it's bent." [4]

I firmly believe that if Martin Luther King were alive today, he would have us remember some of the black and white men and women who sacrificed their lives in the struggle for civil rights: James E. Cheyney, Michael H. Schwerner, Andrew Goodman, Viola Liuzzo, William L. Moore, Medgar Evers, Reverend James Reeb, Jimmy Lee Jackson. He would have us remember that he was an educated man; that he was conversant with the great minds of the ages-Plato, Aristotle, Einstein, Galileo, and Euripides. He would remind us that material goods are but temporary and can be repossessed, but no one can take away your dreams. He would ask that we love one another, and that we not destroy our frail bodies with cocaine, marijuana and amphetamines. He would ask that we prepare well for the world of work and higher learning. He would ask that women say "No" to men who would use and abuse them. He would ask that we end the cycle of children having children, that the family unit be strengthened and that we take pride in who and what we are, He would ask that we improve our minds and our self image within our communities, the nation and the world. He would remind our children that anyone who can recite the lyrics of Stevie Wonder, Beyonce, Janet Jackson and Justin Timberlake has the ability to recite Shakespeare, to build another Colossus at Rhodes or Lighthouse of Alexandria, to again make beautiful the Hanging Gardens at Babylon. Finally he would ask that we make real a new symphony extolling the brotherhood of man.

The Washington March was not my final participation in protesting the rights and wrongs of this country that I love dearly. Even though African Americans have endured centuries of hardship and inhuman treatment in this country, America is still the best country in the world to achieve success and happiness, no matter how limited the opportunity or sophisticated the forces, invisible and visible, that would deny us the full privileges of citizenship. Just as Dr. King spoke out against the Vietnam War and Muhammad Ali refused involvement on religious grounds, Jules Levy and I found time to participate in two anti Vietnam War marches in Washington, D.C. Jules Levy was an art instructor at John Bartram High School. He was well read, highly literate and somewhat a scholar conversant with English literature. He was also fascinated by some of the poets I loved i.e. Yeats, Hopkins, Browning etc. We often had long conversations about the plight of humankind, while we shared remembrances of past deeds. I was committed never to serve in the armed services again as expressed in the following poem I authored after the Korean War:

## Patriotism Revisited

In war, all men die!
Some live only to die again,
While stubbornly remembering
The moment when death struck
The trench line clean, but allowed
An escape hole for squeamish
Patriotic wimps to slip through
Into a destiny of unrealized tomorrows,
Our conscious killing was unconsciously
Emotionless. Whatever moved or stood
Booby trapped in dung-strawed villages
Was annihilated without remorse---men,
Women, children—all gooks in padded,
Musty uniforms.
Would God pleasure me to kill again?
Is my theology, my belief, my love
Strong enough to resist the urge,
The patriotic yearning to procrastinate
That God allows evil.
Even evil may appear unblemishingly
Perfect, as we force our wills,
Dispositions beyond what God has intended.
The next time I die, I shall uphold God's
Commandment to love mine enemies,
Then, I will be free and wholly God-like.

In other words, never again will I become an unthinking killing machine, as I was during the Korean War; thus I protested alone among hundreds of others. Only this time the crowd was quite different. Very few minorities were present. Conversations were sparse, intelligent, but the logic of speech was almost meaningless. We waited; we heard rallying speeches; we waved plaque cards prepared by various agencies and then departed to our separate ways. Nevertheless, we made our statement, and the sense of internal pleasure in participating in an activity that required self commitment and unselfish courage was worth the trip. Twice we protested Jules and I, while the war droned on rendering its capable veterans somewhat crippled and maimed from participating in yet another war to end all wars. Even today I as drive past veterans begging for handouts at the exits of our Florida highways, I am angered by the incessant inability of leaders of all nations to forge peaceful relationships. Still I recall the Marine Corps general speaking to the troops as we waited to board the troop ship to Korea stating, "A little war is better than none at all."

Now that I am very mature (in age only), I wonder why we continue to march. How sad and debilitating it is to have to continue to march in this America for which I was once willing to give up my life in the pursuit of unrealized dreams. How sad! Sad, because some thirty years after the Washington March, I found myself participating in yet another protest gathering in Washington, D.C.. What saddened me most was that this time I walked with my three adult children. It was the Million Man March spearheaded by Minister Louis Farrakhan. Oddly enough, I gave great thought to participating in this gathering of one million men, because I am not a disciple of the Muslim Movement; nor do I condone the philosophies of the Honorable Elijah Muhammad who calls for the hatred of all white people in his book *Message to the Blackman In America*. On the jacket cover of the book *Reader's Digest* commented: "This mild looking man is…the most powerful Blackman in America. He offers a new way of life. Muhammad prompts even his severest critics to agree when he says he attacks 'traditional reasons the Negro race is weak'. The *New York Times* magazine stated: "…It is worth remembering that what Elijah Muhammad is doing to the Negro is, in a sense, what America has done to the immigrant from Europe". However, this same Muhammad wrote: "What can the guilty say when the truth of their guilt is made known?....The origin of sin, the origin of murder, the origin of lying are deceptions originated with the creators of evil and injustice –the white race. I am sick, tired and worn out with sufferings from the persecutions against me and my people by the hands of the most wicked and deceiving race that ever lived on the planet" [5]

One can assume that the so called white press had not thoroughly read the book that they felt was so promising for the Negro race, or maybe they just didn't care as long as The Nation of Islam stayed within its own segregated confines and Temples. However, even Malcolm X, formerly known as Detroit Red, who was recruited as a Muslim in a State prison in Massachusetts, finally found it necessary in 1964, after surviving a three month penalty of silence, to break from the Nation of Islam and left the movement. Meanwhile Minister Louis X (Louis Farrakhan) took over Harlem Temple #7 and eventually became the new Muhammad after the assassination of Malcolm X at the Audubon Ballroom in Harlem February 21, 1965. Therefore, knowing all these things, it was difficult to support a rally and march by an organization that advocated hatred of a given people. Many of the philosophies espoused by the Nation of Islam were contrary to my Christian beliefs. I weighed the pros and cons of attending the Million Man March, but because the focus was on family I decided to go. The issue of the disintegrating family and the high rate of divorce in America, plus the growing disproportionate number of black men and women in our prisons weighed heavily and still does. Therefore, I located a bus group in one of the neighboring cities, Asbury Park, New Jersey, and rode to Washington accompanied by my son Thomas. We planned to meet my son Nicolas and my daughter Beth in Washington during the march. Thanks to the modern invention of cell phones, we were able to communicate and meet at designated places along the march. Even though the march was designated for men, my daughter Beth, an astute psychologist, marches to her own drummer and insisted on being present. My son Thomas, a systems engineer and Program Manager at Lockheed Martin, completed a grid analysis after the march and assured me that over a million people attended the march. Nevertheless, I was totally saddened by the march. In my own head I kept thinking about the fact that I thought the Martin Luther King Washington March would solve all our problems forever. How naïve was I. Now I was marching again, but this time with family members representing a younger generation experiencing prejudices and sophisticated quotas systems of a different scope and sequence. Little did we know that affirmative action programs would soon give way to the indefinable outcry for a nebulous almost meaningless term called diversity. Diversity councils would spring up across America in an effort to define who and what they are, with futile attempts to measure whether or not the work place could be defined under the tenuous objectives developed by committees without a state or national model to hold them accountable.

The Million Man March was indeed a well planned and organized event. Our bus was directed to its parking area by uniformed members of the Nation of Islam. They were at every conceivable cross road directing and ushering the people in a commendable manner. If anyone mistakenly dropped a piece of paper, a member was there to immediately swoop it up out of sight. Marvelously disciplined and immaculately attired, the members assured the safety of all marchers. It was difficult reaching the area where the stage was located. Many notables were on the platform; however, the speeches were long and sometimes uninviting as we awaited the presence of Mr. Farrakhan. When Mr. Farrakhan finally began his speech it was late into the afternoon, and we were somewhat weary from our bus trip. We listened for the first fifteen minutes, and then started to find our way back to the bus by slowly weaving through the crowd. The entire time we were walking you could hear the speech. In fact while we were driving homeward, we tuned in on our portable radio to the rest of the speech while on the bus. As anyone knows Mr. Farrakhan can speak for hours without taking a break. It had been a glorious empowering event just to witness so many members of the African American community coming together in one accord and in singleness of purpose. However, the most endearing moment for me was when a bus loaded with school children passed us as we walked to our bus. Several students leaned out the window of their school bus and shouted, "Thank you for coming". I shall always remember their shout, and will always cherish that one singular moment when these young people recognized that there exists in life a greater promise and respect for the ideas, philosophies and actions of humankind. Their shouts of "Thank you" was my resurrection and assurance that all was somehow or other right with the world—at least for that moment.

Thus, Mozelle Willis Warner's son, Pete, a nobody searching to become somebody, had lived through and participated in one of the most captivating historical times within the development of this great nation called The United States of America. No one called me Pete anymore for I had become Dr. Donald D. Warner, graduate par excellence from The Pennsylvania State University. If only my guidance counselors could see me now. I'm not the carpenter or field hand they advised me to become. Instead I have sought out and achieved three advanced degrees in education and a fourth from the prestigious Princeton Theological Seminary. Along the way I had met and interacted with future basketball stars Wilt Chamberlain, Kareem Jabar (Moylan Recreation Center), Earl the Pearl Monroe( John Bartram High School) , boxers Mohammed Ali (Miami , Florida), Michael Spinks, comedian William Cosby( Temple University and the Underground Club), singers, Teddy Pendergrass, Harold Melvin and the Blue Notes ( Moylan Recreation Center), Patti Labelle (John Bartram High School). Indeed, a true revolution!

# Chapter Six
## FATE, TIME, OCCASION, CHANCE, CHANGE

I f as Percy Bysshe Shelly wrote: " …all things are subject [to] fate, time, occasion chance and change ", then the time arrived when, again, I was led to seek a different kind of agony and a newer, more defined and determined resurrection. [1] Therefore, I applied for three administrative positions, the first in Ann Arbor, Michigan, the second in Trenton, New Jersey, and the third in Willingboro, New Jersey. All three applications were for the position of high school principal. I was invited to apply for the Ann Arbor position by a former Philadelphia colleague, Dr. Fred Holliday, who had accepted a recent promotion there as School Superintendent. At the time, Ann Arbor was touted as a very progressive school system; however, it presented personal challenges in terms of totally uprooting the family and moving a long distance from our Pennsylvania roots. On the other hand Trenton Public Schools were closer to home, and similar to Philadelphia in its urban setting and educational challenges.

Much to my surprise Willingboro High School also needed a principal, and I was somewhat familiar with the town given my recent travels and study of gang leader Norman "Bus Head" Allen and his family. The community was undergoing rapid changes in growth, and the high school was on a split shift as had been John Bartram High School in Philadelphia, where I was employed for the past twelve years. Fortunately, as time and fate would have it, I applied for all three positions, and was eventually accepted as the number one choice candidate at all three locations. Eventually, I accepted Willingboro, primarily because they made the first offer, followed by Trenton and, lastly, Ann Arbor, Michigan. At the time my preference was the Michigan position because I knew the superintendent personally, plus the system differed greatly from the socio-political bureaucracies that I survived in Philadelphia. However, Willingboro made the first contact and presented an early occasion to meet with a committee of citizens, the superintendent and finally the Board of Education. In addition, Willingboro's school population was 87% white, and I became its first African American high school principal.

Almost one week after accepting the position and signing a contract with Willingboro, Ann Arbor, Michigan contacted me followed by Trenton, New Jersey three weeks after Ann Arbor. In fact the Trenton Board was so disturbed by my decision to seek employment elsewhere, that I took the time to meet with them to explain. Needless to say, I was thrilled to relocate my family and begin anew in a school system extremely concerned about its changing demographics, and a potential gang problem which few citizens understood. At the time, my self confidence was very high as I had successfully managed split shift scheduling, worked closely with street gangs and possessed decent interpersonal skills necessary to working with students, staff, parents and community.

Interestingly on my acceptance of the position in Willingboro, New Jersey, the *Philadelphia Evening Bulletin* printed a newspaper article authored by Claude Lewis on Wednesday, September 22, 1971 which read:

### *"SIGNS of PROGRESS in WILLINGBORO*

Too often we spend so much time complaining about the injustices in our lives that we overlook the signs of progress which exist right under our noses.

Take Willingboro, N.J., for instance. Once it was a hotbed of racial hostility, making headlines almost daily over a controversy based on color. A dozen years ago, Willingboro, then known as Levittown, was proud of its all white community. But through court rulings –and experience— attitudes changed dramatically. And no where has the new posture been more apparent than in the town's school system.

A week ago, the community of 50,000 (11% non-white) saw a black man get the job of principal of its only high school with neither fuss nor fanfare. 'I think it is a demonstration of a town's growth', said Donald D, Warner, principal of John F. Kennedy High School. 'It would appear to be an endorsement of America's promise to allow a qualified man of any color to rise in the system based strictly on his ability.'

Warner, an affable 38 year-old has assumed the top job at 'Kennedy' where the student population of 2700 is 87% white. The faculty is even whiter with less than a dozen black instructors on a staff of approximately 155.

'I came to do a job', Warner said in his office recently. 'I'm satisfied and gratified that the Board and the superintendent saw fit to judge me strictly on my background and my ability. It was a new and different feeling.'

A Pennsylvanian, Warner was vice

principal at Bartram H. S. in Philadelphia and has been an educator for twelve years. He beat out 84 other applicants for the position at Kennedy and expects to receive his Ph.D. next June.

Superintendent of Schools Dr. Peter J. Romanoli is as much responsible for Warner's appointment as any one. 'The decision was quite simple', Romanoli said, 'Don was the best qualified man. I recommended him to the board. I was very pleased that he was approved unanimously—9-0.' (The board, which is elected by the residents has three black members including its president, Ted Reid. In addition, Emerson Smith is a vice principal at the modern Willingboro Memorial Junior High School and Ron Webb is principal at one of the town's elementary schools.

'One of the things that attracted me to Willingboro', said Warner, 'is its obvious dedication to education. The students and the town seem genuinely concerned about enlightenment and that has to be an attraction to anyone concerned about the business of education.'

All this is not to say there are no problems in Willingboro. Like almost every other system, there is the problem of drugs and there is some racial strife. Indeed several educators were shifted away from Kennedy High School to make way for Warner, who would surely have faced racial hostility from some of his own staff.

Warner is different. In an effort to learn about the town's drug problem, he talked with one of the local undertakers. And he says he is not threatened by a parent who wants to sit in the classroom to see what his child is being taught. 'I like that. I think a parent who will take that kind of initiative will help his child, because he's concerned about what his youngster is being taught.'

Asked if he was hired because he is black, Warner smiled. 'One really never knows about that', he said. 'But I've got the credentials. I've sat in every chair in my old school and I've got the credentials. I've been a teacher, a motivation coordinator, acting vice principal, vice principal, deputy principal. I think I bring good credentials, but one never knows what other people's motivations are. I've a feeling, though, that I was hired for my ability.

Willingboro has demonstrated that it wants to be fair. It's given me a somewhat unique opportunity, and I don't intend to fail. If I improve things, they will approve of me. What more can I ask?'

Board member Ken Anderson says he sees Warner's appointment as very important to both blacks and whites. 'I think whites need to see blacks off the baseball diamond and football field as well as on. Warner's role will help bring mutual respect. I think what Willingboro has done has made the entire country a little stronger'.

Twelve years ago, Willingboro asked only one question about a man: 'What's his color? Today it's asking: 'What's his competence?'

That's what I call progress." [2]

However, several challenges presented themselves almost immediately. On the first day at work, 8:30 a.m. sharp, a Mr. Bentley appeared in the main office seeking an appointment of great urgency with the new principal. My secretary, Kay, approached me and apprised me of the situation. As one who believes in an open door process, I instructed Kay to invite him into my office. He calmly entered the office dressed in a light, blue business suit. I said, "Good morning, sir, how may I be of assistance?" I offered him a seat, however, he refused to be seated; therefore, I too stood to receive him. He firmly stated: "My name is Mr. Bentley and I represent a citizen's organization here in Willingboro. As their representative, I am here to tell you that we do not want a black man here at John F. Kennedy High School serving as principal!" My first reaction was one of shock and dismay, after all this was my first day at work. I had just relocated with my family. Not only that, but I had the choice of two other school districts who wanted to hire me. The Philadelphia side of me and the U.S. Marine Corps side of me wanted to jump over the desk and attack him unmercifully; however, instead I remained very calm, placed both my hands in my pockets so as not to mistakenly use them and said, " Mr. Bentley are you finished speaking?" He responded, "Yes". I added, "Then you may leave now!" Mr. Bentley exited the office, and I went to the outer office window and watched him leave the school property. Then, I left the school building, drove a few miles to the district superintendent's office and informed him of what had just happened. I stated very clearly that in the interviewing process there had been no mention of racism and or prejudicial concerns existing within the community. For the first time, he explained to me the make up of the community, its divisions into ten separate towns and the socio-economic uneven distribution of limited resources in each town. He also made reference to the increasing racial divide and the changing demographic that tended to create multiple tensions within the schools and community.

It was now too late to accept a position elsewhere; therefore, I returned to the school, and began the task of administering a dual shift school in the midst of racial tensions, faculty and staff ambivalence within the framework of a school board whose primary concern was to protect the individual towns and parks from which they originated.

As principal, I spent the majority of the school day in classrooms, observing teachers and students, walking the school corridors, and patrolling the outside perimeters of the building and fields before and after the school day. Seldom, if ever, did I have to depend upon secondary information, because the majority of time I was available and "Johnny on the spot" when disturbances or controversies of any nature occurred.

During my second week at the high school, after class dismissal, I was patrolling the outdoor perimeters of the property when a fight broke out between two rather large students, one white, one black. Utilizing the "walkie talkie" to summon help, Mr.Trama, Vice Principal on assignment in an adjacent area, appeared and we were able to calm the two young men and break up the fight. We then escorted the two young men, accompanied by Mr. Cosby, hall monitor, to Mr. Trama's office, where we questioned them to determine the cause for the altercation and to see if we could settle the dispute amicably. During the interviewing process, John Grimes, the white student, stated clearly with great determination: "My mother told me not to take any shit from any of these niggers!" He was speaking to the vice principal, but staring me directly in the face. Subsequently, I explained to John and the other student that fighting on school property was against school regulations, and that they were suspended from school and could reenter only after a meeting with their parents.

After the boys left the office, Mr. Trama, the vice principal began to explain that John, a senior, and his brother were both members of the football team. They had been in altercations at the school previously, but given the ugly disposition of their mother, had never been suspended. It seems that school administrators were afraid of the wrath of Mrs. Grimes. Claire Grimes was reportedly the most vocal bigot in the town. Her prejudices relative to minorities were well known in the community. Furthermore, the school superintendent was aware of her noted dispositions and supported the high school administration in its actions or lack there of as regards the Grimes family. I thanked Mr. Trama for the "heads up" information and suspended John Grimes indicating that the conference would occur with the school principal and not the usual meeting at the vice principals level.

The very next morning, 8:00 a.m., Mrs. Grimes telephoned the main office requesting an immediate conference or she would take her concerns to a higher level. Even Kay, my secretary, knew of Mrs. Grimes' reputation, and appeared to be rather flushed as she explained the urgency apparent in Mrs. Grimes' voice. We scheduled an appointment for 10:30 a.m., and patiently awaited her arrival. Upon arrival, we met in the vice principal's office where all staff members' heads turned as she abruptly entered appearing quite anxious and perturbed. I greeted her with warmth and all the courtesy and gallantry Mozelle, my mother, had taught me throughout the years. Throughout the dialogue, I responded with "Yes, ma'am" and "No, ma'am. It is my intention Mrs. Grimes, to treat every student fairly, firmly and with respect. I will do all in my power to help our students achieve academically and socially; however, there are rules and regulations stipulated in our school handbook that every parent has seen and signed. Your son, John, has violated one such rule and must now adhere to the consequences listed. I will not make exceptions when rules are broken", I explained. Because I was present at the scene at the time of the fight, Mrs. Grimes was agreeable to the suspension and mentioned that this was the first time her boys had ever been suspended. We shook hands, and I thanked her for being present to show interest and solidarity where her children are concerned. Mrs. Grimes left the office politely saying, "Thank you, Mr. Warner". The two vice principals plus all the on lookers were surprised to see that Mrs. Grimes left the premises calmly and without commotion. Interestingly, as the days and months passed, Mrs. Grimes became one of my staunch supporters. She was present at most of the parent teacher meetings, and expressed support for the new educational climate at John F. Kennedy High School.

Nevertheless, as the town demographics

changed and a greater influx of people moved into the district from Philadelphia and Camden areas, the number of racial skirmishes in the school and community increased. As the incidences increased so did the presence and vigilance of the Willingboro Police Chief and his officers. Especially interesting were meetings with the Police Chief. Whenever he held a conference with me , he always stood with his right hand resting atop the revolver holstered on the right side of his waist. Of course, each time he twitched or performed other involuntary body movements, I too shifted positions in an effort to stay prepared for any inevitability. I was never certain as to his thinking, attitude and disposition regarding juvenile delinquents. Even today I twitch when I reflect back on our numerous meetings both at police headquarters and in my office. In spite of the situations listed above, my tenure at John F. Kennedy High School was refreshing and satisfying. I had the distinct pleasure of having experienced similar situations on my prior job in Philadelphia. For example, I knew more about gang structure and the reasons for ganging than the majority of people in the community, especially chosen leaders including the police department. Also, I had served previously at a high school involved in changing demographics. John Bartram High School, Philadelphia, had changed during the years 1960 to 1970 from a majority white school population to a majority black school population. Willingboro was in the process of changing in 1971, and today, 2007, the schools are predominately minority based. Given my experience in coordinating the Motivation Program in Philadelphia for students who needed extra resources to achieve, coupled with skills in Developmental and Remedial Reading, I was well prepared and equipped academically, socially and politically to deal with schools operating educational programs on split shift schedules. However, the population in town increased so rapidly that a second high school had to be built, and I was assigned as "clerk of the works" to give oversight and management to the construction of the new Willingboro High School.

This new assignment coupled with my daily responsibilities as high school principal was exciting in that I had the opportunity to know and approve every nook and cranny of the building design, plus was given the responsibility for developing a new, innovative curriculum for a model high school. This assignment was given with the approval of the district superintendent, who delegated authority to the Assistant Superintendent for Curriculum to assist and approve total planning and initiation in cooperation with the School Business Administrator, Mr. Elmer Corda, a force unto himself. However, one of the most exciting aspects of the new responsibility was the task of choosing staff members for the new school. There were many guilt pangs as I interviewed the best staff members from John F. Kennedy High to transfer with me to the new Willingboro High School. In one sense of the word, I was robbing the best of the best to serve the children from the best. Little did I realize that one of my staff members, Mrs. Evelyn Lewis was the mother of the now famous Carl Lewis, track and field star, who attended Willingboro High School. There was a distinct difference in the location of the new high school as it was located in the wealthiest section of town. In fact, the superintendent had purchased his home there. As mentioned earlier, there were distinct economic differences within and among the various towns and their respective locations. As any educator "worth his salt" will tell you, there is a noticeable positive correlation between wealth and educational achievement.

The school years went quite well at Kennedy High and students were achieving and attending colleges and universities in increased numbers. The community supported school programs, and increasingly our reputation as a quality school moved forward in a positive fashion. One particular incident bears mentioning. It was graduation time, and as usual one had to make the decision whether to hold graduation inside the building gymnasium or outside at the large football stadium. Naturally, the preference is outdoors as ticket distribution is unlimited and students can invite as many relatives and friends as they wish. In the meantime, administratively, one must prepare for both circumstances as sometimes, even on the clearest days, the rain comes unexpectedly. Such was the case at the second graduation ceremony at John F. Kennedy High School. The weather was absolutely gorgeous, and we were at the point of calling names and distributing diplomas when suddenly the skies darkened and the rain poured down. At this point everyone moved to our secondary location to continue the ceremony. However, before leaving the stage, a nattily attired woman approached the stage and screamed: "You ball headed son of a bitch, didn't you know it was going to rain?" I stood speechless for a second and then responded, "No ma'am," just as Mozelle, my mother, had taught me. The woman was somewhat startled by my respectful reply to her bombastic outburst, and she left the area without saying another word. Once inside the graduation was completed in good order and we all retired from the premises, but I carried home with me an unforgettable tongue lashing from a disappointed spectator parent.

The following year Willingboro High School opened and our educational program moved along in an aura of excellence. I had a wonderful supportive staff and my vice principals and department heads were the best in the state. Little did I realize that the Board of Education was undergoing difficulties with the superintendent, until I read in the local newspaper that he was to be suspended without pay for mismanaging the district. This in and of itself was not particularly disturbing as Boards often have disagreements with their educational leaders. However, the big surprise was that on Friday afternoon, I was summoned to the Board office where the Board of Education was meeting in emergency session. Why me, I wondered?

My encounter with the Board was very brief. Once inside the meeting that was closed to the public, the president invited me to be seated and made the following statement: "As you may be aware, Dr. Warner, the superintendent of schools has been suspended without pay , and you have until 10:00 a.m. tomorrow morning to make a decision to serve as Acting Superintendent of Schools in his absence. If there are no questions, we will expect to see you in the morning." I left the building pondering the challenge and wondered the majority of the evening why they had not chosen any of the present central office staff to take the position. There had been situations where business administrators served in dual capacities; also it was my opinion that both the secondary and elementary assistant superintendents were top notch administrators. Why weren't they asked to take this position? Internally, I knew that I had been a highly visible respected school principal in the district and the community was well aware of my educational attributes, but the challenge was beyond comprehension. However, after a sleepless night, I met with the Board of Education and arranged to become Acting Superintendent of the Willingboro School District at a salary commensurate with the task. " Fate , time occasion, chance and change" had entered my life again causing another new resurrection, only this time I was rising to a whole new world of intrigue and accompanying complications and contradictions. Instead of standing in defense of one high school, I now had a multi-million dollar district to be held accountable, ten elementary schools, two junior high schools and two high schools. In addition, who was I to trust in central office and where were their allegiances, with me or the suspended superintendent? As expected everyone was cordial, but cautious in their working relationships. I had learned over the years never to disclose personal information with colleagues as it will come back to haunt you; therefore; beyond the normal information found on applications and personnel files I kept all personal information to myself and never shared. My technique was to be a good listener, but never to share information of a personal nature.

On Monday morning I arrived at the Superintendent's office for work at 7:00 a.m. hoping to avoid central office staff, but also hoping to observe their work habits once they arrived at 8:00 a.m. When I entered my office two board members were waiting, Alice Martello and her friend, Pat Harper. They represented two different towns in the community; both usually ran on the same school board ticket. They had with them a lengthy written agenda concerning the district, inclusive of individual teacher behaviors and central office business practices. Their direction to me was to investigate the matters listed and inform them in writing once completed. They were my first lesson in central office diplomacy with board members. Later I was to learn that there was a third member of their team, one Delores Gross who differed only slightly in her perceived pursuits of district needs. The entire time I was present as Acting Superintendent, Alice and Pat were present in my office at least three times a week prior to my arrival, waiting with a list of event, actions and investigations requiring action. Because of their constant presence, I started an activities log on which I listed the names and purposes for visitation of all persons with whom I had contact during the day. Later, this log became very important in documenting individual behavior and legal matters within the district. Interestingly, Alice was a seamstress and curtain maker who had business with many homes in the community, and in the course of doing business knew many people in town and their concerns about the school district. Her campaign motto when running for school board elections was "Alice Knows". Even though she and Pat could be perceived as "royal pains" in the derriere, they became my strongest supporters on the board. In fact, during my tenure as acting superintendent, they suggested that I attend the National School Board's Conference with them in Miami, Florida. Having never experienced a national meeting, I decided to attend; however, I learned through the board secretary's office where they were staying in Miami and made a purposeful decision to locate a different hotel with the excuse that their hotel was sold out for the conference. Therefore, I booked a hotel in Hollywood, Florida about a thirty minute drive from Miami. This worked to my advantage and provided necessary relief, rest and restoration out of sight from their daily vigilance. After they accepted the avoidance, we attended dutifully the conference, then Alice suggested that we visit her mother in Orlando, some five to six hours drive from Miami. After the conference, we rented a car and drove to Orlando during the bug mating season. We arrived at her mother's and were greeted warmly, and given separate accommodations for the evening. The next day, Alice, Pat and I purchased tickets to Disney World and enjoyed the day of fun and relaxation. However, there was a slight problem with some of the rides. I especially remember one amusement ride in which the cars were rather small comfortably seating two persons, but a third was near impossible. As the cars loaded I waited in line with Pat and Alice until it was our turn to load. Pat and Alice were rather large size women. When they entered the conveyance, I hesitated as obviously no room was left for seating in the car. Suddenly Alice called out loudly, as only she could, "You bald headed S.O.B., get your black ass in this car!" I ran and jumped in the car, and thank goodness the ride didn't require a seat belt, because I had one buttock in the car and a leg hanging out the side. One thing for certain, they both had dynamic unforgiving personalities.

Before my five year tenure ended in Willingboro, I attended a second school boards conference alone in Miami, Florida, and this time I stayed at the Fontainebleau Hotel. My scheduled stay was for four days. On the second day while standing in the lobby around 10:00 a.m., the double doors swung open and a rather large figure accompanied by Barry White, the musician, entered the hotel lobby. Much to my surprise it was Muhammad Ali, the championship boxer. He shouted, "Who wants to watch me box? If so, come with me. I'm the greatest in the world!" Several people in the lobby, including me, boarded the bus that awaited us outside the hotel. They drove to the Fifth Street gymnasium where Muhammad Ali was in training for that famous fight against the "gorilla in Manila". The boxing area was similar to what I had witnessed in Philadelphia, only this time there were ladies surrounding the boxing ring in white mink jackets. Unbelievable, because this was a time of very warm weather. The women of all races and nationalities stood two to three deep surrounding the ring. While there, I spoke with one young woman who was a student from California who admitted to following the champ from location to location. About a year later, I read where this young woman had become one of his wives. I am not certain whether she was the second or third.

Nevertheless, I watched the champ as he skipped rope in warm up exercises, and then hit the punching bag for a period of time, the entire time talking and bragging about who he was. Dundee, his trainer, was there trying to keep Muhammad on task as he playfully sparred with young people surrounding the ring. Then he invited a few young students of elementary age into the boxing ring with him. He sparred with them and pretended to be hurt when one of the children landed a blow. I was mesmerized by his showmanship and particularly pleased at his ability to captivate his onlookers and numerous fans. When I returned to the hotel, I learned that Mr. Ali was living on a houseboat tied in the dock area while training in Miami. I was so impressed that years later, I wrote the following poem:

## AH LEEEE

Pummeled into submission
Beaten by a pair of
8 ounce gloves,
Puffy- eyed , defenseless
Cassius Clay,
Muhammad Ali,
the man who would be king, pathetic human bee
without a sting,
no longer dreaming new dreams,
but caught up in the timeless truth

of an infants' babbling
"what goes up, must come down",
Caught up in the malaise of
Crumbling statuary,
Crumbling pyramids,
Falling monuments,
Changing deteriorating shapes.
Ah LEEE! Ah LEEE!
The crowded throng
Shouted, egging the champion on-
Stick, jab, rope-a-dope,
Faint of heart, he failed to answer
The bell.
He fell into the endless river of illustrious company:
Louis, Joe, Dempsey, Jack and the like,
Never to rise again.
But in the splendor of his youth,
Neither human nor animal,
Dared stalk him as potential prey.
He danced through controversial Vietnam,
Praised Allah until his second wife,
Jabbed through the world of champions,
Shouted clumsy adieus
To mink clad ladies
At training camps galore,
Autographed thousands of handkerchiefs,
Napkins and notebooks for elementary students,
Who boxing in his 10 by 12 training ring
Went home to tell of sparing
With the champ.
Falling star,

# Resurrection

You are family to me.
You dared to be different,
You hung precariously at the top.
Fall softly, sweetly-
Into deep, dark earth
Where roses , fresh fruits
And orchards grow,
And know that out of the ashes,
And clay of crumbling civilizations,
Indifferent man
Has pointed skyward
Cathedrals with glass domed roofs
That reflect the sun's glow,
And send heavenward
Messages of AH LEEE, AH LEEE
Ah LEEEEEEEEEE!


## Higher Ground

My tenure as acting school superintendent of the Willingboro Public Schools started abruptly with one day's notification by the school board. It ended just as abruptly, only this time there was no closed session meeting to address the failure of the charges against the former superintendent to be validated at the State Board of Education level. Therefore, without notification, the former superintendent was back at work, and I was dismissed and sent back to Willingboro High School to the former position of principal. Seldom did the superintendent communicate with me prior to his dismissal, and now all communication was either through one of the assistant superintendents or via memoranda. As a means of retaliating against me for serving as acting superintendent, the former superintendent made every effort to strip me of all power within the district. One of the major actions was to remove all custodial workers from the high school and leave us with an unsanitary building. My first reaction was one of dismay and disgust; however, I knew I had to have a plan to survive in the district or be fired for incompetence and insubordination. Given the ever changing nature of school board composition this is always a possibility at any given election. Therefore, I devised a plan, a strategy, and called a meeting of my vice principals and department chairs together to discuss the plan. They understood the predicament and promised to support my action plan. The plan was simple, but powerful. In order to keep our building clean, the three administrators led by me and the department chairs, when possible, would clean the building. My plan was to telephone the Burlington County Times, our local newspaper, and have them send a reporter to witness our dilemma. The next morning, we put our plan into action. Immediately as classes were passing the students and staff members were upset questioning me personally as to why I was cleaning and vacuuming the school floors. A reporter arrived on the scene and posted a lengthy article about the lack of services at the high school. They interviewed students and staff.

When the newspapers were published the next day, the situation at Willingboro High School became apparent to the entire community, and that night we were given a full emergency crew to clean our building and all services were immediately restored. That was the final visible act of retribution fostered upon the school; however, I knew it was time to relocate and seek employment in another district. As time, fate chance, and change would have it, a gentleman I had never met telephoned my office to let me know that the Red Bank Regional School district was seeking applications for a school superintendent and would I be interested in applying? I later learned that the gentleman caller was one Dr. Larry Kaufman a professor at Rutgers University who had heard of me through the New Jersey State Principal's Association. Yes, I applied for the position, was accepted and submitted my letter of resignation to the district superintendent.

The community at large was surprised at my resignation and sponsored a farewell dinner in celebration of my tenure in the Willingboro School System. I in turn made the following remarks at the dinner:

"It will not be my intention to discuss my recent $4000.00 drop in salary, or the National Honor Society speech made in defense of a student who the committee failed to recognize and admit. Nor will I discuss the recent administrative comment which said: "Blame Warner for everything wrong in the district. He's leaving". Nor will I comment in reference to the direct confrontation to me stating: "Perhaps you fight for too many things."

If you call fighting to improve the curriculum, fighting for budgetary control, fighting for preventative maintenance and improved custodial services, fighting for uniqueness, fighting against mediocrity and apathy, fighting for improved grades and scholastic aptitude test scores, fighting for the best staff in the state of New Jersey, fighting for improved elementary classrooms, fighting for recognition of our students within the community and the state, then perhaps I fought too much.

It was unfortunate that for 4 ½ years I was evaluated as an excellent administrator by certain people in power positions and then suddenly, after leaving the acting superintendency, I was perceived as extremely threatening. Suddenly communications ceased or were reduced to a barrage of memos-- memos that in fact became needless justification and CYA (cover your ass) garbage.

It was whispered that I made three mistakes: (1) You did your job too well, (2) You failed at courtesy consultation with the suspended superintendent, and (3) You didn't back a salary increase for top central office administrators.

Some people thought I desperately wanted the superintendency on a permanent basis. The early decision that I had to make was one of "You're damned if you do, and damned if you don't". I had no regrets with the exception that I discovered so many small minds who began to stoop to petty nuisances as a means of justifying and maintaining their positions.

I am eternally grateful to those board members, who followed their convictions of equal opportunity for all in the Willingboro School District, and who continued to support my endeavors and/or seek my advice on issues involving the well being of the Willingboro school system. Unfortunately, some board members have been misunderstood and blamed for my leaving the system. The very people who were perceived by some members of the community as being bigoted and prejudice were the very people who came to my rescue. Board members who were perceived as having no empathy for the minority culture were the very people who when questioning business firms stated: "Do you hire blacks and women and if not will you in the future; if not we don't want your business?"

None of the so called liberals took this approach, yet the information stemming from those liberals tended to purposely taint and confuse even the most militant of the black community into thinking negatively about those items most affecting their well being.

It was never my intention to permit trade offs or any type of bargaining with board members that would in turn endanger the well being of the students or teachers in the Willingboro School District. Consequently when the pressures and the "blame Warner" syndrome became prevalent and obviously manipulated to the point of allegedly using police tactics to question my teachers, and finally withdrawing and withholding the principal's newsletter, because it spoke truthfully and honestly about custodial issues, I knew it was time to leave. It was your dissatisfaction with the system that represented my greatest administrative challenge. The community was urged to maintain its dissatisfaction, for the lack thereof leads to mediocrity. Mediocrity, interpreted by some as "I was here when you came and I'll be here when you're gone", lends itself to intense apathy. Apathy, in turn, leads to failure for the young people of Willingboro.

I love this community, the teachers, the

students and the many citizens who supported my ideas and concepts about what quality education is all about. Witness the strange conglomerate of individuals from all walks of life, all present tonight supposedly in tribute to me. But the tribute is yours, not mine. You gave me the opportunity to work with your youngsters. You gave me support in the midst of adversity. You insisted that the wrongs be made right. You demanded educational excellence in leadership and teacher ability. You had the courage and raw guts, especially those of you who are employed in the schools, to come out tonight. I shall never forget you. You have touched me deeply. And in the words of Ralph Waldo Emerson: 'If a man write a better book, preach a better sermon, or make a better mouse trap than his neighbour, tho' he build his house in the woods, the world will make a beaten path to his door'." [3]

That evening I received a prestigious award and certificate from the Willingboro Teacher's Union, thanking me for my commitment to the teaching learning process. I'll forever cherish that award which hangs in a prominent place in my home today. It was so unlike the impression one receives when reading the story of the Union Dog:

Donald D. Warner

# A Union Man's Dog

Four workers were discussing how smart their dogs were. The first was an engineer who said, his dog could do math with calculations. His dog was named T Square, and he told him to get some paper and draw a square, a circle, and a triangle, which the dog did with no sweat. The accountant said his dog was better. His dog was named Slide Rule. He told him to fetch a dozen cookies, bring them back and divide them into piles of three, which he did with no problem. The chemist said that was good, but his dog was better. His dog Measure was told to get a quart of milk and pour seven ounces into a ten ounce glass. The dog did this with no problem. All three men agreed that this was very good and their dog was equally smart. They all turned to the Union Member and said, "What can your dog do?" The teamster member called his dog, whose name was Coffee break and said, "Show the folks what you can do". Coffee Break went over and ate the cookies, drank the milk, shit on the paper and screwed the other three dogs and claimed he injured his back while doing so, filed a grievance for unsafe working conditions, applied for Workmen's compensation and left for home on sick leave.

# Chapter Seven
## REASSUMING AN EMPIRE

As I left the temporary glory and grandeur of Willingboro, I knew that the time for change was apparent. My dream there was over, and I had awakened to the rhythmic beatings of a new drummer. This time the mission would be fulfilled and controlled by the inner instinctual urgings of my own indefinable soul. The helm would be mine and the ship would either sail or sink given my intelligence, motivation, creativity and drive towards excellence in all with whom I interacted. Again, Percy Bysshe Shelley, the poet, had summarized my condition when he wrote:

" These are the spells by which to reassume
An empire o'er the disentangled doom.
To suffer woes which Hope thinks infinite;

To forgive wrongs darker than death or night;
To defy power which seems omnipotent;
To love, and bear; to hope 'til Hope creates
From it's own wreck the thing it contemplates;
Neither to change, nor falter, nor repent;
This like thy glory, Titan, is to be
Good, great and joyous, beautiful and free;
This alone is Life, Joy, Empire, and Victory." [1]

Indeed, I needed to establish new vistas. I had successfully navigated the mean streets of Philadelphia, promenaded through the boulevards of an increasing belligerency in Willingboro, and the time to move forward was imminent. Forgiving wrongs was easier than forgetting, but defying power was a part of the energies that consumed me; however, thanks to Mozelle, I have always been able to love unconditionally, to hope, to change and maintain the good, great and joyous life which surrounds me. In this manner I am forever beautifully free. Yet, a different journey was about to unfold. The entire application and interviewing process at the Red Bank Regional School District was lengthy and non-compromising. However, immediately after applying for the position, I visited the three towns serving the high school and talked with passer-bys on the streets about their perceptions of the town and the school systems, elementary and secondary. One of the places I stood to meet people was in front of the Pilgrim Baptist Church, where I later became a member and

Associate Pastor under the leadership of Reverend Milliard Harris. Nevertheless, there were three community panels desiring to interview and possibly recommend or deny my candidacy, prior to meeting with the school board for a first and final interview. In fact several Red Bank Regional Board of Education members actually drove to Willingboro to witness my job performance and to interview selected persons in the district. The automobile visitation was led by Dr. James Parker,Jr., a prominent black physician who later allowed our family to live next door in his father's home, rent free, while our house was under construction. It was a large home complete with former business offices where his father, a former physician, had once lived. Much to my surprise, the underground oil tank held 1000 gallons, when the average large tank for home owners was 500 gallons. The only mistake I made while living there was to call the police to arrest Dr. Parker, Jr. because at 5:00 a.m. in the morning when I heard noise next door, I assumed burglars were trying to break into the home, when low and behold it was merely Dr. Parker depositing trash in one of his metal garbage cans. How was I to know that his office hours started at 5:00 a.m. to accommodate clients who had to work.

Soon after visitations from board members to Willingboro, I was hired and attended the meeting accompanied by my wife, daughter, Beth, and three sisters. Our strategy was to position my sisters in various sections of the audience so that they could listen to comments and then report back to me after the meeting. It worked beautifully. The surprise of the evening was to see three board members from Willingboro, Alice Martello, Pat Harper and Marty Townsend , who had come to support my candidacy and respond to questions , if necessary. After the meeting, we all met at the local diner in Red Bank and discussed the meeting. All comments were favorable. Within a week "The Buccaneer", our school newspaper had printed the following article:

### Dr. Donald Warner to be Superintendent

With emphasis on teaching the three R's, Dr. Donald Warner will take over as superintendent of this school on November 17 (1975).

" If I find there is a need for strengthening the basic skills, then I will recommend it and it will become my first priority," he said.

Dr. Warner is the first black superintendent of a Monmouth County School, something he said he was not aware.

He comes here from Willingboro High School in Southern New Jersey, where he was principal. He said, "I remember I was the first black principal in Willingboro and during an hour long press conference , I spent 45 minutes talking about my blackness. I don't really think that matters though, because what people really want to know is, are you qualified? Do you know what you're talking about, and can you do your job? That's all that matters."

The present superintendent, Mr. Harold Shaible , will retire Dec. 31, and will act as consultant to the superintendent from November 17 until that time.

"I've always taught as an administrator", said Dr. Warner, "and I think administrators should always keep their hands in teaching, even if it's only as a resource person".

"My administrative style is very open", he continued. " Sometimes that is hard for people to accept, but that's the way I do it. I like to be approachable; I don't like to learn things second or third hand. If you have to deal with things that way, then you have problems".

He will receive a salary of $35,000 a year, $3,000 more than he was making at Willingboro. He said his decision to come here was based on the community's and the school board's attitude.

"I came to town, he said, to look around and I found citizens were proud of their community and a board of education that talked about education rather than individual personalities. That's the way a school board should operate".

He was one of the 93 original applicants for the job. Seven of the applicants were given in-depth interviews.

William E. Graff, president of the board of education, said there was no one or two reasons that Dr. Warner was picked for the job. He said he could "go on for hours" as to why Dr. Warner received the job.

Dr. Warner is a 1958 graduate of Temple University with a major in English. He received his Master's Degree from Pennsylvania State University in 1970. His doctoral degree was awarded summa cum laude from there in 1972. He is a member of several professional organizations, and has received awards from the Rotary Club, Veterans of Foreign War, and various educational groups. Most recently, he received an award for outstanding educational leadership from the Kinsmen, a local community service group in Willingboro.

Mr. Graff said that since the statewide achievement tests were down last year that perhaps more emphasis should be placed on the fundamentals.

He said that the board expects Dr. Warner to be active in developing ideas and new techniques in education as well as evaluation, discipline, negotiating, and budgeting.

"We are looking to make this high school the best in the state", said Mr. Graff, " and we want our students to have a better education when they leave here".

Dr. Warner is married and has two school age children."

## The Sophisticated North

My mother, Mozelle Emily Willis Warner was born in the south, Newport News, Virginia. She once mentioned to me that she had certain preferences for the south, because in the south, as a black person, you always know where you stand; however, the north has a more sophisticated form of hidden prejudice. This became very clear to me when I applied at the local bank, Colonial First National, for a mortgage. I was merely requesting a cross mortgage, because my home in Delran was sold, and I had the money to transfer into a second home in the Monmouth County area. The lending officer refused my application for unstated reasons; therefore, a week later I requested to meet with one of the banking officers. They assigned a vice president and I met with him and gave him an option. I first told him of my application and the refusal from the lending officer; then I reminded him that the Red Bank Regional School District had invested a multi million dollar business with the bank and if I did not receive a loan from the bank, I would request the board withdraw all its business and seek another bank. In a matter of two days I was notified that my application was approved.

The second minor shock came when the school's union leader Joan Lockhart requested a meeting with the superintendent as teacher negotiations were scheduled and she wished to begin sessions on an amicable basis. I agreed to the meeting as I, too, hoped for a positive and early settlement. We sat down to talk, and her first statement was, "You know, Dr. Warner, I have never worked for a black superintendent before". My immediate response was, "Guess what, Joan, neither have I , so I guess we will just have to find out how it works". It was a brief meeting, but I imagine her fears and anxieties were satisfied. One would think that in 1975, the interactions between races would have changed a bit, especially after the Civil Rights Movement of the 1960's. However, on a personal level, when we first moved into our new home in Tinton Falls, New Jersey, a little five year older, my neighbor who was white, came to visit while I was sweeping the driveway. He said, "Mr. Warner, my mother said you are a nigger. Are you a nigger?" "No", I answered, "My name is Mr. Warner, what's yours?" About 10 years later on the same property the young man was very helpful in shoveling the snow from my yard and doing other small tasks for which he would not accept compensation. We had become good friends.

The final northern admission was from a

newspaper journalist for the Daily Register, who had interviewed me several times on the telephone after I had accepted the position of superintendent. He called to say, "Gee, Dr. Warner, in the two to three conversations we had in the past, I never realized you were black until I actually attended the last board meeting". I never responded to that particular comment; however, I imagine I failed to meet his mental perception of how a black person should articulate over the telephone. Again, this was 1975 and in 1997, Colin Powell, former Chairman of the Joint Chiefs of Staff, addressed the National Volunteer Summit in Philadelphia where he stated: "The great American poet, Langston Hughes, talked about a dream deferred. There are still Americans who are not sharing in the American dream…. For too many young Americans that dream deferred does sag like a heavy load that's pushing them down into the ground, and they wonder if they can rise up with that load. As you're heard, up to 15 million young Americans today are at risk. They are at risk of growing up unskilled, unlearned or, even worse, unloved. They are at risk of growing up physically or psychologically abused. They are at risk of growing up addicted to the pathologies and poisons of the street. They are at risk of bringing up children into the world before they, themselves have grown up. They are at risk of never growing up at all. Fifteen million young lives are at risk, may not make it unless we care enough to do something about it….And so let us join in this great crusade….Let us save our children." [2]

That same year Fran Lebowitz spelled "it out in black and white". She stated, " If you're black, don't you say to yourself, 'We've been here for a zillion years, and here are all these people coming along, acquiring power by saying they're powerless- acquiring power by equating their lot with ours.' Blacks are the standard of oppression…the truth is that the farther you are from being black, the more likely you are to assimilate, to be more like white. The more you are like white, the less trouble you have-because the more you are like white, the less trouble you are…..The way to approach it(the solution), I think, is not to ask, 'What would it be like to be black?' but to seriously consider what it is like to be white. That's something white people almost never think about. And what it is like to be white is not to say, 'We have to level the playing field', but to acknowledge that not only do white people own the playing field, but they have so designated this plot of land as a playing field to begin with. The advantage of being white is so extreme, so overwhelming, so immense, that to use the word advantage at all is misleading since it implies a kind of ' parity' that simply does not exist….yes, it is true that 50 years ago a black person with an I.Q. of Isaiah Berlin would have been a janitor, and now look: we've solved the problem of what to do with the black geniuses—they have the same opportunities as the white geniuses. But we don't need affirmative action for these people and we never did. The problem of the talented tenth was actually solved by the civil –rights movement. It is to create parity between the untalented 90th and its white counterpart that we require what are perversely called racial preferences. ---I say perversely because surely we all know which race is preferred, talented or not. We will have equality when dopey black people get into Harvard because their chair-endowing grandfathers went there. We will have equality when incompetent black people buy their way into the Senate. We will have equality when larcenous black union plumbers start not showing up in greater and greater numbers. We will have equality when the unjust deserts and ill-gotten gains are spread around impartially. One Clarence Thomas is not enough." [3] And so, the contentious problem of race in America continues even today.

In 1975 within the state of New Jersey there were 600 independent school districts. Of the 600 districts only 10 to 12 had black superintendents. In Monmouth County, I was the only black superintendent. I didn't realize this until I attended the monthly county district superintendent's meetings. Nevertheless, the Red Bank Regional Board through the years of my tenure usually had one or two black representatives serving on the board of education. Three who made notable contributions to the children of the regional school were Dr. James Parker, Jr., Mr. Jesse Garrison and Mr. Art Palmer. They served with distinction representing all children within the district, as the major student population came to the school from three towns Little Silver, Red Bank and Shrewsbury. Economically speaking, the student body ranged from students who were on the list to receive free and reduced pricing for lunch, to the very wealthy. Because I taught in certain classrooms and roamed the corridors the majority of the day, I was able to communicate with a majority of the students on a first name basis. One young lady, Suzy, in particular criticized my outfits on a weekly basis, and insisted that my clothing was a bit old fashioned for the times. It was a delight to see her coming even knowing that she and her group would say, in a nice way, uncomplimentary things about my dress code, especially my colorful neckties.

## A Place Where Everybody Is Somebody

The Red Bank Regional School System was uniquely shared by three municipalities, Red Bank, Little Silver, and Shrewsbury. Each town or municipality had its own separate elementary school system. The four districts each had its own school board and operated independently of one another. Several attempts were made during my tenure to have meetings with the four boards and administrators; however, it was a tedious and tenuous process at best with each district protecting its own special interests. In years to follow the Red Bank Regional High School District initiated a Performing Arts school within a school and students eventually were registered on a tuition basis from 33 different districts in Monmouth County. However, historical demographics weighed heavily in determining the educational achievement levels of the incoming students from the three sending districts- Little Silver, Red Bank and Shrewsbury. Both Little Silver and Shrewsbury boasted of proven excellence in education as determined by achievement test scores, while Red Bank traditionally suffered with poorer academic results than the other two. This concern is exemplified in an Executive Summary submitted by the newly formed Charter School, when it was attempting to establish an alternative path for students in Red Bank who did not wish to attend the struggling elementary system. Coincidentally, the majority of black and other minority students lived in Red Bank.

## Executive Summary

"Red bank is a diverse community with a rich history and exciting future. Situated along the banks of the Navesink River, Red Bank benefits from the daily exposure to the wonders of nature's beauty. Long a commercial center, Red Bank has a historic downtown that is renowned throughout the state for its architectural splendor, thriving commerce and devotion to the arts.

Our community is blessed with a population as diverse as that of our country, from the first generation immigrants to families who can trace their ancestors from the earliest settlers and Native Americans. It is this diversity that gives Red Bank its strength and character. This diverse and thriving community was built, maintained and expanded by the proud graduates of a then healthy public school system. While our community has in the past relied upon the strength of our public schools to insure its growth, this reliance is now threatened. The failure of the Red Bank public school system threatens the future of our students and our town.

Red Bank shares a regional high school with the neighboring towns of Little Silver and Shrewsbury. A comparison of the 1996 Early Warning Test (EWT) results of the regional communities clearly reflects how the failure of the Red Bank school system has reached crises proportions. EWT scores indicate that between 96% and 100% of eighth grade students in Little Silver and Shrewsbury were competent in mathematics, reading and writing. In Red Bank only 28.3% of eighth grade students were competent in math; 30.4% in reading and 8.7% in writing…..

The EWT scores at the eighth grade level demonstrate that the Red Bank Public School System has been ineffective in providing an education to the children of this community. Consequently, a majority of Red Bank students fall within the State's mandate for remediation…. Moreover, when such poor academic achievement is left unaddressed for many years, as it has been in Red Bank, it is a costly process to rectify.

The primary responsibility for this remediation has been falling to the Red Bank Regional High School. Dr. Donald Warner, Superintendent of Red Bank Regional has stated that the EWT results present "difficult concerns for us and the allocation of our resources. It impacts every attitude and behavior in this building". Dr. Robert Nogueira, principal of the Red Bank Regional High School, has explained that the EWT scores have " a bearing on the scheduling on the number of remedial classes and the number of aides hired". Clearly, a change must be made to break this continuous pattern of poor achievement….

Attempts to reform the system from within have not produced acceptable results. Concerned Red Bank parents and community members have tried to work within the existing educational system to correct this disturbing educational decline. Other residents possessing the economic resources to do so have chosen to place their children at private, parochial or out-of-district schools. Still other parents have chosen to home school their children. As a result student enrollment in the Red Bank Middle School continues to decline….."

The above mentioned Executive Statement from the Charter School clearly stipulated the academic concerns within the district; however, the divisions within the three school communities could easily be witnessed simply by touring the high school building and witnessing which classes were laden with minority students, who had been tracked into remedial and lower academic level classes. The other area to witness separation was in the school cafeteria where the majority of black students sat with other black students and the majority of white students sat with white students. Occasionally, a mixed more diverse group might be seated at a cafeteria table, but these were usually sport's team members.

## Homework Contracts

As a means of overcoming the racial divide, I attempted a special event similar to what I attempted while teaching at Fitzsimmons Junior High School in Philadelphia, where I first started teaching. As you recall, I visited the homes of the children in my classes. This time, however, I would visit the home of every student in the school system. At the time this merely meant 1100 to 1200 visitations. As I planned the home visitations I was very much aware of a quotation attributed to Mark Twain: "For every complex problem, there is a simple solution and it's usually wrong." However, Frederick Wilcox once said that "progress involves risk; you can't steal second base and keep your foot on first." I also knew that to try is to risk failure, but risks must be taken, because the greatest hazard in life is to risk nothing.

In my thinking homework has always been an integral part of the school curriculum. It's an idea that is as old and acceptable as "motherhood and apple pie." From an educator's viewpoint, homework has always been viewed as (1) a factor contributing to a student's ability to learn, (2) a means of enhancing independent study, and (3) an enrichment activity specifically designed to enhance the classroom lesson. Yet, based on informal discussion with parents, my own children's school experience and literature espousing homework as a part of the thrust towards improving the basics, it would appear that in many districts homework had lost its importance in the classroom.

Parents, however, still worship the so called "old norms". Witness the following statements: "

As children we always had homework, and after all didn't we turn out all right"; or " No school is worth its salt unless homework is applied as a vital part of the curriculum, especially today when the almighty switch isn't applied to the vital part of the anatomy as a means of enhancing learning."

The idea of initiating homework contracts originated with the Superintendent's Advisory Council, a group of approximately 50 parents from the three districts. During one of the well-attended monthly meetings, parents began to ask basic but difficult questions. Do teachers assign homework? How much homework is given in each subject, and do assignments vary from teacher to teacher? I actually groped for possible answers, but promised to investigate and report the findings at the next meeting.

My investigation revealed inconsistencies on the part of teachers in assigning homework. In addition, there was little, if any, direction given to teachers nor was there a board policy governing homework assignment. Therefore in order to promote Board of Education support and sanctioning, I prepared and recommended a Homework and Independent Study policy which was adopted on May 18, 1977. The policy stipulated the reasons for homework, consideration in length of assignments and the caveat that homework not be given for disciplinary reasons.

The next concern was to give meaning to the policy in a positive fashion without undermining the classroom teacher's academic freedom, while at the same time providing a necessary service to students and parents. It was at this point that I devised a program called "Project H.I.P" (Homework Improvement Program). It was a contract of the school with individual parents. At first the Superintendent's Advisory Council cautioned against using the term "Contract", suggesting that a school district could not bind parents with a legal contract. After an informal session with the board attorney, it was decided to add one sentence: "This is not a legal contract" The contract to be signed by parents read as follows:

"We agree to adopt the following homework contract for the benefit of our son/daughter for the 1977-78 school years.

(A) Set aside a minimum of one hour for preparation of homework assignments.

(B) Eliminate T.V., telephone calls and any other distractions during this period.

(C) Check daily to see if work has been completed

(D) Check teacher corrected assignments to find areas of student weakness.

(E) Encourage and recognize any achievement or gains our son/daughter attained.

The final step involved enlisting staff volunteers to tour the three communities, to visit the homes of students, and to request the return of homework contracts that had been mailed to every student's home. Unfortunately, after two weeks, the list left in the main office for staff volunteers remained unsigned. Nevertheless, I was determined to tour the communities alone, when the Title I Coordinator and an English teacher telephoned to volunteer. They spoke with the Teacher's Association President who also volunteered. In the remaining few days, a vocational education teacher, the school social worker and a guidance counselor joined the interested group. Not one administrator or department head volunteered. A legalistic principle narrowed staff involvement, as teachers operate under a rather strict contract that tends to frown upon activities unrelated to extra work extra pay activities that are not a part of the teacher's contract.

Our plan was to visit homes the entire month of November for three nights each week. After receiving a computerized student address listing, and arranging for press coverage by our local newspaper, the grand tour began. We decided to visit homes between the hours of 7:00 p.m. and 10 p.m. We carried flashlights to see house numbers, sticks to ward off dogs and necessary rain gear when appropriate. We were generally received in homes with courtesy and enthusiasm. Once inside conversations ranged from homework to general school problems. Some parents expressed general disbelief that the school superintendent and staff members were actually visiting homes within the community. In two of the three communities, students were telephoning ahead to let other students know we were in the community. After a month had passed we found that 72% of the contracts had been returned by students or mailed. Many parents and students sent letters directly to the Superintendent in support of or contrary to the concept of homework contracts:

Student #1: "I consider this an affront to my scholastic achievements. I have always considered homework an important part of the educational process...I can see that you want to improve the academic standard and heartily agree, however, you are forgetting people who put in long hours of time for teachers like......."

Student #2: "I do not feel that either I or my parents should have to sign a homework contract because I feel that I am old enough to know whether I should watch T.V. while I'm doing my homework or turn it off. I spend more than one hour doing my homework anyway."

Student #3: "I do not feel that either I or my parents should have to sign this contract . Since I have three honors courses I do at least two hours of homework every day without having to sign any kind of contract."

Parent #1: "Please note class rank. Signing this would be an insult to Barbara's present study habits. (The parent did sign.)

Parent #2: "Could this form letter mean that our son is not meeting his academic requirements? We have been very happy with the reports we have been receiving. Have we been mistaken in reading his report card? If so, we will certainly work to improve his record."

Parent #3: "Please note: last year math labs were poorly staffed."

Parent #4: "It has always been our custom to see to it that our children did their homework at night without television or telephone interruptions."

Parent #5: "We both agree that it is better for high school students to assume responsibility for their own learning without undue parental pressure."

Parent #6: "We appreciate your establishing standards for students and back you all the way."

Parent #7: "Both my husband and I would like to thank you as well as congratulate you on your Homework Improvement Program. We feel your efforts should be respected by all parents as well as students."

Parent #8: "I think it would be a good idea to consider moral standards in the school instead of homework contracts. Instead of punishing all the young men and women, get rid of pregnant girls who corrupt the morals of their friends and acquaintances. I never heard of allowing a pregnant girl to finish high school. It's a disgrace. You educators should wake up to the real problem."

Parent #9: "I am sure that my son's academic record proves that it is not necessary for him or me to sign a contract."

Parent #10: "I would like to express my approval of the approach you have taken to improve the quality of education at Red bank Regional High School."

Parent #11: "We are extremely pleased with the new effort to make discipline and study a part of the curriculum. Your goals are ours."

Parent #12: "Please give me your assurance that your teachers/staff will meticulously demand completion of every assignment."

Parent #13: "I expect my children to take their homework seriously and they do."

Parent #14: "I find this difficult to do as very few corrected papers are brought home."

Parent #15: "We are sending this homework contract unsigned because it is in opposition to our method of child raising."

Parent #16: "My daughter has very little activity now, and when she comes home she does her school work first above anything else."

President of Red Bank Regional Education Association: "Your outstanding work has gone beyond the boundaries of Monmouth County and the Teacher

Organization of the State of New Jersey in recognizing you for your outstanding administrative procedures and outstanding community relations."

A graduate student involved in university research on homework inquired as to whether or not the contracts resulted in improved grades. It was difficult to isolate homework contracts as the sole contributing factor to improved grades at the high school since several new programs were instituted at the same time. These included in-school suspension, a policy on graduation standards, reinstitution of final exams, structured study halls tied into academic grades, and finally homework contracts. However, the total academic climate of the school changed significantly. The concept of academic excellence turned the school around. Finally, parent members of the Superintendent's Advisory Council were astonished that communications between students and parents related to school concerns had either increased or become a priority for the first time since elementary school.

As things worked out, Homework Contracts did not cure the racial divide, but was an initiative that increased dialogue between the school system and all participants within the high school district. In fact the program was so widely accepted that the Daily Register, our local newspaper, printed a very large cartoon display of our efforts with homework contracts. Yet, in the midst of change and innovation at the high school, the quiet unspoken sophistication of race and its divisive misunderstandings continued in the school system. In some ways our quiet dilemma reminded me of Plato's work *The Republic* and "The Allegory of the Cave". [4] In this cave allegory, Plato describes a deep, dark and noticeably damp cave. In the midst of the cave there is a fire. The light from the fire casts shadows on the wall. The fixtures consistently remain fixed and comfortable in their limited existence. However, one day one of the shadows begins to move, and in doing so discovers light, discovers the mouth of the cave, and discovers freedom. Having found a new world, a new beginning, the shadow descends back into the depth of the cave to offer the others a new existence, but the others continue to remain fixed in place, content to remain in the shadows and dampness and limited comfort of their meager existence.

We might conclude from this allegory that when it comes to ameliorating the racial divide in our school systems, many of us are afraid to come out into the light, afraid to risk the inconsistencies found in debating the great issues: affirmative action, diversity, welfare, income disparity, immigration, the future of the economy, the expanding prison culture, religious fanaticism, dysfunctional families. Thus, even today, April, 2007, Imus, a popular radio/ television commentator, humorously labeled the Rutgers, New Jersey girl's championship basketball team as a bunch "of nappy headed 'ho's ( whores)". The question that looms outside our hidden caves is: When will we, as a nation of intelligent individuals, have the courage to come out of the caves of our limited destinies and dialogue about the great issues of the day? Why can't we as Americans persist until we settle once and for all the race issue? It takes persistence, but we have multiple examples of persistence. For example, there is scarcely a bar in Beethoven's music that was not written and rewritten at least a dozen times. [5] Gibbons wrote his auto biography nine times and produced *The Decline and Fall of the Roman Empire* in twenty years.[6] Even Plato, one of the world's greatest writers, wrote the first sentence in *The Republic* nine different ways before he was satisfied. [7] Burke wrote his conclusion of his speech at the "Trial of Hastings" sixteen times, [8] and Butler his famous "Analogy" twenty times. [9] It took Virgil seven years to write his *Georgics,* and twelve years to write the *Aeneid.* [10] Why then, can't we persist and answer our racial problem in America? Surely, we care about our children and future generations! Our children are at risk!

## CHILDREN AT RISK

Each day across America thousands upon thousands of children of all ages, descriptions, ethnicities and origins can be seen romping on our playgrounds, swimming in tiled community-sponsored pools or running under water splashing from fire hydrants on hot city streets. Many are uniformed participants of community based baseball, soccer, football and basketball teams. A lesser number learn to play tennis and golf and are privileged to participate in the golden opportunities of the "land of the free and home of the brave" called America. Others learn play and socialization skills in large empty cardboard boxes, that once held refrigerators and washing machines similar to the ones used at the Laundromat. They play half ball with broom sticks and one half of discarded tennis balls. Some boldly shoot craps (throw dice) in the middle of abandoned streets, and in a few cases, streets whose adult community are too frightened to take command of their neighborhoods. Still others are seeking temporary highs while smoking cigars filled with marijuana (blunts) or ingesting illegal drugs and imbibing top shelf liquors and wines. A number are raiding the closets of their parents, stealing money and saleable goods from home to support illicit habits. Many have taken to body piercing, baggy trousers, rainbow colored dyed hair, black lipstick, stark white Draconian facial powders, spiked neck and wrist collars.

The above descriptions know no particular race, color or creed, but represent children who are seeking, striving, trying to find themselves in America. Many come from wealthy home environments, others can be classified middle class; many are recipients of food stamps or free and reduced lunches in our schools, but all are being socialized into the diverse and complicated fabric of American society. Unfortunately, too many fail to survive the throes of childhood, and become burdens to society in general and our nation as a whole. They become our helpless and our homeless. They help to fill our mental health facilities, and populate our overcrowded jails and other incarceration institutions inclusive of juvenile detention centers.

The bleak scenario painted above does not aptly, dutifully or appropriately acknowledge the fact that a large majority of our children do succeed. They become meaningful caretakers of our values and attitudes, and adhere to the democratic principles of "liberty and justice for all", and in fact fulfill the American dream. However, I am concerned with the thousands and thousands of children categorized dispossessed, disenfranchised, and misplaced. African American children are no exception, and in the minds of many become the rule for all negative behavior experienced in the larger society. This socialization norm is reinforced by images depicted on T.V. shows such as MTV characterizations of Mims, Fat Joe, Huey, Crime Mob and others whose cultural means and methods of communication differ from the larger societal norm. Thus, African American children are faced with a greater risk challenge than other ethnic groups, because of the ever increasing bureaucracy of opposites, i.e. poverty vs. wealth, intelligence vs. dullness, existing in a society with an ever increasing gap between " the haves and have not's". Schools, hospitals, court systems, mental health facilities, child care institutions all are faced with the realities of the bureaucracy of opposites.

When reviewing some of the crucial descriptions associated with our school system in Monmouth, you realize that no single town or municipality in America can compare to the beauty and magnificence of our surroundings. Monmouth County, New Jersey's beauty is enhanced by a 27 mile coastline bordering two well kept military installations, municipalities composed of 35 boroughs, two cities, 15 townships, one village, Brookdale Community College, Monmouth University, 187 public schools, 28 parochial schools, 13 private schools, several charter schools and 13 vocational wings. The county abounds in natural resources enhanced by an abundance of parks and recreational facilities. Hendrik Hudson, founder of Monmouth County, would have been proud to witness our many seashore resorts, and prospering industries exemplified by electrical machinery plants, businesses dealing in chemicals, farming, horse breeding, large insurance companies and communication corporations.

At first blush Monmouth County exemplifies all the old tried and true traditions of what America can and must be – diversity, success, high employment rates. Yet, even in the midst of prosperity and changing demographics, Monmouth County and the nation's educational systems face a continuous problem of preparing all our citizens for entry into a highly competitive, skills driven labor market. Our present educational policy and practice will result in many of our youth entering the 21st Century unprepared to meet the demands of the future. Specifically, are minorities who have been historically discriminated against prepared through effective training to participate in an ever changing economy; or will we be satisfied with a permanent underclass, disproportionately African American, incarcerated and/or remaining in the same socio-economic stratification generation after generation? Further, what are the implications relative to economic parity and racial equality?

The above mentioned question causes one to reflect upon both local and national circumstances surrounding family life, educational patterns, preparation for the work force, the disproportionate number of minorities concealed behind locked doors in our jails and juvenile detention centers and the social impact of our religious institutions in driving the direction of our children.

Shakespeare's Hamlet aptly describes the overall dilemma facing African American children:

"To be or not to be, that is the question;
Whether 'tis nobler in the mind to suffer
The slings and arrows of outrageous fortune
Or to take up arms against a sea of troubles, and
By opposing end them." [11]

Few realize or articulate the true meaning of the soliloquy quoted above. It can be classified as one of the most militant expressions of hopelessness existing in the world today. Nothing said or written in *The Autobiography of Malcolm X* reflects the potentiality for violence and destruction as does the eventuality of taking up "arms against a sea of troubles", so enmeshed in the ongoing relationships of African Americans in the land of freedom and opportunity—the "good ole U.S.A." [12]

Sociological concepts and belief systems which center around theoretical notions of "being" and "becoming" loom heavily over many aspects of the African American community. There is a constant struggle existing in the tried and proven adult community which is sometimes passed down from generation to generation, father to son, mother to daughter: "You ain't never going to be nobody, until…." This negative notion of "being" vs. "becoming" is many times ingrained within the inner fabric of young men and women who must contend with tenuous, sometimes temporary family relationships, while simultaneously dealing with the historical question of the individual and his/her place in the larger American society. All children are faced with this concern; yet African American youth everywhere face a dual-edged sword in contending with on going negative forces at home which are reinforced in our institutions—schools, jails, religious institutions. One aspect of the dual-edged sword can be found in differences of perceptions of the acceptability of language patterns. For example, at a recent Sunday morning service at a local Baptist church in Red Bank, the choir sang three beautifully arranged songs. The lyrics were as follows:

Song #1: "When I woke up this morning, I didn't have no doubt."

Song #2: "I gotta new walk over in Zion and it's mine, mine, mine."

Song #3: "Steal away to Jesus; I ain't got long to stay here."

It should be noted that many, if not most, of the predominantly African American churches were probably singing songs with similar lyrics and grammatical construction. Congregation members internalize the meanings of these songs, and, in fact, hum and sing the lyrics during the week. This is an acknowledged part of the culture, just as is "talking back" to the preacher during the sermon and standing, clapping, "making a joyful noise to the Lord" throughout the sermon.

Religious institutions are only one medium through which language is learned and culture is defined. Other "stop-overs" for language and culture such as M.T.V., the music of R. Kelly, Akon, Diddy, Bow Wow, Beyonce and Shakira further complicate the learning process. These artists and their music are heard over and over again on popular radio and T.V. stations. The language, dress styles, behavior and attitudes of these modern folk heroes are imitated and emulated in homes and on the streets. In many cases children are rapidly inculcated into the perceived normative behavior of the popularized artist, and, in turn, play out in realistic ways the perceptions of tunes and lyrics whose full intent may be pure fantasy. The above behaviors are especially dangerous when certain role models become first time felons. However, this depiction of culture is in no way reflective of the entire African American community; nevertheless, the daily ritual of contending with the strange duality of language and culture is prevalent in most, if not all, segments of our society.

Yet, the "war" begins on Monday morning in most school districts throughout the nation where we immediately witness a clash of cultures in the classroom. Neither the acceptable language pattern nor the behavior exhibited in the religious institution is tolerated in the school classroom or corridors. The young person who attended the local Baptist Church and/or other predominantly African American churches must now put aside the poetic language of the church and experience a rigorous set of established behaviors traditionalized as acceptable by the larger society. Many students are unable to adjust to the different normative behavior, and are consequently placed in special designated classrooms as punishment for unacceptable actions. Not all African American students are unable to make the necessary accommodation to change, but far too many rebuff the system without understanding why.

This tragic clash in cultures and learning styles is readily realized when one compares the continuing saga of deficiencies in predominately minority schools vs. schools whose clients are predominantly white. A sample illustration from Monmouth County's Early Warning Test and High School Proficiency Data revealed the following:

| District | School | Percent passing | | |
| --- | --- | --- | --- | --- |
| | | Reading | Math | Writing |
| +Asbury Park | Middle School | 78.8 | 40.9 | 64 |
| Deal | Deal | 100 | 94.1 | 100 |
| Howell Township | Middle School | 98.3 | 92.9 | 95.9 |
| Little Silver | Markham Place School | 100 | 100 | 100 |
| +Long Branch | Middle School | 84.8 | 64 | 72.9 |
| Monmouth Beach | Monmouth Beach Elementary | 100 | 100 | 100 |
| +Neptune Township | Middle School | 86.1 | 75.5 | 72.2 |
| +Red Bank | Middle School | 83.4 | 65.1 | 69.2 |
| Wall Township | Wall Intermediate | 98.2 | 93.9 | 97.4 |

+ Predominately minority school population

# High School Data

| District | High School | Percentages | |
|---|---|---|---|
| | | Drop Out Rate | College Bound |
| +Asbury Park | Asbury Park High School | 13.7% | 44% |
| Holmdel | Holmdel High School | 0.1% | 98% |
| +Long Branch | Long Branch High School | 3% | 76% |
| Rumson Fair Haven | Rumson Fair Haven High School | 0.5 | 94 |
| Shore Regional | Shore Regional High School | 0.8% | 95% |

+ Predominantly minority population

The cycle of poverty, so aptly described by Oscar Lewis' *La Vida*, and its impact upon the health, safety and welfare of our nation and our communities must become an integral part of our state and national agenda and become prioritized by our county and local governments. [13] Most important are the ever increasing numbers of Juvenile Commitments for youth.

One of the most devastating reality checks happened a few years ago, when I served as Chair of the Monmouth County Visinage Committee. Our task was primarily to serve as a "watch dog" citizen's group for the county court system. On one occasion we were given a tour of the Monmouth County Jail System. The facility is clean, attractive , well equipped and furnished, secure, complete with recreational and food service facilities; yet, in the midst of all that appeared comfortable, there existed a sea of incarcerated humanity, most of whom were African Americans who once walked our school corridors and isolated themselves in the corners of our classrooms. Most embarrassing were the many persons who shouted out to me by name, saying: "Dr. Warner, what are you doing here?" These were my former students that somehow we as educators and the rest of society had let slip through the cracks. We failed to inculcate them in the knowledge of right and wrong. We failed in so many ways too numerous to mention. I am still sickened by the thought of the tour, plus the intelligent gentlemen I met in one of our state prisons, who were all serving life sentences.

The Monmouth County Court System possessed a cultural ethos dominated by values/ ideals unique to the complicated bureaucracies which direct their viability. Fortunately, the court system's Chief Executive Officer, Assignment Judge Larry Lawson, understood the existing sub culture of the court system and those forces, direct and indirect, which tend to shape the direction of the courts. Yet, if we recognize that a strong cultural imperative is necessary to properly care for the young, transmit knowledge and limit external and internal conflict, then our courts must move from the perceived closed system syndrome to an open system which includes public scrutiny at the highest level of decision making. Fortunately, the Supreme Court of the State of New Jersey established a Standing Committee on Minority Affairs which provided a model for our county. Their task, simply stated, was to eliminate discrimination within the justice system. A portion of the viable action plan included but was not limited to (1) community based volunteers, (2) active processing of grievances against the judiciary, and (3) an ongoing training and career development programs designed to fairly and effectively sensitize court personnel to the needs of minorities.

While establishing commissions on juvenile justice was laudable and commendable, the increasing incidences of school violence remained an issue. According to Weist and Warner, " incidence of violence as early as 1949 was relegated to lying and disrespect, however, reports of the 1990's include physical assaults, rapes, homicides. Today's violence is categorized by the increasing use of weapons. A high percentage of students in the inner city has witnessed someone shot stabbed, robbed or murdered". [14]

Along with indicators mentioned above that impact our ability to properly educate our children, there exists the ever imposing problem today of deteriorating neighborhoods, a phenomenon accepted by the larger society as a constant, imposed upon a certain segment of the society and then forgotten. The unfortunate result is that many persons view the place where you live or "come from" as synonymous with your ability to succeed. Your economic worth and even your potential for success are measured by perceptions of those in control, who may lower their expectations for you based on preconceived notions of what constitutes "middle and upper class". The perception is that if you reside in "x" community and "x" neighborhood, then "you won't amount to much". This attitude prevalent in all areas of the larger society weighs heavily upon our children who are sensitive enough to know that many of those in control of their destinies fail to value them as other than the lesser of necessary evils existing in a particular community.

Kuykendall deals with the perception of differences stating: "We are products of our own cultures. We see people and all things in the way we were conditioned to see them. All too often, innocently and inadvertently, we draw conclusions about others based on our own limited perspectives.. For example, a teacher raised believing that people who wear glasses are smarter than those who don't, would, inadvertently, engage in behavior which would reveal to students those feelings and beliefs. Similarly, a teacher raised to believe that an "only" child is more likely to be a "loner" and underachiever than a child born of a large family is likely to make inference and behavioral choices which reflect that belief". [15]

## The Stakes

I began this segment wrestling with the multiplicity of problems associated with an increasing society of children at risk, and now I pose the question: What are the stakes? Clearly, the future of our nation and the well being of the local community where you reside will depend upon our willingness to provide necessary, meaningful and challenging opportunities for all inhabitants of the land. The nation's economic stability and eventual competitiveness in the global arena demand a wise use of human resources, especially African Americans and other minorities who are at risk of being a liability to the general welfare rather than an asset.

From a practical point of view, who will support the social security needs of our ever increasing aging society? Even more challenging is the notion that an uneducated, social misfit may be the only service worker available in our nursing and rehabilitation facilities. Will he or she be responsible and responsive enough to administer medications, or for that matter, take care of the multitudinous physical needs of the once revered senior citizen?

If predicted birth rates for African Americans, other minorities plus the influx of immigrants increase above majority culture participants and we fail to educate and provide for mental and physical health needs and continue to incarcerate in disproportionate numbers, what then will be the predictable results for the American society? Without positive programmatic interventions, a gloomy future replete with abject hopelessness and its potential for disruption and revolt rests in the shadows waiting to explode and or "take up arms against a sea of troubles". [16]

Applicable to African Americans is the notion once posited in a cartoon by Jim Borgman printed in the Newark Star Ledger. The cartoon reiterated an old popular adage: "It takes a village to raise a child". However, the cartoon suggested several questions requiring discussion: (1) What if the village is on crack? (2) What if the village is ruled by gangs? (3) What if the village doesn't know it's a village? (4) What if children don't know that they're children anymore?

It has not been my intention to argue the historical merits and failures of equal opportunity, affirmative action, community segregation or the failure of urban education. Instead we must focus on the future global economy whose varied competitive structure will demand a world economy where the less educated person will find himself characteristically destined to remain in low paying jobs without tenure, without seniority and with little or no means of advancing via a career ladder. Given the predictable continuing growth in areas such as computer service technicians, programmers, electrical engineers, insurance, medical, physical and occupational therapists, mechanical and electrical engineers to name a few, it follows then to be in our best interest to prepare effective workers who know how to allocate time, money and materials, work on teams, acquire and evaluate information, apply technology, think critically and be decision makers imbued with integrity and honesty. Thus if the nation and our local communities are to move from status quo and laissez-faire to progress and initiative, then we must reexamine public policy positions and initiate programs and partnerships that give recognition and action to the dilemma faced by the larger society, inclusive of the plight of African American children, and focus on eradicating the social and political ills directed at human resources outside the mainstream.

## PIGEON OR STATUE?

The average length of time a person stayed in a school system as superintendent was approximately five years, after which it was usually desirable, if not forced to resign, to seek a position in another school district. However, in 1975, historically I was breaking ground as "the first" African American in every Administrative position held. Therefore, other than the few urban districts that hired black superintendents, where was I to go? Nevertheless, being aware of the risks in the superintendency regarding board- superintendent-staff relationships, community perceptions and student achievement or the lack thereof, I applied for a position as Chief School Administrator in Washington, D.C. In my thinking, the system there was sorely in need of revitalization, and I had developed the necessary skills to turn it around. Interestingly, my interview took place on the same day John Hinckley, Jr. attempted to assassinate President Ronald Reagan. In fact, it was the very same hotel, the Washington Hilton, where they held my interview later that afternoon. When I arrived the assassination attempt was over and police officials and others were surrounding the premises. The cab driver could not drive into the hotel area, but had me exit the cab a short distance from the hotel. Approximately three hours later after the scheduled interview was finished, I felt confident that I would be one of the top contenders as I had proven experience in all the areas questioned. Later I was contacted and notified that a person inside the school system was appointed to the position. Immediately I surmised that the position was taken before applicants applied, and that the interviewing process was merely held to meet the required legalities associated with board policy regarding administrative vacancies.

If ever asked to explain the job as superintendent, I would reply: "Some days you're the pigeon, and some days you're the statue." During the majority of the twenty-three plus years of my days as superintendent (Willingboro and Little Silver, New Jersey), I was a pigeon flying high. In the Afro-American community there is a musical form that I love called the "blues". B. B. King once sang one of my favorites entitled "Ain't Nobody's Business What I Do." [17] At first blush the title rings with a sense of unbridled freedom and is suggestive of an unbridled soul high on life, devoted to the carefree nuances of an individual running free in a society that continues to shackle, both figuratively and literally, my ability to reach, obtain and maintain any semblance of manhood and respectability. It is as though the blues singer was saying, "I'm tired of being the statue, with all its implications, and because opportunities for becoming the pigeon are limited or void, allow me the momentary privilege of casting aside the worries and hardships of daily living, for "It ain't nobody's business what I do!"

Strange how I love that blues song. It is an internalized part of my culture, and yet I know that the suggested lyrics move beyond the predictable of genius, property, difference, accident, and species cited by Aristotle, and way beyond the counsel of the biblical prophet Elijah and Micaiah to the evil King Ahab. [18] For you see, it is your business what I do! Therefore, I reject that part of the culture which calls for reckless abandonment of the social order. I must abide by a greater destiny as exemplified by a musical instrument I once saw in the Metropolitan Museum of Art. This strange instrument has a dual bank of strings composed of two layers, five strings on the top and fifteen strings on the bottom. When you pluck the top strings, the bottom strings vibrate in harmony and support of the top strings. They are called sympathetic strings. The power structures in our respective communities are symbolic of the top strings of the musical instrument. Each power broker has a network of bottom strings, human resources, that can be plucked--people who understand the debilitating effects of the drug culture, people who understand the ills associated with disintegrating families, people who know the truth and value of education, people who will stand up for right and justice. Collectively, we need to strike those strings, and send them forth into our local communities, the state and the nation. Have them carry the good news about each individual human being. Have them concentrate on our similarities. We must begin a new revolution; one that rejoices in the knowledge that love is, love was, and love always will be the true revolution. That's the mission of superintendents, boards of educations and our multitudinous teaching staffs.

As time passed in the Red Bank Regional District, I managed to pluck a few strings by being engaged and active on many community boards including but not limited to the Monmouth Medical center, Riverview Hospital, Brookdale Community College, The Women's Center, Urban League, N.A.A.C.P., New Jersey Administrator's Association, Rotary Club etc. Over the years I was privileged to receive numerous awards of recognition from organizations, the governor's office, county freeholders, the Holocaust Center, school boards, religious organizations and churches. The greatest of the awards and tributes was the dedication of the twenty million dollar Student Life Center at Brookdale Community College in my name. The occasion was a glorious tribute, and my greatest joy was being able to whisper to Thomas S. Warner my son, a Program Manager and engineer: "You once told me I should stick with the philosophical crap, and you would stick with mathematics and science. Now, hopefully, you will understand the rewards of philosophical crap!"

A few years earlier the *Asbury Park Press* carried an article in its Community Profile section of the newspaper entitled: "Hands-on Educator Shapes Lives". In the article the reporter, Chanta L. Jackson, expressed some of my philosophical action plan. She wrote:

"Growing up as one of eight children in the town of Crestmont, Pa., population about 5000, Donald D. Warner was influenced by the many "invisible" faces who shaped his future. For instance there was Mr. Chapman, the store owner who gave him the $6.00 he needed to buy a book when he was a college student at Temple University. The store owner's face may have faded from Warner's memory, but his generosity has left an

277

indelible impression.

"He is one of those faceless individuals from the past who helped me become who I am today," Warner said.

Warner, 61, was recently honored by the Black American Cultural Association, a student group at Red Bank Regional High School. The award is given to those who exemplify high standards of scholarship and mentoring as set by former head coach and teacher, the late Howard Tyrone "Ty" Lewis, who died in 1990 of chronic myeloid leukemia.

The group aims to raise the awareness of the accomplishments of contemporary black leaders, build student pride, school spirit and positive attitudes, and promote racial harmony and service to the school and community.

Shalabda Nix, 18, association president, said the group selected Warner because of his determination and his dedication to the students. "Dr. Warner takes a personal interest in the students and everyday, you see him walking around the hallways", said Nix. " If students have a problem we can go to him first because he makes everyone feel comfortable. Instead of discouraging us, he makes everyone feel human and helps us realize that's it's OK to make mistakes, but its how we handle them that counts," she said.

For Warner, it's a role that comes naturally. "I always try to help people or do the things that are asked of me because I constantly think 'Who else is there that will help?'" he said.

"People need to examine themselves to see if they are a product of themselves and the answer, of course, is no. A lot of invisible faces along the way help, so it's now our obligation to be an invisible face to someone else."

Warner often draws on experiences from his early life for insight into situations he faces today. "My mother taught me to never give up on an individual," he said, his voice cracking with emotion as he called his mother's faith in an older brother who was often in trouble with the law.

"I was 10 or 12 and I use to ride the bus alone to Atlantic City with bail money for my brother tied to me", he said. "When I got to the precinct I would try to reach up over the high counters to let them know I was there with the money. These trips taught me something about dealing with people.

In 1951, Warner enlisted in the U.S. Marines and served on the front lines during the Korean Conflict. "I was trained to become a killing machine there and after my tour was over, I had to overcome that so I could get back into mainstream society.

He learned another important lesson when he returned to the United States and was one of the few black Marines stationed in Portsmouth, Va.

"One day we were returning to the base and the bus stopped to pick up myself and the other servicemen", he recalled. "They told me I had to go to the back of the bus and my friends, who were white, said that if I had to go to the back, then we would all get off the bus. The base was 10 miles away and we walked the distance because the guys felt we didn't go to Korea to fight for this country to return home and have one of us have to sit at the back of the bus," said Warner, explaining that he used the experience as a motivator to not let anything stand in the way of reaching his full potential.

After serving in the military, Warner used the G.I. Bill to pursue his lifelong dream of going to college. He earned a Bachelor of Science degree from Temple University, Philadelphia, and a Master's Degree and doctorate of education from Pennsylvania State University.

Only three of my brothers and sisters graduated from high school and I was the only one to go to college, but they all rallied to help me."

From his vantage point as superintendent

of schools for 18 years, Warner sees the need for greater emphasis on instilling values in young people. " We need to go back to some of the ways of the past and start outlining for our children what is appropriate and acceptable behavior", he said. " For some students the high school is the final chance for them to determine what society is all about."

"One of the most important things we can do is to instill in youth self-assuredness, because everything adds up to how they feel about themselves", he said. "If we can get them through the drug culture, then everything else is workable. We just have to take this opportunity to mold the students while they're in our safe haven."

For Edwin Hood, a 17 year old junior, Warner has served as a role model. "Dr. Warner cares about the students and, even though we've had our problems at the school, he has done a lot to make us feel safe," said Hood, a student in the Performing Arts Program. "He knows almost every student and one of his main concerns is our grades. And if we have a problem, he helps us."

"He's very into school spirit and is present at almost every school-sponsored activity. I don't think even the teachers take that much interest." Marion Fitzgerald, 18 of little Silver, said she is thankful for his caring concern. "I think the students here get the feeling that we are Dr. Warner's kids because that's how he treats us," Fitzgerald said. "He comes over and talks to you personally and makes everyone feel special and that's an important feeling to have in a school with such a diverse population as ours."

Shelly Lewis said she was having problems in several classes and received help and encouragement from Dr. Warner. "Dr. Warner stresses to the students, especially the minorities, that if we are not successful it's not because we can't be, it's because we don't try", said Lewis, who will be attending Brookdale Community College.

Warner also takes an active role in the community, as a member of numerous organizations .... In what spare time he can find, he enjoys gardening, reading, writing poetry and chauffeuring his youngest son Thomas, 18, back and forth to school at the University of Pennsylvania where he is a sophomore.

"A few weeks ago I was called for jury duty and,

Even though I was unable to serve on the jury because I knew one of the involved parties, it was the first time I had a chance to read three books," he said with a laugh.

Warner lives in Tinton Falls with his "grandest supporter" and wife of 37 years, Mercedes, who is a kindergarten teacher at Mahala Atchison School, Tinton Falls.

Despite his achievements, Warner is reluctant to take full credit for his own success. "It's embarrassing to deal with an interview when you are talking about yourself, because what's important in life is beyond self," Warner said. "It's about the people who define what you are and what you'll become." And whenever the going gets tough, he looks to a sign on his office wall. "I take each day one at a time and the sign behind my desk, (saying ) 'Don't let anyone take your joy' keeps me going." [19]

The newspaper article mentioned above was an excellent testimony to my efforts to stabilize a school community and the community- at- large relative to our individual beliefs and attitudes about other human beings that was many times out of joint with the biblical commandments to love. But one must view life in its largest perspective, for just as I was enjoying the benefits of hard work and commitment to others, the news of my mother's death reached me. As mentioned earlier, my mother, Mozelle Willis Warner was the motivation for all that I accomplished. Usually she required a telephone communication from me each evening at 6:00 p.m. sharp, and whenever I missed, she would telephone to inquire of my health. The answer was simply that on some days I was still busy at the office or in the community and not able to call; however, I could never use that as an excuse to her. At the time of her death she resided in Crestmont, Pa., almost a three hour drive from Tinton Falls, New Jersey where we lived. Yet, when she was hospitalized I drove the two turnpikes almost daily to visit. We discussed many varied topics ranging from family history to the economy. As a boy I was always reluctant to kiss my mother, because there were eight of us and I knew that "Momma",as we called her, loved us all and I didn't wish to get in the way of her hugging all the rest of her children. Eight kids require a lot of hugging, and I think she understood my reluctance for on one of my hospital visitations she asked me to lift her in the bed. Now my mother was a very tall and somewhat large woman, close to six feet in height and maybe 200 pounds. I think she knew the impossibility of my lifting her in the hospital bed, but it was her way of getting me to give her those final few hugs before death. I did so, struggled at the lifting which I never accomplished and kissed her on the forehead.

On just about every drive on the New Jersey turnpike and the Pennsylvania turnpike I would, in my solitude , cry along the way as I knew the end was near. On the date of her funeral, there were no tears, because I had already emptied myself after all the trips and visitations. Therefore, I celebrated in the midst of everyone else's sorrow. I carried with

me a secret memory, for on one occasion I asked
my mother what her favorite biblical scripture was
and she told me I Corinthians 13 and then she began
to recite the scripture line by line. Never will I
forget her final recitation:

"Though I speak with the tongues of men
and of angels,
and have not charity I am
become as sounding brass or tinkling
cymbal.
And though I have the gift of prophecy,
And understand all mysteries and all
knowledge;
And though I have all faith, so that I could
remove
Mountains, and have not charity, I am
nothing.
And though I bestow all my goods to feed the
Poor, and though I give my body to be
burned,
And have not charity, it profiteth me
nothing.
Charity suffereth long, and is kind; charity
envieth not;
Charity vaunteth not itself, is not puffed up
Doth not behave itself unseemly, seeketh not
Her own, is not easily provoked, thinkest no
evil;
Rejoiceth not in iniquity, but rejoiceth in the
truth;

Beareth all things, believeth all things, hopeth

All things, Charity never faileth: but whether there be

Prophecies, they shall fail; whether there be tongues,

They shall cease; whether there be knowledge,

It shall vanish away. For we know in part, and we

Prophesy in part. But when that which is perfect

Is come, then that which is in part, shall be done

Away. When I was a child, I spake as a child, I understood

As a child: but when I became a man, I put away childish

Things. For now we see through a glass darkly; but then

Face to face: now I know in part; but then shall I know

Even as I am known. And now abideth faith, hope, charity,

These three; but the greatest of these is charity." [20]

It was in the midst of these verses that I sat at the funeral alone, but not lonely, because her God had set me free and because staff members from Red Bank Regional High School were there at the funeral in large numbers, three hours from home , strangers in a strange land.

Upon arrival back at work, the occasion of their presence at my mother's funeral prompted me to address the staff at our first faculty meeting using the following analogy stating: "Today is August 10, 1992. It's 4:00 p.m. and Oprah Winfrey is on television discussing "The plight of political prisoners". Yet, I can't seem to concentrate on Oprah, because my mother recently passed. She was a powerfully humble woman, perhaps like your mother, whose full passion for life was one of loving others. Her total 86 years of experience was one of sharing.

As long as I live I shall never forget approaching the First Baptist Church of Crestmont, Pennsylvania, where my mother was to be funeralized. I saw representatives from every unit within our staff. A few vigorously shook my hands to console, others dared hug me and light a kiss on my darkened cheeks. Still others stood nearby, smiled and silently indicated by their presence, "I'm here not because you're black, or white, or Hispanic, but because the human condition requires that I sacrifice a full Saturday to be with you, when I could be at home, on the beach, or at the theatre.

My home is gorgeous today, because it's filled with expressions of sympathy from those of you who knew of my sorrow and wished to share a moment of my agony. The beautiful cards, flowers and baskets of fruit are neither black nor white, but instead reflect a multi-colored variegated magnificence. They speak no hatred, no animosity, no envy, no jealousy—just plain old fashioned human kindness.

Yet, as I view the expressions of sympathy, I think of you, my staff, 'old heads, beginners, middle aged' and wonder why as reflected in our end of the year 'Joys and Pains', many of us managed to see pure black and pure white. A few polarized "to the death" to defend with hatred and animosity the beauty of each definitive culture.

Our professional staff is composed of 116 persons, 12 are African American. Simply stated, our mission is one of teaching and caring for high school students. Yet, as Rodney King cajoled after the Las Angeles riots, 'Why can't we all get along?' What are the suspicions and allegations that tend to rip asunder our hardened veneers. Why are some of us frightened by the very students we have pledged to teach? Why does the large tri-colored flag in Brandon's classroom create near panic? Should we allow an African American club to coexist with our Spanish, Latin and French societies? Should the Black American Cultural Association be allowed to sell Malcolm X t-shirts, and is that the same as Students Against Drunk Driving and /or the Student to Student clubs promoting their activities?

Why are African American staff members viewed as anti-white when they conduct a luncheon to laugh and joke and listen to 'soul music', and should the school superintendent attend this luncheon if he is to represent us all? What other club or school organization has invited the superintendent to attend a social function? What factors contribute to the change from an integrated cheerleader's squad during football season to a predominantly black squad during basketball season? Why was there a problem or misunderstanding between staff members when one African American wore a black armband in recognition of a historical celebration and another white staff member found this objectionable and questioned the reason for the armband?

Do we devote too much time, energy and human resources to the continuous academic and social dilemma of Red Bank borough students who historically enter our hallowed halls academically disabled? Do our lower level, segregated classrooms reflect unintentional institutional racism?

What about our curriculum? Are there similarities and differences between the actions of Hamlet and Malcolm X? How should Renee approach this topic? How will Steve treat the issue of immigration as he discusses United States policy towards Haitians and other groups? Does BoBo regard the issue in the same manner and does it make a difference? How will Brian explain the United States of America's position and role in providing aid and substance to the people of Bosnia as compared to the people of Somalia? Will Ginny treat it differently and does it make a difference? As

Gerry discusses chemical dynamics and the nature of reactants, will he relate the bonding of chemicals to the bonding of human relationships? How will Tim and Pierre treat the same topic and does it make a difference?

Is there a place in the curriculum to discuss ancient civilizations and their impact upon today's society re: hieroglyphics, the calendar, sun dials, water clocks, pyramids, irrigation, Pythagorean Theorem, embalming and medicines? What approach will Janine take, and will Lou teach it differently; and does it make a difference?

And when T.J. teaches the rhythms of the people of the universe, will it differ from Sara's biology class when the rhythms of life and death are taught? Will it make a difference?

Will Joe's drama productions begin to give full consideration to the new changing demographics, and does it make a difference?

Is there a relationship between the African American slave who sealed himself in a wooden crate in Virginia and shipped himself to freedom in Philadelphia, an unknown land, and the Lord Odysseus, who experienced misfortune and could not reach Ithaca? How will Mary Todt teach this and will it differ from Erika's version and does it make a difference?

Finally I believe in our staff, your competence, intelligence and capabilities. True, this can be a difficult year re; the economy, changing values, and teacher negotiations, to mention a few. You will probably deliver to me the usual "hell" reserved for and deserved by all superintendents, yet, as we, like Cyrano de Bergerac, thrust, parry and drive home our beliefs, I will quietly re-read the multi-colored cards and expressions of love—especially the Mass cards which extended to me and my mother, a universal acceptance of the worth of humankind and the subsequent dignity of all human beings.

At Grambling State University there is a gymnasium built to honor Ed Robinson, football coach, who trained so many fine athletes, many of whom play professional football. Emblazoned across the top of the building in bold letters is the logo: *"A Place Where Everybody Is Somebody"*. That's the kind of home my mother insisted on and that's also my vision for Red Bank Regional High School students, staff and community *–"A Place Where Everybody Is Somebody"*.

# Chapter Eight
## It's Me; It's Me, Oh Lord...

One of the traditional religious classical hymns sung by our congregation at First Baptist Church in Crestmont, my home town, was "Standing in the Need Of Prayer." The familiar lyrics that I recall were: "It's me, it's me, It's me o Lord, standing in the need of prayer, not my mother, nor my father, but me o Lord standing in the need of prayer. Not my brother or my sister, but it's me o Lord, standing in the need of prayer". [1] That song was a song of hope, a song of restitution, a song of justification, repentance and resurrection. There were many occasions when I hummed that tune and repeated the lyrics silently as I stood before the caskets of our loved ones in churches and funeral parlors. First, my father, Robert "Deddy" Warner, Junior, then Robert Warner, the third, my brother, followed by my sister Dorothy Deans Vaughn, then Norman L. Warner , youngest brother, Charlotte Warner Robertson, younger sister, and finally Audrey Marie Warner, the sister who escorted me to first grade. Now, I stand alone surrounded by the freshness of memories of family, and the inability to communicate to them my responses to our lifetime of interactions.

In earlier chapters I discussed the bureaucracy of opposites, my intense love for Mozelle, my mother, and my quiet subdued hatred of Deddy Bob, my father. Each family member was uniquely positioned in my life, and offered lessons to duplicate and utilize to confront the realities of life. First my older brother and hero, Bobby, followed by quiet reserved sister Dorothy, the brightest of us all. She managed to give life eight wonderful children whose reluctant fathers hid their identities under the trestles of the railroad tracks behind our home on Washington Avenue. Audrey, the sister who nurtured my soul, caressed my limited energies and helped me to understand the arrogance of the visiting nurses, who interrupted our poverty with their unwillingness to understand the dimensions of being poor and black in America. She was a collector of affordable antiques, and in strict accordance with the biblical principles of love and commitment raised her three children independently unsupported by the former men in her life who called her preciously endowed with wisdom and integrity. On the other hand, Charlotte, my younger sister, stood on the sidelines and managed to embrace the American culture in full regalia of truth fashioned by a devoted husband and daughter who understood the expediencies in life that mark our shortened destinies. However, younger brother Norman energetically lived life to the fullest, and along the way challenged the credibility of unresolved passions that witnessed the blossoming of two beautiful children, one of whom was a mystery until I found her sobbing relentlessly in front of the funeral casket in the only church in the area who would accept his precious remains. And yet, even though I stood in the need of prayer, my prayers have been answered through the maturity and faithfulness of Mercedes , beloved wife, who fashioned a new tomorrow for all our children while maintaining the rigors of a home environment whose ambiance sometimes took on the rigors of a mother whose one dominating concern was that all the children be successfully planted in worthy professions . It was the blossoming of the lives of our children that counter balanced the on going intrusions of death in our midst.

Beth Suzette was our first child. At the time of her delivery, I was employed at John Bartram High School as a vice principal. Early in the morning, when labor pains began, we were at least an hour and thirty minutes from Einstein Hospital South in Philadelphia where our pediatrician had privileges. How convenient, thought I. In my stupidity, I drove to the hospital without any perceivable problems, admitted Mercedes and drove to work in Southwest Philadelphia. Around three o'clock in the afternoon, I received a call from the hospital announcing the birth of a baby girl in good health; therefore, I finished my work day and then drove to Einstein Hospital to visit my wife and view the new born baby. To this day, I have not been able to live down the fact that I did not stay at the hospital with my wife to await the arrival of our first child. Actually, I too regret having, in a sense, figuratively abandoned my wife to work at a job that could have awaited my presence given the special circumstances surrounding child birth. Nevertheless, Beth matured into a marvelous young woman, adhering to the principles of life as taught primarily by her mother, because most of the time I worked two jobs in an effort to provide for the family. Beth was totally involved in school activities during her school years inclusive of cheerleading , National Honor Society etc. ; however, the early years were somewhat trying for us as parents. Before Mercedes was able to stop working as a teacher, we employed a neighbor to care for her and discovered that certain unsupervised physical accidents were occurring such as smashing her right hand in the automobile door. Therefore, we engaged the volunteer services of my sister Audrey who lived in Philadelphia to care for Beth while we worked. Each weekday morning at 6:00 a.m., Beth was strapped into the back seat of my automobile, and we drove into

Philadelphia where I left her in the care of my sister Audrey, and then drove to Southwest Philadelphia to work. This solved our baby sitting problems. The years passed quickly and Beth was admitted to Brown University where she met lifetime friends. She and her friends are somewhat the intelligentsia of today; however, The Brown group, as I affectionately call them, all possess individual independent personality traits. For example while at Brown, Beth thought it proper to wear men's boxer shorts on public transportation when traveling home on study breaks; also much to my surprise one of my Little Silver Board of Education members, Flo Apy, was delighted to report to me that she saw my daughter Beth at her son's graduation at Brown, and that Beth and her group were in the midst of climbing over the six foot security fence to gain free admission during the event. Today the trend continues, only Beth is blessed with achieving a Ph. D. in psychology and besides being employed by the University of Maryland, enjoys a growing and successful private practice.

After a few years of unsuccessful attempts to conceive, Mercedes and I decided to adopt a child. First, we visited a few agencies in Philadelphia, but came to the conclusion that life was for sale and the adoption agencies were more interested in earning dollars than placing children. Their attitude and disposition reminded me of the stories I had read in the past about auctioning slaves in early America. Therefore, we successfully found an agency in

Philadelphia, through the welfare department, who directed us to the proper office. They sent representatives to view our home and then granted us the adoption of our oldest son, Nicolas S. Warner. The agency recommended that he receive special services for his stuttering, but we knew that once he was involved in a loving and caring environment, that the stuttering would cease. Such was the case, for after a year the stuttering ceased. Meanwhile we sought out an attorney in Norristown, Pennsylvania, Mr. Charles Smith, and legal papers were drawn officially changing his name and status. Nicolas was not only an excellent student, but he excelled in track gaining the Monmouth County title record for the 440 yard run. Later he attended West Point on a scholarship, transferred to Monmouth University, and then completed a graduate degree at Temple University. He is now a licensed lawyer, who married Susan, a lawyer, and they gave us three beautiful grandchildren, Alexandria, Gabriella and Sophia.

We were extremely happy with the ideal nuclear family, when ten years after the birth of our oldest daughter another son was born named Thomas S. Warner. His birth occurred in Mt. Holly, New Jersey, while I was employed as Acting Superintendent of Schools in Willingboro, New Jersey. What a wonderful tribute to the beauty of life, for behold, unlike the small delicacies of his older sister, Beth, Thomas matured to become 6 feet four inches tall and over two hundred pounds. After graduating from the University of Pennsylvania, he became a Network Engineer and Program Manager after obtaining a stable position with Lockheed Martin in Orlando, Florida, where he found true love and married Ingrid, a beautiful, intelligent woman. One of the honors associated with both my sons, Thomas and Nicolas was that as a licensed minister, I was able to officiate at both their marriages and counsel them in the Word of God regarding the sanctity of marriage.

Once again as I stood in the need of prayer, God balanced the continuing saga of family deaths, by giving us new life and new beginnings in the precious beings of our children and grandchildren.


## SURRENDER

Surrendering had never been a part of my vocabulary, yet the time had come when after twenty two years as Superintendent of the Red Bank Regional High School District it was time, once again, to fold up the tent and become involved in a new aspect of life; therefore, I submitted my resignation. The Board of Education flattered me by accepting the letter "with regret". We had made many positive strides together over the years, and had accomplished much re: the initiation of a new Performing Arts program that attracted tuition students from as many as 33 other districts; academic achievement had improved significantly with our students gaining admission into the most prestigious colleges and universities in the country; racial harmony was improved and fewer students were being classified as special needs students strictly on the basis of disciplinary concerns shadowed by discrimination of color. One commentator had stated that "Politicians are like diapers. They need to be changed often and for the same reason"; however, we had managed to so engage our local municipal mayors in such a positive manner that when appealing the defeated budget to the city council, a mayor was heard to say: " Give Dr. Warner whatever it takes to run the district". What a positive testimony of faith in action. Finally, our teaching staff had matured to become one of, if not the best, academically prepared staffs in the state, resulting in students who were well prepared for higher education pursuits or entry into the business/ industrial complex.

As I moved towards retirement, I reflected on a paper my oldest sister Dorothy had pressed into my palm while she was receiving treatment in the hospital prior to the final cauterization that ended her life. It was entitled *Desiderata*. It was reportedly found in old St. Paul's Church, Baltimore, Maryland (1692) and reads:

"Go placidly amid the noise and haste and remember what peace there may be in silence. As far as possible without surrender be on good terms with all persons. Speak your truth quietly and clearly; and listen to others ; even the dull and ignorant; they too have their story. Avoid loud and aggressive persons, they are vexations to the spirit. If you compare yourself with others , you may become vain and bitter, for always there will be greater and lesser persons than yourself. Enjoy your achievements as well as your plans. Keep interested in your own career, however humble; it is a real possession in the changing fortunes of time. Exercise caution in your business affairs; for the world is full of trickery. But let this not blind you to what virtue there is; many persons strive for high ideals; and everywhere life is full of heroism. Be yourself. Especially, do not feign affection. Neither be cynical about love; for in the face of all aridity and disenchantment it is perennial as the grass. Take kindly to the counsel of the years, gracefully surrendering the things of youth. Nurture strength of spirit to shield you in sudden misfortune. But do not distress yourself with imaginings. Many fears are born of fatigue and loneliness. Beyond a wholesome discipline, be gentle with yourself. You are a child of the universe, no less than the trees and the stars; you have a right to be here. And whether or not it is clear to you, no doubt the universe is unfolding as it should. Therefore be at peace with God, whatever you conceive him to be, and whatever your labors and aspirations, in the noisy confusion of life keep peace with your soul. With all its sham, drudgery and broken dreams, it is still a beautiful world. Be careful. Strive to be happy." [2]

Thus I entered the end of the beginning and the beginning of the end. A rather large celebration of my retirement was held with friends traveling from many states and representative organizations to wish congratulations, but not farewell. Reluctantly, I graciously accepted the awards and precious gifts and commentary from community leaders, parents and students. Most encouraging was the presence of my Uncle Fred, the last remaining family member on my mother's side of the family. He is a good Catholic, and we stay in touch on a weekly basis.

Christine Federico, *Asbury Park Press* newspaper reporter published the following:

"Donald D. Warner started his career as an educator in the Philadelphia schools 40 years ago when teachers rode the trolleys to escort children to school and where he would visit the homes of each child who misbehaved that day.

He's ending his career at the end of June when he will retire from Red Bank Regional

High School after leading it as superintendent for 22 years.

The Board of Education sat quietly for a few moments before moving to accept Warner's letter of resignation last night. None of the members wanted to be the one to move it forward. One member, Florence Apy, even abstained from voting to show how much she wanted Warner to stay.

"I feel grateful to have such a fine school for my kids to go to and a lot of that gratitude I owe to you" said Leslie Taylor, another board member," We are going to have to try to fill the seat, but I know we are never, ever going to replace you", said board President Barbara Cottrell.

The board adopted a resolution increasing Warner's $129,923 salary by $3,000 for the 1997-98 school year. Warner will donate that increase to a scholarship at Pilgrim Baptist Church in Red Bank and to one of this year's top graduates in the senior class. He dedicated his last year's raise to scholarships as well. The board approved his retirement package which is a payment of 70 percent of his accrued sick time and remaining vacation time, Warner said. The payment figure was not available last night. Warner, who turns 65 in March, is popular in the community and the schools three towns-Little Silver, Shrewsbury and Red Bank. The ninth through 12th grade school which now has more than 1000 students started its performing arts program under his leadership.

Warner also serves as chairman of the Brookdale Community College board and on the board of Monmouth Medical Center. He has been a member of the board of the Monmouth County Urban League and was chosen as one of New Jersey's "100 Most Influential" by the City News of Newark earlier this year.

Warner said he believes Red Bank Regional is one of the best high schools in New Jersey. "People who have homogenous populations may be able to brag of their accomplishments, but when you have a population as diverse as ourselves and you are able to do the things we are able to do, then you have to be proud," he said. The Tinton Falls resident said he has no retirement plans as of now, but will continue serving many of the community's organizations.

In addition to starting the performing arts program, Warner remembered other highlights, like the time in the mid 1970's when he visited each student's home and asked them and their parents to sign a commitment to do homework. And then there was 1988 when the school had five National Merit Scholarship finalists.

304

Warner said the students haven't changed in his 40 years in education, but the external influences on them have, and they are faced with many more life-threatening decisions that could result in afflictions such as drug addiction and AIDS.

"You had a solid family structure (then)," Warner said. "Everybody was not always working all the time so youngsters could go home to a dinner table. So that is very different from today...As well meaning as we want to be, if we are not there for our kids, it becomes difficult, and that young mind , which is very flexible, can go in many directions, and that is a very difficult and dangerous change."…..

Even the *Asbury Press* editorial page carried a tribute: *"A LOSS TO EDUCATION"*. Much of the previous article was reiterated adding:

"The departure of a beloved and highly respected educator, whether an administrator or classroom teacher, is wrenching for any school district. Warner's departure is particularly painful for the Red Bank Regional Board of Education, which has come to rely on his success in helping students to learn and his devotion to their well being....Apy(board member) praised Warner …as a strong leader and educator with " a capital E"—who is sensitive and compassionate and a gentleman in the true sense of the word. "He is a man who truly reaches for the stars, both in his professional goals and in his personal life," she said. "He came to Red Bank when the school's reputation was at a very low ebb. Under him Red Bank Regional has become the respected institution it is today. " I think he has accomplished this because he strives for excellence and he expects this of all the professional and non professional staff and the students," she added. "He's been a role model for everyone with whom he's come into contact".

This is a man who....has successfully melded children entering the high school from widely divergent households and academic backgrounds in little Silver., Shrewsbury and Red Bank into an achieving student body that regularly graduates all its seniors. Any students found to be trailing their peers in studies are given the extra help they need to catch up.

Warner will be difficult to replace. But he won't be bowing completely from the public eye...The Monmouth County community is fortunate, indeed, that it will still be able to benefit from Warner's insight, knowledge and wisdom for some time to come, even if he will no longer be at the helm of Red Bank Regional High School after the end of the school year."

Thus in the midst of community and personal accolades, I was able to retire to the warmth of a home and family that over the years I delicately sacrificed time and energies in employment related activities. Now I was free to enjoy, to travel, to write and, if I so chose, to do nothing. However, I stayed active in several community activities and my church, where I was committed to teaching adult Sunday school each week to an interesting and enthusiastic group of adult students. As it would appear Sunday School had always been a part of my life since a young boy when Mozelle insisted on all the children attending.

## Affirmation

Mentally I was wrestling with the "what ifs" that define whether or not my life had made a difference to others in society who needed someone to serve and direct them. Actually, I questioned as did Anselm of Canterbury: Why Did God Become Man? Anselm, as you recall was "one of the great teachers of medieval scholasticism" and in a few words found in the Eugene Fairweather's book *A Scholastic Miscellany:Anselm to Ockham,* a debate occurs between Boso, a monk and then abbot of Bec( 1124-1136):

Boso. "While the right order requires that we should believe the deep things of the Christian faith before we undertake to discuss them by reason, it seems careless for us , once we are established in the faith, not to understand what we believe. Therefore since I think by God's prevenient grace I hold the faith of our redemption so firmly that nothing can shake my constant allegiance, even if I can find no reason to help me grasp what I believe, I beg you to show me what many, as you know, seek with me. Tell me what necessity and reason led God, although he is almighty, to take upon himself the lowliness and weakness of human nature in order to renew it."

Anselm. "What you ask from me is above me, and I am afraid to handle 'the things which are too high for me' (Ecc.3:22). If someone thinks or even sees that I have not given him adequate proof, he may decide that there is no truth in what I have been saying, and may not realize that in fact my understanding may have been incapable of grasping it". [3]

And so like Boso and Anselm, I began the search.


## Feet Planting on Higher Ground

As time and fate directed my path, late one night I had an unusual dream. Unusual, primarily because I seldom if ever dream. In the dream I was asleep on the bed, when I awakened to see Rev. Milliard

Harris, my pastor at Pilgrim Baptist Church, Red Bank. He was seated in a chair dressed in a black suit, white shirt, with his ankles crossed. I continued to rest in a fetal position attired in white under clothing. Opening my eyes and noticing Rev, Harris, I questioned, "Where are you going?" He responded, "I'm going to preach, but you're not ready yet." I awaked after a period of time, recalled the dream and ignored the experience. Then on September 17, 1998, two weeks later, I had a second dream. I was visiting the Red Bank Regional High School library, that had been named in my honor. I was seated waiting to speak with the secretary. Suddenly seated next to the secretary is a person, who showed me a religious text, stating: "The next time you speak, I want to hear you." Then she proceeded to wrap the soles of my right shoe with a soft cloth. I examined my feet and noticed that she had wrapped only the right foot and not the left. I awakened and wondered about the nonsensical dream; however, for the period of one week I had pain in the arch of my right foot for a reason I could not understand. In analyzing the first and second dreams, I decided that the two dreams each indicated a sense of incompleteness and unpreparedness. Then in a third dream, I was given a parchment, a large scroll half eaten, similar to the vision of Jeremiah 36 and the scrolls. In the final dream, dream #4, November 15, 1998 at 12:46 a.m. a gentle hand was laid atop my head. It was very gentle, mesmerizing to the point of numbness, and a voice shouted, "Who wants me? Who wants me?" At that point I awakened startled. In the next few months I began to search for a seminary where I could study for the ministry. I searched the internet, spoke with my pastor and several friends and visited three campuses on the east coast. After checking the various campuses and researching the backgrounds of the staff members, it appeared that many of the professors at the various campuses had been credentialed at Princeton Theological Seminary, plus Princeton, according to my research, had a superior library in religious studies. Reluctantly, I discussed with my wife my decision to attend Princeton, and applied for admission. Because I did not have the courage to commit Mercedes to move to the Princeton campus, I commuted each day of class 1 ½ hours each way until graduation. There were many days of inclement weather when the drive was twice as long; however, I purchased a new automobile with my sick pay payoff and engaged in the daily commute. While there, I became a daily fixture at the library, as I wished to finish as much of the academic work on campus before returning home each day.

As you may have guessed, I was then 66 years of age, the oldest student on campus. Most of the students were in the age grouping from 25 years of age upwards to one or two second career people in their early fifties or late forties. At least 40% of the students were women. Women, even today, struggle for positions in our various churches.

What was I doing attending seminary at such a late stage in my life? When I was a young boy, Uncle Eldridge died. My mother informed me that he had left money in his will to give to anyone who wished to train for the ministry. Never will I forget my reaction as I told my mother, "Mom, that's the last thing on earth I would like to do!" Ironically, my statement and declaration rings with elements of truth.

In my required biographical essay to Princeton Theological Seminary, I mentioned that it was during my final year at Temple University that I studied and discovered Gerald Manley Hopkins and the poem "God's Grandeur". [4] It was this poem that reminded me of humankind's fallibility. I was forced to acknowledge the presence of the all powerful God in my life. The poetic image of God brooding over mankind like a mother hen brooding over her baby chicks had stayed with me even today. Finally I realized why my mother had dragged me off to church three times a day each Sunday, plus Baptist Youth Fellowship and Sunday school.

Reflecting over the past forty years in the various roles of teacher, administrator and school superintendent, I was able to effectively minister to students, staff and community in a compassionate and encouraging manner. It was my love and compassion for positive human relationships that motivated me and drove me forward in pursuit of and commitment to Jesus Christ. In fact, my personal administrative style was always one of risk taking; however, risk taking involves analysis and commitment to positive change in my life and others with whom I interacted.

Time and time again I found myself involved in community organizations such as the Monmouth County Human Relations Commission , the County Vicinage Committee on Minority Affairs, and the Women's Center. Hope rests in the eventual triumph of good over evil; thus, the power of the church is the saving of lost souls as stipulated through the life, death and resurrection of Jesus Christ. Historically, much has been accomplished, yet the work of the church remains as paramount importance to the overall well being of a society confused by a life of vacillating standards. Hopefully, eventually a united church, one body united in faith and love, will make a substantial difference in a world culture yet to be determined.

Thus the rigorous study of the omniscience and omnipotence of God began in full force. I had a distinct advantage over many students, because many of the course papers required knowledge of the world and experiences about which to write and reflect. I was never without an experience to draw upon. In particular in one classroom I was able to bring to class an old wind- up victrola and recordings of people like Bessie Smith and other artists of the past. More importantly, many husbands and wives on campus sought me to counsel them in their marriages. In many cases the wife was sacrificing her career while the husband was pursuing a theological degree on a limited scholarship with few financial resources, thus creating hardship, emotionally and financially, for one if not both of the partners. However, I met many wonderful friends, and was honored to stand as best man in a wedding for one of my Korean friends, Steve. Steve and the now venerable Rev. Wonjae Choi became my closest friends on campus. Steve had a physical handicap requiring him to use a wheel chair for all activities. He was very independent and on many occasions refused to accept my help in pushing him around campus, and assisting him into the various class rooms. I always refused to listen to him and told him I was going to push him anyway, as he was not going to deprive me of my blessing. There was one particular day when Steve was trying to navigate his way into one of the school stores that was not handicap accessible. He was obviously stuck. This was the most pleasurable day of my life on campus, because he had to admit that he needed help. I, blaspheming, shouted out to him: "Vengeance is mine sayeth the Lord, but I've got you now sucker. You can't make it without me!" What joy! On other occasions, we toured Philadelphia and ate at the various restaurants having a wonderful time!

One of the highlights of the training at Princeton Theological was the actual field work internships designated for two experiences, one at a church and the other a hospital The church that accepted me was an inner city church in Trenton, New Jersey , Raritan Baptist Church, and the hospital where I served as Chaplain was Centra State Hospital in Freehold, New Jersey. Each position presented different challenges. The Raritan Baptist Church was organized under the leadership of the Rev. Samuel Hazelton, a former Princeton graduate and advisor at the Seminary. My attendance in Trenton was required at least two nights during the week for Bible Study, instruction, plus various never ending activities i.e. special services, and meetings with designated congregational groups .

Raritan Baptist Church was uniquely located off Martin Luther King Boulevard in an ever changing socio-economic division of the city. Judging from the surrounding homes and the populace who attended the community Saturday morning breakfast/ brunch handouts, every conceivable segment of the community was represented. Outside the building there was a permanent security guard stationed in the parking lot and around the premises to insure and provide a sense of security and safety for members and visitors. The guard, Mr. Amos, was a necessary and permanent fixture on the premises, but he constantly complained about money and his salary to anyone who would listen. However, given my years of experience in Philadelphia, I was cautiously at ease in my entrances to and from the property, especially in the late evenings. A few activities were as follows:

**September 20, 2000--** Met with Reverend Samuel Hazelton, Senior Pastor, who explained the needs and goals of the church as (1) reorganization and leadership, (2) the future initiation of a funded Nursery School, (3) an assignment to teach Adult Bible Study class, (4) the initiation of a Leadership Workshop. As explained to Pastor Hazelton, I felt most comfortable in areas of group dynamics and interactions with congregants; however, the first major hurdle was learning the names, capabilities and talents of the various congregation members.

**September 24, 2000--** After an hour and thirty minutes drive , I arrived at Raritan Church at 9:00 a.m. where I was greeted by the security guard and ushered into the pastor's office. The pastor explained that 21 years ago, he was asked to preach at this church as a favor until a new minister could be found. Subsequently, there was a split in the congregation membership. The head deacon was very supportive at first and the pastor was paid from the collection plate. Finally, a contract was arranged paying him $200 a week until such time as the membership increased, as he was involved in full time prison ministry. Since that time they have only had one church meeting, however, the agenda was not mentioned. The church building had been refurbished, but the pastor expressed deep concern relative to the human resources within the church which were at best "questionable". Mrs. Hazelton served as lay minister; however, she does not sit on the pulpit, but sits directly behind, managing all aspects of the service as regards late comers, prayer requests etc.

This service was soon followed by Family and Friends Day. I was requested to read the scripture and the other Princeton student rendered morning prayer. There were no deacons or trustees present and a strange woman took over clerical responsibilities. A three piece musical group provided the morning music, and the organist seldom played in the right key and was seldom in tune with the voices. Many of the songs were initiated by the pastor, who also read the announcements.

**September 27, 2000--** Met with the pastor and the other student to iron out responsibilities within the church for the academic year, where I requested a Sunday School manual to prepare for the class that someone else was teaching in a very dictatorial style. Class participation was discouraged and little if any discussion took place. Only eight members were present.

**October 1, 2000--** Arrived for Sunday School at 9:30 a.m. and noticed that the regular teacher had been replaced, with only five students in attendance. One senior member of the class tended to constantly argue points of scripture with the instructor.

At the 11:00 a.m. communion service much time was spent engendering the call of the Holy Spirit. Preaching lasted for at least fifty minutes followed by communion that had been reorganized . Unlike Family Friends Day , there were only about 150 people present. Also, the evening "Foot washing" ritual had ceased and was no longer apparent in the service. I arrived home around 4:00 P.M. after receiving a Sunday School manual from the pastor's wife, Evangelist Hazelton; another woman, Minister Joseene, served as worship leader and was also in charge of educational ministry with children on Wednesday evenings.

**October 3, 2000--** It was interesting to learn that the organist who played off key and about whom I complained was the pastor's son. I learned to observe more, before attempting to be critical of the institution. I arrived at 6:45 P.M. for a scheduled Men's Club meeting to observe the pastor's teaching. Instead the group was composed of 14 members, including the pastor's wife Evangelist Hazelton who was busy walking around the perimeter of the sanctuary invoking the call of the Holy Spirit. The rest of the group sat quietly reading the scripture or praying. Four of the faces were familiar, two ministers and two others; however, all others were unfamiliar. Finally, the pastor began teaching from "I Timothy" and provided excellent examples for today's Christian to follow. At one time during the presentation, he corrected the perceptions of his wife re: how to deal with pastoral care issues. Several persons testified to personal events that had occurred during the week which served as examples for the lesson. Our next meeting was scheduled for Saturday morning to participate in an anti-drug march, plus a scheduled supervisory meeting where I requested to teach in the pastor's absence.

**October 7, 2000--** Participated in the Anti-Drug march along with 50 to 75 young people, plus Rev. Hazelton, two ministers and several adult church members. We canvassed the surrounding neighborhood distributing literature, singing, marching and ministering to the people. This was street ministry at its best. Also, each Saturday people are fed by the church, provided free groceries sometimes after waiting for indeterminate lengths of time. The pastor and I spoke of arranging a program whereby we would minister to them first and then provide the groceries. Some of the anti-drug rally speakers included the policeman who accompanied us on the march, a nurse and a youth minister who had previously experimented with drugs. The children asked excellent questions such as: "What happens to a policeman who uses drugs?" and "Do cops beat people with their night sticks?" God blessed us that day!

**October 12, 2000--** An evaluation meeting was held where I discussed the uniqueness of the congregation , some of whom were unable to read, a few couldn't manage mortgages, rent or food payments, while others were state workers, teacher aides, secretaries—a very diverse population. The church service takes on Pentecostal aspects in its worship service under the stated denomination of Baptist. Praise service is a high component of worship and devotions. One always had to be prepared and ready to lead various aspects of the service--prayer, scripture reading, singing etc. As God is in control of the universe, Pastor Hazelton directly controlled his flock. Interesting dynamics were at play in the congregation re: the pastors wife, the ministers, Sunday School youth programs, community feeding programs and the empty building owned by the church that was used by another unidentified congregation. Interestingly, there are more churches than bars on Martin Luther King Boulevard, a rare phenomena in today's urban centers.

Later that day we delivered a refrigerator and washer dryer to a neighbor of the church who was in need. When we left a Jamaican gentleman had arrived late missing the grocery gifts, but the pastor promised to return later.

The next few months yielded a series of observations and lessons in human interactions: (1) The ministers met "to be of one mind in Jesus Christ". We discovered that many members originally on the membership list had either gone to another church or their telephone numbers were incorrect. The pastor insisted that every one on the list be checked. There would be no more "assumed" membership. (2) A required leadership course would be offered for ministers and church officials. Ministers should be able to officiate at all ordinances of the church. (3) No service would be held just to raise money. (4) The majority of programs with meals drew large crowds from the community. Regular services drew 125 people with 25% of the congregation entering the sanctuary late. (5) Sunday school attendance was usually limited to eight or nine persons with one adult student challenging the instructor until he absented himself. The instructor's methodology was usually lecture and dictation. Most participants left the class in quiet lock step defeat.

The Trenton Internship continued up through August, but the overall program of the church became routine, and reflected a sense of ritualistic control emanating from the pastor's office and implemented through the fellowship by his wife, who served as caretaker of the flock in subtle ways that protected the leadership control of her husband pastor in a manner that inferred God was directing the path and direction of the church. The culture was different in that foot washing and "laying on" of hands became daily ritual. Noticeably, one rather large woman always came to the altar for prayer and laying on of hands. Always she fell at the touch of the pastor in an auto hypnotic trance and stayed on the floor of the sanctuary through most of the service, somehow or other reviving herself prior to her time to sing a solo before the congregation.

After the experience at Raritan Baptist Church, I spent a second internship at Centra State Hospital, Freehold, New Jersey as Chaplain under the leadership of Chaplain Lancaster, one of the most dedicated servants of God I have ever encountered. I had previously served on two hospital boards and was familiar with the inner workings of hospitals from an administrator's point of view, but never had I experienced direct on the floor interaction with staff and patients.

After meeting Wynetta, a second Princeton student intern at the Red Bank train station, we drove to the hospital in Freehold. The drive was very familiar to me as I had spent the last 25 years in the environs; however, Wynetta was commuting by train from Princeton each day at a great sacrifice, as just getting to the railroad station in Princeton was an arduous task. Nevertheless, we arrived at the hospital at 7:45 a.m. and met with Ellen, Service Improvement Specialist, who explained the benefits and salary package, mission statement, quality assurance reporting and the patient rights privileges relative to the right to refuse medication, the right to have a translator, and the right to initiate advance directives for care and hospitalization. Then she ushered us into Security where we were assigned identification numbers, photographed, given parking passes and the emergency code number. Following that our applications were processed and medical procedures took place inclusive of protective inoculations and other necessary explanations of health precautions. Ten to fifteen days later we entered the hospital, a relatively cold almost frigid building. As we toured the premises, I observed that the patients were primarily of the

Jewish and Catholic faith, with very few Protestants receiving care. We were given extensive readings to complete in terms of hospital language, acceptability, and emergencies. There was much to learn in a short period of time. My initial comfort level at the hospital was at best questionable.

At 10:00 a.m. we met with hospital staff composed of several nurses, and physical therapists to review patient histories, physical, mental states and dispositions. All appeared knowledgeable about various perspectives and conditions of the patients; however, the individual lingo was mind boggling as every specialty area had its own symbolic language to describe in "short cuts" the condition of the patients. There was a set staging to determine the suitability and appropriateness for discharge from the hospital. Later I was assigned to the Cardiac Care Unit and given a Hepatitis B Inoculation at the end of the day after completing rounds with Chaplain Lancaster.

My first and only patient that day was an elderly woman, who spoke of the Freehold Reform Church where she participated in missionary work and volunteer service with the Salvation Army. She had previously been a patient at Robert Wood Johnson Hospital, but did not like the size of the hospital. She reminisced about Ann Arbor, Michigan and asked to be remembered to the other Chaplain. For some reason, I could have prayed with her, but did not, as I felt somewhat uncomfortable with her in her present state of undress. Her husband was present and very pleasant at the age of 84.

Week one beginning June 2, 2000 was somewhat frightening and uncertain. I felt secure in my religious beliefs, but unsure of my ability to fully understand the brutal and real agonies of patients staring at me at every level of existence. I walked past one room where the woman was shouting "God help me." Another patient requested a drink of water from her cup, which I could not give, because I feared that one drop of life sustaining water might yield disastrous results to patients whose chemical regimen demanded "no liquids." I hastened to request water from the nurse, who felt no urgency in responding to the needs of this patient, whose condition differed from the needs of the 90 year old woman who requested to be lifted back into the bed. In this particular case, the nurse said, "We just got her up; she needs to stay mobile, ambulatory and devoid of bed sores."

By Friday, the last day of the work week, I felt alive, in touch with myself and God. Even though one major emergency ended in the death of a patient, and the hospital room scene was one of grieving daughters peering through tears at their pale, ashened mother that death had taken, I was able to endure and comfort others. This was the second death for the girls in so short a time frame, one month. The mother's body lay with mouth stretched open as though gasping for final air. Her head was thrown back on a thirty degree angle as though the neck had been broken. Tubes were still attached to the body with visible shunts no longer housing life giving fluids. It was painful to witness, yet I could accept it. Interesting, because the day before, I became physically ill after enduring three days of naked helplessness of patients whose total life was now determined by strangers who probed their background histories to determine their limited futures. Many of the patients were allowed to return home, yet with the exception of the maternity ward , most of the patients were at or nearing the geriatric stage. Decisions relative to homecare, nursing homes, extended care, and occupational therapy were prevalent in the minds of families who have hard decisions to make. Do they continue the aggressive treatment of wires, tubes and pumping machinery, or do they pull the plug to allow death with dignity? Delay or enhance? It was not a question of nobility. There is no nobility, just dehumanization and lifelessness. From Tuesday to Friday, I had matured, come to grips with my God, even though I was unable to stand the pain, the loneliness, the crippling helplessness of patients. I still love God and humanity, yet a little bit of me died with each patient, a small piece of me rested in each hospital bed. God bless the doctors, nurses, staff members and all who champion the needs of the sick, and God grant peace and love, eternal love to the chaplains who bring visitation and comfort into rooms that house the last vestiges of humanity longing to understand its mortality.

Fortunately, I was granted a few days away

from the hospital, and was able to visit Scotland and Ecuador with Brookdale Community College, where I served as Chairman of the Board of Trustees. Brookdale had established an International Study program in both countries. Upon return from Scotland, I felt very comfortable about the original tensions associated with hospital care. Once again I attended the rounds in the Cardiac Care Unit and Step Down, a division for cardiac patients who are improving in health. Each day I visited at least 16 to 20 patients. The nurses were exceptionally busy, and could not leave their stations. We had to speak in low, sometimes inaudible voices in an effort to maintain patient confidentiality. As we discussed the various patients, I was impressed that Dr. Weinstein was present to participate in the patient's analysis documentation. After the discussion I visited five additional patients, one of whom was classified psychotic, but I could not discern why the patient was classified as confused. One patient in room # 139 refused prayer, but was amenable to my reading Psalm 129, which I read daily in an effort to come to grips with my mission and search for identity in the hospital setting. Chaplain Lancaster was very helpful in all questionable matters involving hospital personnel and hospital ethics. Patient after patient each had a specific story to be heard ... I quickly learned to pray with Catholics and say the necessary Hail Mary, and to pray with Jewish patients carefully citing Old Testament prophets. One of my greatest challenges was a woman Buddhist patient, whose son sat with her day after day for very long hours, but would never utter a word. His mother was totally intubated and the first day I visited I asked the son if it was okay to pray for her. He mentioned that he was not a follower of Buddha and I had his permission. Each day after prayer I would have a one way conversation with the mother, even though I knew she was unable to speak. Each day upon hearing my voice, she moved and grunted. The son took this to be a sacred sign, and when I entered the room, he would bow down before me and grab me hugging me around the legs. He was a grown man in his early thirties. I inquired of him: "Do you ever speak with your mother?" He responded, "No, because she has tubes down her throat and the only time she moves is when you enter the room". I responded: "Just because she does not speak, it does not mean that she can't hear or understand". Again he insisted, "But she only moves when you appear". I explained to him that I was not a God, just a minister and servant doing the will of God; yet each day he insisted on bowing and hugging my legs in submission.

By the end of June I was assigned to both Cardiac Care and Oncology. Oncology was somewhat devastating as many of the patients were terminal and without hope. Nevertheless, my daily schedule included as many as 25 patient visitations per day on three floors, plus emergency calls. As acclimated as I had become, I was still cautious about hand washing after each visitation. Some patients insisted on privacy and closed their curtains prior to my visitations. Many women patients were in a state of undress and exposed to any passerby. Various private acts such as urinating in vessels without privacy was embarrassing and trying in situations where any member of the public could witness the act. Also, Jewish patients were reluctant to accept ministry from an interfaith chaplain. Both patients and family members present certain verbal nuances which convey in sophisticated ways their reluctance to accept representatives of New Testament theology. It was disconcerting that their professed religion allowed little connectivity beyond the strict parameters of all that represents Hebrew culture and custom. Today I visited 29 patients (all floors), yet I was unable to connect theologically with enough people. I didn't feel threatened and was aggressive enough to enjoy the sophisticated rejections, yet God has called me to minister to people in various diverse manners. I continued to accept the call to humble myself helpless before God, but empowered in the knowledge that through Christ all things are possible. I shall have joy in the bad times and joy in the good times. I will sing his praises and glorify his name. O Holy God, O sacred Spirit rest in me, thanks for the peace that abounds in you, and the relationship from you to me and back again. O how I love Jesus. Majestic God, keep me humble!

The next day I unknowingly walked into a room

and was confronted by two police officers, one reading and the other resting beside the window at the base of a female patient's bed. The patient looked distressed and requested prayer. I prayed for healing and questioned my superior as to why male police were assigned for a female in hospitalization? Perhaps prisoners give up all their rights to privacy upon incarceration. Where was God in the midst of this demise, I asked myself? This was a shameful manner of suffering, plus her name was never listed on the hospital status sheet.

Reflecting late in the afternoon, I thought of the chaplaincy at Centra State Hospital as a continuous rendezvous with death and dying. However, in the distance I heard the refreshing cries of very young pre- kindergarten children rushing through the corridor, and I found pleasure and strength in the revelation of their loud penetrating sounds that reverberated and bounced rushing off brick and metallicized walls. Anxious death was temporarily dismissed. The inevitable was temporarily placed on the back burner for a few moments of joy. "I can do all things through Christ which strengtheneth me" (Philippians 4:13 KJV). [5]

Just as there was joy in the midst of hearing the loud laughter and cheering of the pre-kindergarten children running through the halls of the hospital, there was immediate grief in the passing of the Buddhist woman. It was coincidental that at the time when I finally began to read the assigned grief manual, *How We Die,* that Mrs. Che died. [6] She never once spoke to me, never smiled, just gestured once, the one time I saw her eyes opened. And yet when she passed, died, I cried because I had known her through her son. The son was anxious, concerned, fully involved with his mother, who was transferred from the Cardiac Care Unit, to the floor, and back to die at 8:00 a.m. on the date of her death. The manual prepared me to grieve, but the tears wouldn't go away. In my own personal demise I rushed to the floor to visit patients as though it would help me forget Mrs. Che, but immediately upon withdrawing from room 104 my eyes welled again. "What's taking me so damn long?" I asked myself. She wasn't a member of my immediate family; never once spoke, just stared upward for only a few seconds. Intubated, she couldn't smile or frown, only gasp for life preserving oxygen. I feel better now, ready to move on to the next situation; yet in so short a period of time I grew attached to a motionless body and a mother's son whose language (Chinese) and religion(Buddhist) I have yet to understand. At the end, God triumphed, stole Mrs. Che at the midnight hour causing both the son and I to grapple with our fragile mortality.

Near the end of July, my favorite nurse left to take a position in a private doctor's practice, where she told me her salary would be considerably increased. The last words I heard from my favorite caring nurse in the Cardiac Care Unit was: "I've got to go empty some pee". Although apparently somewhat the language of the streets, she realistically described the inner workings of dedicated hospital staff whose major tasks range from intubating patients to necessary cesspool antics expressed by the nurse. This particular nurse, Sylvia, somewhat of a miracle worker had just motivated a silent, sullen, depressed man to walk again and get on with his life. Now he too can go pee with dignity and without the assistance of care givers, whose 12 hour shifts reflect their ability to energetically service patients whose hope and future destiny rests in their ability to resurrect their helpless bodies and fragile minds.

Yet, "the beat goes on" by stopping intermittedly, for on July 21, 2000, I lost Janice Ringo. Janice was admitted to the hospital on my first day of the chaplaincy. She had written an advanced directive which called for "no resuscitation, no aggressive treatment", but her husband ruled against the advanced directive. They took her off the ventilator at 7:30 a.m., and I watched the monitor as her vitals rapidly deteriorated. She died at 9:00 a.m. God knew her dreams, her actions doing extensive volunteer work in the community and most of all her heart. God also knew and understood her heart of hearts, Mr. Ringo, and her sons, daughters and caregivers. To the end, I am happy in thee O God. I rejoice in thy name. Thou hast blessed me with days beyond my asking. I was diminished with the death of Mrs. Ringo, and yet my bowels were lifted up to the Lord. Thank you for the peace you gave to Mrs.

Ringo. Thank you. We praise you; we magnify you; we glorify in your name. Amen

After two weeks in the oncology ward, I felt depressed and thought it time to make a move. The patients in oncology are struck by potential grief, hopelessness emanates throughout, conversations are more guarded, patients are angrier or unknowledgeable about the future and their eventual destiny. It was on the way out of the oncology unit that I met Paul who was sobbing in distress in the Chapel. I stopped to speak with him, and learned that his father was dying in the cardiac care unit at 86 years of age. The father, loved by his family, had visitors from all parts of the country. I spoke with Paul about God's presence in all things, including death. He appeared to be somewhat comforted and I left the hospital seeking fresh air and freedom from pain with a desire to embrace life, meaningful or otherwise. Finally, during my last week of internship as Chaplain, I heard an emergency call over the hospital loud speaker system for a Catholic Priest from the operating room. Knowing how priests schedule their visitations, I knew that a priest would more than likely not be present in the hospital. It was 4;30 p.m., and I was on my way past the uniformed security guards and out the front door. The announcement caused me to stop in my tracks. I turned around and asked for directions to the surgery wing. When I arrived, the doctors informed me there was a woman ready for a scheduled surgery, but would not go forward without seeing a priest. I asked for permission to speak with her. When I spoke with the woman, I explained to her that I was not a priest; however, I would be happy to pray with her and extend the blessings of God and to recite the Hail Mary with her. She was very delighted that I had come. We prayed together and she waved to the surgeons in the next room that she was ready. This was the most blessed and exhilarating experience of my chaplaincy, and I rushed home thanking God for his presence in my life. The next day I inquired of the patient, and it was reported that she was doing well and improving. From there I rushed back to Princeton, where the mysterious God was shackled, reinvented, turned upside down and inside out, then put together again, packaged as it were in myths, fables, beliefs and unbelief, until the power of God came down and delivered us, professors and students alike, into the glorious avenues of the streets charged with a commitment to support the Great Commission with love and obedience.

The religious instruction at Princeton Theological Seminary was fast and furious, and graduation had come and gone before I realized the time had passed. Meanwhile, the local Sea Coast Minister's Association at home was caught up in its own bureaucracies, and the question of my being ordained was paramount. It would appear that various contingencies within the local structure were insisting that I serve in one of their churches to be mentored in the inner workings of the ministry. Given my long term service as an administrator, plus internship at Raritan Baptist Church and the chaplaincy at Centra State Hospital, I felt I was more than ready to serve as a pastor. In addition I had multiple experiences as a speaker at various community functions, and was better prepared educationally in Christian Education and Theology than some of the persons who had been ordained previously into the ministry. Fortunately, my mentor, Reverend Milliard Harris, had the courage and vision to have the ordination supervised by the American Baptist Church, a national organization with roots and powers beyond the purview of the local association. I was well prepared and presented written answers to multiple questioning prior to the oral examination before supervisors and peers. I have always loved the engagement and badinage between professionals in the field, and I emptied my God given intellectual and spiritual being before them in "sacrificial obedience. What a wonderful hallelujah occasion! What was lacking in the local pastor's group was what Eugene Peterson describes in *Living the Message as* "Intense Imagination". While walking through the streams and forests of Maryland he states: "The first hours of that walk are uneventful: I am tired, sluggish, and inattentive. Then bird-song begins to penetrate my senses, and the play of light on oak leaves and asters catches my interest. In the forest of trees, one sycamore forces its rootedness on me, and then sends my eyes arcing across trajectories upwards and outwards. I have been walking these forest trails for years, but I am ever and again finding an insect that I have never seen before startling me with its combined aspects of ferocity and fragility. How many more are there to be found? The creation is so complex, so intricate, so profuse with life and form and color and scent! And I walk through it deaf and dumb and blind, groping my way stupidly absorbed in putting one foot in front of the other, seeing a mere fraction of what is there".[7]

Such was and is the case of the Seacoast Ministers Association. There are many new humans dedicated to God to be found and nurtured to carry out the Great Commission: "Go ye therefore, and teach all nations, baptizing them in the name of the Father, and of the Son, and of the Holy Ghost" (Matthew 28:19 KJV). Yet, there are times when they just place one foot in front of the other, blindly ignoring the truth that is set before them.

Once ordained and licensed, I served as Interim Pastor at Pilgrim Baptist Church in Red Bank for approximately two years, and Mt. Pisgah Baptist Church in Asbury Park, New Jersey while they searched for a pastor for a little over a year. Both churches are now blessed with competent God fearing men.

# Chapter Nine

## Where's The Horse For A Kid That's Black?

In 1942, Langston Hughes authored a poem entitled "Merry-Go-Round" depicting a colored child at carnival. As a young boy living in Crestmont, located one-half mile south of the Willow Grove Amusement Park, I hitched a ride on the merry-go-round almost daily. Most of the time my buddies and I waited until the merry-go ride was in motion, and then we jumped on without purchasing a ticket; therefore, I was familiar with the images presented in this poem as it reflected upon "Jim Crow" with all its ugliness.

Donald D. Warner

## Merry-G-Round

Where is the Jim Crow section
On this merry-go-round,
Mister, cause I want to ride?
Down south where I come from
White and colored
Can't sit side by side.
Down south on the train
There's a Jim Crow car.
On the bus we're put in the back-
But there ain't no back
To a merry-go-round.
Where's the horse
For a kid that's black? [1]

Imagine for a moment that you are that small
child brought up in the land of plenty called
America. Imagine the merry-go-round as the world,
and somewhat like this youngster you want to find
your place, your niche in the world. You want to
ride! However, full of historical awareness, you
know that in this so called land of opportunity your
forefathers had been trained and obligated to take
their designated seats at the back of any vehicle that
moved-train, bus, or cattle car. The first time in
your life you visit the carnival, see the merry-go-
round with its entire musical splendor, its colorful
horses, sculptured with the rainbow in mind. For the
first time, you can't find your designated place and
you shout to the world: "Where's the horse for a kid

338

that's black? Where do I as an hyphenated American find my place in this nation that espouses freedom for all? Who am I? I want to ride! Am I considered an outsider based on the fact that my ancestors arrived here at a time when human labor was an economic necessity called the slave trade. A part of me identifies fully with the legacy of Africa, its great people, great civilization, great kings.

In the midst of all that I am, I remember Dr. King in 1965 urging the United States to order sanctions against the cruel and brutal government of South Africa. I remember that his voice was ignored, as he spoke to our mistaken involvement in Vietnam. I remember how he knowingly and symbolically thrust blacks into the lighthouse of the world, when he accepted the Nobel Peace prize. Yet, the question remains: "Where is the horse for a kid that's black?"

Even today as I listen to political rhetoric about possible oil sanctions and view third world countries, I'm fascinated by their ability to control the economics of world politics. I am equally fascinated with the growth of Japan since World War II and its impact upon American lifestyles re: computer technology, televisions, automobile tires, and farm tractors. Conversely, I am dismayed with the federal government's inability to control the influx of drugs entering our country, and the alleged laundering of billions of dollars through some of our most prestigious banks and businesses. Little recognized is the fact that all of the above, even from an international perspective, affects the political, socio-economic growth of blacks as a people. I struggle painfully to identify with efforts at parity in Africa; yet I applaud our efforts to provide relief in dollars and human resources. Still I ask where in this country is the horse for kids who are black? For you see as much as I identify with poverty in Africa, I also identify with poverty in North Philadelphia, New Orleans, New York City, Orlando, Florida and in almost every municipality and hamlet in America. I've walked the outskirts of Puerto Rico, and witnessed life away from the advertised white beaches and plush hotels. I've ventured outside the plush areas of renovated Atlanta with its glass skyscrapers. I've walked through the outskirts of New Orleans even before the Katrina disaster. I've watched carefully the plight of black Americans in the suburbs and cities of Red Bank, Asbury Park, Philadelphia and Atlantic Highlands and still I ask: "Where's the horse for a kid that's black?"

I've sat in our courthouses and witnessed a large number of high school drop outs waiting to be incarcerated. I've seen a few of our graduates pleading for mercy before social workers, visiting nurses and judges who render justice, but who acknowledge in their own minds that justice, proper health care, and hospitalization must be purchased in this country. One must pay for good health care. You must pay for the best attorney. Our country revolves around economics, green power, which unfortunately the black community lacks and suffers the consequences, whether it be in our schools or your back yard and mine.

Where do we move from here? The future of our nation, our community, rests in our ability to properly inculcate values, judgments, morals into the youth of the nation. We are failing for many reasons. You might suggest: "Heck, I'm not failing. My children are excelling in school, involved in community activities, mannerly at home, communicates, are not taking drugs, smoking crack, standing on the corner at ridiculous hours, and have friends who have purpose and direction. If so, then you are an exception, for nationwide the increasing number of families experiencing difficulties is overwhelming and best expressed in increasing divorce rates and children born out of wedlock. For years I've argued that one good woman in the home may be more valuable than a nuclear family without a responsible male figure. Yet, I know from personal experience that there are times when our children need the collective experiences of both parents to help explain or overcome the complexities of life.

Last year on Valentines Day, people throughout the world celebrated the rites of love and courtship, but times have changed. Each year an increasing number of adolescents experience pregnancies and births. In many cases we have babies having babies, with young mothers becoming grandmothers with the accompanying cycle of poverty. Couple this with the fact that prison construction, along with its disproportionate numbers of blacks incarcerated, has become one of our largest growth industries, and we begin to recognize a divisive and shameful problem in America. Therefore, we must acknowledge that every youngster in America must be able to freely ride the merry-go-round of life , be it international, or on the home front, but must do so with a high school diploma in his hand, with the knowledge that the family of humanity supports his endeavors with self esteem, with a sense of direction and control, with a sense of self in relation to the larger world, with concern for those less able, with optimism for the future, with the belief that they can build on the accomplishments and achievements of their ancestors. Then each citizen in the United States, of every race, creed, ethnicity and persuasion, can have a horse to ride.

Much of the above statement depends on our ability to provide effective educational programs for our children. Dr. Hugh Scott, Dean of Education, Hunter College states: "Educators frequently proclaim that our society seeks to provide equal opportunity for all, regardless of genetic structure, condition of birth, color or previous condition of servitude. In practice most black Americans have neither experienced equal educational opportunity nor have they been the beneficiaries of a quality education." (Black Consciousness and Professionalism: Implications for Leadership in mainly Black Schools) [2]

As one of the educators so disdainfully referred to in Dr. Scott's statement, I've dedicated my life to making every conceivable effort to reverse the notions of reality mentioned above , especially since my early elementary years of education took place in a predominantly black school. The quest to provide effective education for all students was critical in every fiber of my total being. My final confrontation with a school system was in Asbury Park, New Jersey. At the time Asbury Park schools were devastated by all the predetermined indicators of failure; however, when hired as Interim Superintendent, I sought the impossible in hopes of initiating positive change to a school system with deplorable educational results. Very few of the negative outcomes of the system were caused by students, but rather the adults, paid professionals and politically motivated volunteers, who controlled the learning environment, purse strings and decisions affecting standards leading to quality education.

My very first contact with the Asbury Park School system was approximately fifteen years prior to June 2002, when I received a telephone message from Mr. Howard West, President of the local National Association for the Advancement of Colored People (N.A.A.C.P.). At the time I served as a committee member of a state imposed monitoring team to evaluate the school system. However, the most recent visitation was two to three years ago to serve as guest speaker at the senior high school for Dr. Martin Luther King's birthday celebration.

The telephone communication from Mr. West was a request to serve as community volunteer with expertise in administrative affairs, and to coordinate evaluations of the superintendent previously made by board members. My task was to complete an analysis of their written comments, and submit the package to the board of education. Seven of the nine board members had submitted the necessary forms, with two members absenting themselves from any comment for reasons not shared.

Upon completing the task, I contacted the board secretary's office to arrange a meeting with the board and was given a date. However, upon arrival at the meeting, I was told that only the personnel committee would be meeting. This abrupt change in understandings caused me to exercise caution in my dealings with this unknown entity; therefore, upon entering the meeting I asked whether or not the superintendent had been served with a "rice" notification? The response I received was "No, but he knows about the meeting". I repeated the same question and received a similar response; therefore, I asked to speak with the board attorney. Why the attorney had not given the board proper instruction relative to evaluating personnel was beyond my imagination. Given the fact that proper notification of the superintendent's rights under the law had not taken place, I submitted the evaluation report to the board secretary and immediately left the meeting. That was my first interaction with the board, who were divided in their mission within the district and were at odds with replacing the superintendent, who was later improperly suspended without pay, plus inadequate documentation.

Once the superintendent was suspended, I was then sought out by the board president, sanctioned by a state department of education member, and asked to interview for the interim position. After a lunch meeting with the president and two other board members, I interviewed for the position and was accepted as interim superintendent while the position was vacant. I was retired and made a difficult decision. After checking with several state department of education types regarding my pension, I began working for a divided board. Two of the board members were staunch advocates of the former superintendent and worked diligently to override all positive efforts of the board to move forward. As I had learned many years earlier in Willingboro, New Jersey, I immediately established an activities log to keep a record of all contacts and conversations with board members, parents, teachers, staff personnel and students.

My first day on the job was cordial, but one of low trust. It was as though the central office staff had been mesmerized by yet another change in the district. Everyone was very low key in their efforts to not be discovered in the positions for which they were being paid. Especially silent were the two administrative power brokers, one in charge of curriculum and the other a wheeler and dealer in human resources and personnel matters. My only open resource was the business manager, and I had learned many, many years prior to be wary of those who approach you first as friendly entities in the midst of disintegrating systems. Nevertheless, I was also aware that the business office or those who controlled the purse strings were empowered to know the most about the efficiencies of the district, as regards its overall management, organizational styles, strengths and weaknesses. Therefore, my first order of business was to establish a trust relationship with the business manager. Immediately I requested a voucher system whereby no requisition for money would be signed and approved by me, unless it was first reviewed and approved by the business manager. This angered one of the business manager's secretaries, who had in the past given all requisitions and vouchers to the previous superintendent prior to approval from the business manager. It took several communications and denials from my office before she realized that she could not override the new procedures. Consequently, she became a very embittered personality within the district, and wore the typical long face, don't bother me attitude her entire time at work. Even though she was to report all financial actions and entries through the business manager's office, she had seen at least three business managers released from the district and had therefore established her own system for running the district independent of supervision.

All professional staff member within the central office knew and understood their individual roles and job descriptions, but in the midst of board member dissension, factionalism and public bantering, the professional staff members had developed their own individual survival techniques, and had honed to a state of excellence an aura of independence that no evaluation instrument could surmise. For example, the second most powerful position, next to the superintendent of schools, was the Director of Curriculum, who ran the district, made decisions for the former superintendent and had bonded closely with the Administrative Assistant to the Superintendent in charge of personnel and human resources. Seldom, if ever, did the Director of Curriculum visit the school buildings where the principals, teachers and students under her charge suffered daily with discipline problems, inadequate teaching methodology and psychologically crippled teaching staff members. Instead her total thrust for the district was to present meaningless multiple training workshops and central office meetings, while she manipulated state department managers who controlled the finances within the district. One of the all time areas of negligence within the district was to discover that the district had let squander millions of dollars of state money reserved for the district by never applying for the funds in a timely manner. This became evident when I attended a state department meeting in Trenton to discuss future funding for the district. In fact, one of the greatest hardships perpetrated upon the children of the district was the fact that the curriculum director spent at least 45% of her time at the state level attending various workshops, and was not available within the district to effectively manage her job description responsibilities. In addition, there appeared to be unproven collusion between the director of curriculum and the director of the Information Technology Center, making it difficult for the business manager to properly oversee grants, vendor replications and general management of that division. Therefore, when the so called ITC Center was repeatedly "running its business operations in the red" over a period of three consecutive years, the nature of the problem was muddled by the protective machinations existing between the two entities –central office curriculum director and Information Technology Center (ITC) management personnel. Several meetings ensued designed to ameliorate the deficiencies of the ITC Center as it related to a systematic inventory of materials purchased and the utilization thereof by the Technology Coordinator. One such example dealt with the purchasing of Larson's Interactive Math Series Software with three options totaling in excess of $44,000.00. The district technology coordinator insisted that the materials purchased for high school students were inferior, and not at a suitable level for secondary students.

Secondly, the program was replete with unanswerable technical problems, and thirdly no program data had been gathered to prove the program worked. However, in response to the technology coordinator's complaint regarding one program the ITC manager sent damaging memoranda to the coordinator, with written copies to the business manager and the curriculum director stating: "I have messaged you three times now requesting specific information about your procurement of software for your program . I find your refusal to provide the source, vendor, date the order was mailed from District, number of copies ordered, place of delivery and name of person receiving items very troublesome. The fact that you processed this order and for that matter all your orders without ITC review is yet another concern. The ITC has been performing a lot of damage control because of mistakes noted in pricing, compatibility, space mapping, electrical and network requirements...." Thus the blame game continued while the ITC manager deliberately engaged the technology coordinator in meaningless meetings designed to protect his own alleged inadequacies, while supported by the curriculum director through written substantiation copied to the business manager.

Meanwhile, because of the districts failure to properly manage financial and curricular matters the State Department of Education, through the County

Superintendent's office, assigned a full time resource person to the district to oversee district matters and advise central office staff. In addition, the State also assigned a financial specialist to assist and monitor the business office operation and expenditure of funds. The State also confided that a new district organizational chart should be proposed for central office staff, but must first be approved by the local board of education and forwarded to the county office. In order to accomplish this task, I began daily meetings with individual staff personnel to determine job feasibility, and finally to make recommendations for consolidation of positions within the district. In total, 27 persons were interviewed, along with an extensive analysis of the functionality of their individual job descriptions.

Yet in the midst of quiet, delimiting work ethics at the central office, very little meaningful education was occurring in the school buildings. As a superintendent in previous districts, I always spent time in the schools and whenever possible taught classes as visiting lecturer or as teacher substitute. I continued this trend in Asbury Park. Each day I visited at least two schools on a rotating unannounced basis. Teachers were very welcoming and delightfully surprised that I would spend time in their classrooms. Many of the classrooms were staffed with as many as three professionals per room. The extra staff members were placed there to provide instructional aid to individual students; however, in most cases the teacher aides were situated in hidden places in the classrooms, seldom seen helping students and in many cases nearly asleep in their seats. Taxpayers and the State were providing the extra financial resources, yet the program was ineffectively organized and utilized by the principals and supervisors charged with the responsibility of educating students. Not only was the Middle School in total chaos relative to discipline and education, but neither the principal or vice principal could ever be located outside their offices, with one principal having an office hidden on the second floor of the building behind a series of closed doors. On any given week, there were as many as eight to ten students and their parents and guardians referred to the superintendent's office from the Middle School for Superintendent's hearings and disposition relative to remediation of poor behavioral patterns. A typical listing from the Middle School vice principal in charge of discipline revealed the following:

**Student #1 (C.C.): Found in possession of weapon-suspended 4/8- 4/22/04**

**Student#2 (D.M.): Found in possession of a weapon-suspended 4/7-4/19/04**

**Student #3 (M.B.): found in possession of a weapon-suspended 4/7-4/21/04**

**Student#4 (L.S.): found in possession of a weapon-suspended 4/7-4/21/04**

**Student#5 C.R.): found in possession of a weapon-suspended 4/7-4/21/04**

**Student#6 (J.O.): found in possession of a**

weapon-suspended 4/7-4/21/04

Student #7 (T.B.): pulled fire alarm-suspended 4/7-4/28/04

Student #8 (R.T.): pulled fire alarm-suspended 4/8-4/29/04

Student #9 (D.S.): pulled fire alarm-suspended 4/7-4/28/04

Student #10 (T.G.): pulled fire alarm-suspended 4/8-4/29/04

The ten students were comprised of four girls and six boys, all of whom had to appear before the superintendent and his representatives with parents and/or guardians for final disposition, prior to a recommendation for expulsion by the school board or alternative educational placement outside the district at exorbitant cost to the taxpayer, and the state of New Jersey from whom districts classified as "Abbott" receive full funding under state legislation passed to enhance educational support and excellence in economically "poor" districts. In the majority of cases full time counseling with weekly supervision from school personnel and parents solved the problems. Only fully recalcitrant students received limited outside placement. However, the Middle School was and still is in need of serious revitalization in disciplinary procedures, new teaching strategies and effective management. In spite of all the negativity surrounding the school district,t two of the elementary schools, Bangs Avenue, Mr. Mednick, Principal and Thurgood

Marshall, Mrs. Beauford, Principal, were well on the way to becoming schools of excellence. In fact, Mr. Mednick was so persuasive in his insistence that teachers perform in an outstanding manner, that a small group of minority teachers submitted a petition complaining about his administrative style and accusing him of racism. Both matters were eventually settled and the complainants finally learned to adhere to new and exciting classroom teaching expectations.

In an effort to salvage the perceived problems at the Middle School, I met with teacher union representatives, and then held a faculty meeting at the Middle School under the general heading of "Take Back Our School". It was obvious that the students were in charge of the school day. Classroom teachers and administrators were merely pawns in the students' games of manipulation inclusive of lateness to school, unsupervised absenteeism, defiant behavior on premises, bringing weapons to school, pulling fire alarms, etc. You name it, the students claimed it. Directly influencing student behavior were the many drug salespersons operating on the corner surrounding the convenience store across the street from the school. I was personally approached for a possible buy while visiting the school at 10:00 a.m. on a Friday, after I had ushered several late students into the school building. Obviously it took a combined task force of municipal government officers, citizen and parent committees, police officers and community organizations to ameliorate and solve the problem. Therefore, I began a series of meetings with the various groups in the community starting with the minister's council, the municipal government's business manager and the police chief, who was a personal friend of mine with similar background and expertise in working with urban gangs. Most of the citizen groups were grateful for the contact stating they had never been able to work with school officials in the past. Unfortunately, my few months' position as Interim Superintendent ended abruptly with a one day notice stating that the suspended superintendent would be returning to the district as the board had violated his rights. I am in possession of a volume of litigation referring to the suspension, and the costly endeavors associated with his removal. However, it should be noted that after returning to the district, the superintendent sued all the black board members who voted for his suspension, but failed to sue the one white board member who voted for his suspension. Today, 2007, that same white board member is president of the board, and one of the superintendent's strongest supporters now has her daughter working in the central office. Also note that the superintendent has again been suspended by a different board of education and the State Department of Education and Attorney General's office are investigating his departure. The following article was posted in the Asbury Park Press dated May 4, 2007:

## " Asbury Schools are Served New Subpoena"

The state Attorney General's office served a new subpoena on the school district for certain personnel records Thursday as part of the ongoing investigations into the districts operations that began last August shortly before the Board of Education suspended Superintendent Antonio Lewis with pay, school officials said.

The subpoena was limited in scope, compared to a raid by state authorities on Feb. 22, when investigators filled a truck with boxes and computers. The search warrant at that time covered both the district's central business office on Lake Avenue and its computer and technology center on Park Avenue.

School board officials in recent weeks have expressed frustration that the state has not been able to get to the point in its investigation to help the board resolve the issue of Lewis' suspension.

"We have been putting pressure on the investigative agencies to move the investigation along as best they can," said Alan J. Schniman, the school board attorney.

The board early last September wanted to buy out Lewis' contract, but the state

Department of Education intervened and did not let Lewis get the money he had agreed to---$600,000.

State education officials have been overseeing district expenditures and working closely with school administrators since September."

Thus the Board of Education, after two suspensions and three interim superintendents and as many business managers, under state directed funding and supervision has not moved forward in its basic mission to provide excellence in student education, nor have they achieved success in changing the leadership dynamics of the district. As writer/observer, I could fill a book on the dynamics of a disenchanted ever changing school board existing in the midst of a powerless community, whose anger constantly erupts at public board of education meetings requiring security and police protection; however, the continuing chaos is clearly documented in the continuous barrage of documents associated with the No Child Left Behind legislation and its multiplicity of requirements in curriculum revision, parental involvement, student discipline, academic performance in language arts literacy and mathematics, all buttressed with high teacher/staff/administrator turnover rates.

My tenure as Interim Superintendent was short, lasting from the end of January until early June when a state official called to say I had one day to pack and leave the district. Packing was a relatively simple matter, as everything I owned relative to the district I carried in my briefcase. My one regret was that I was unable to see several seniors that I had met at the high school graduate, but even their graduation was marred in the midst of a scandal allegedly perpetrated by the high school principal and vice principal allowing certain students to graduate who had not met graduation standards. Nevertheless, the County Superintendent of Schools requested that I return to the district to meet with the no longer suspended superintendent. I refused such a meeting as there was obviously very little in educational practice and leadership we had in common.

However, I did meet with the County Superintendent and presented her with an analysis of needs within the district. A summary of observances and recommendations was as follows:

Interference in the daily operation of school affairs ceased upon my arrival after direct instructions to two of the Board members; however, new members who are anxious to make an impact are appearing in buildings, commenting to personnel or placing themselves into spontaneous situations which require misunderstood responses i.e. recent insurance visitations by insurance representatives. However, if new members will focus on the children of the district, they will provide for a smoother transition, provided tensions about life styles (gay liberation issues) and racism diminish. Two board members are seriously evil and engage in ugly open warfare, especially leaking confidential matters to the public press and engaging State Department officials in one sided debate.

Given the lack of cohesiveness in the African American community, the board will change again during the next election and the emerging majority will be the same as this year as the board president will not run again. Further the board must interview candidates within the next week, and must also select new attorneys as the present firm will not receive a new contract. Mr. DeSanto will serve well as president and Mr. Dellaesandro will work to balance teacher perspectives, but must be aware of his new responsibility as a board member. The new insurance proposal will be protested by the union leaders and will probably not receive enough board votes to pass.

There are several serious personnel issues. A strong Middle School principal must be hired without interference from the dysfunctional parent Student Leadership Committee as the president is a serious biased supporter of the former superintendent and will not render an independent recommendation.

Place the Information Technology Center (ITC) under the supervision of the Monmouth-Ocean Educational Services Commission. The ITC is a worthless division with incompetent devious leadership who have been accused of purchasing inferior equipment for the district. They provide limited services within and without the district. They can improve and make a profit, but only with new direction and new leadership. There is constant warfare between the Director of Technology, the Director of ITC conflicted by prior allegiances to the Curriculum Director.

The Curriculum Director is in serious difficulty with lack of time and energy to maintain programs that directly impact parents and families. Too much money is left dormant and unspent. Parents are not engaged. Supplemental services were not started until May of the fiscal year after parents had signed contracts in October. The funds are there; hire a Coordinator Grants person instead of constantly applying for carry over funds year after year.

Although central office personnel are competent, they were very secluded and somewhat devious in their temporary allegiances to the Interim. Thanks to my history in the community, I was able to find true answers to questions where confidences were weak within the administrative staff.

The high school sorely needs different leadership. The principal lacks organizational skills, knows little about scheduling, uses dictatorial language, and has caused the district to lose important key supervisors who state that his "arrogance" drove them to seek other positions. He lacks people skills, as does his assistant who brings her own history and incompetence to the district inclusive of her disbelief in the ability of African American students to learn as witnessed in our Middle States evaluation conference. Our strongest principals are the Bangs Avenue School and Thurgood Marshall School principals. The Bradley School principal needs intensive administrative training, and because the District Curriculum Director barely finds time to be present in the buildings except when state monitors are present, the district goes lacking. We have extensively trained Central Office personnel, but principals and teachers go lacking. The State stinks in this regard. Train, train, train, change, change, change; however, the students improve very little.

Teachers are in need of direct, but helpful supervision on a daily basis, which means that principals and supervisors must get out of their offices and into classrooms at times other than the mandated evaluation period. This is especially important for Middle and High School principals.

The community and parents feel disempowered and lack confidence in the school system. Why? Poor achievement scores, near abusive administrators who practice avoidance and many times are frightened when confronted by parents. Many parents are seeking solutions outside the district and are placing their children in alternative programs. Supplemental services has been a failure, and Title I services are nonexistent in the eyes of parents-many of our problems exist because of poor people to people relationships on our part. For example, under the former principal, parents were not allowed to start a Parent Teacher's Organization at the Middle School; others who wish to help are constantly rebuffed. Parental complaining may be a pain, but our job is to serve.

As to community organizations, I have met and welcomed several: National Association for the Advancement of Colored People, Ministerial Alliances, Gay Community , Municipal Government etc. and have established meaningful relationships with all, even though the fire department fined the school district for excessive fire alarms at the Middle School. The high school depends too heavily on the Black Muslim organization for speakers and presentations which I assume is the principal's way of engaging meaningful "tell it like it is" speakers.

The elementary scores K-4 are improving; however, grades 5 to 12 need lots of work coupled by consistency in leadership and people who believe in them. Each school has its own culture, but hope is alive in Asbury Park. Our focus must change to children and leadership, and not the narrow politics of meaningless self interest.

Strategic planning is an area of great weakness. We need a strong district vision statement, combined with measurable superintendent's goals and objectives to umbrella the diversity of State mandated programs and a strategic plan to implement goals and objectives. Then we will have a viable means of evaluating performance. The State must give the new board an opportunity for training.

Finally, please hire the recommended assistant business manager at once. The School Business Administrator's position has been advertised, but a State monitor must be present during the interviewing process to help eliminate possible pressures for individuals who might further cause the system to diminish in its efforts to provide quality education."

For well over 40 years as teacher, recreation leader, motivation director, principal, superintendent and member and chair of various community boards and organizations, I had experienced every conceivable management and organizational problem imaginable, and yet the complications and chaos surrounding the Asbury Park School system seemed somewhat insurmountable. In the five months serving the system, I had only limited power and allegiances necessary to changing the system from one of mediocrity to one of educational excellence. Even the school business manager, in whom I mistakenly placed trust , was under investigation when I was abruptly given a one day notice and requested to leave the district. I confided in him relative to personnel and management issues as I expected him to properly manage the financial business portion of the district, especially given the state had continuing presence and oversight in the district. However, as things worked out, the consulting firm that he managed within the district came under investigation re: the legalities surrounding utilization of funds and a personal friend hired to implement certain programs within the district. The outcome of that investigation has not yet been made public, and perhaps the recent Attorney General's subpoenas may lend light to the utilization of financial resources within the district.

I am convinced that no board of trustees or school board can adequately evaluate the various central office positions from a distance. Weekly and or bimonthly meetings that depend on information submitted by the very people you evaluate are not sufficient to fairly and effectively evaluate the given bureaucracies of a system, especially one that seldom focuses on the children they serve. And yet, in the midst of personal failure, I realize that the Asbury Park educational system is but a small cog in the wheel of justice or injustice in America that continues to plague urban schools resulting in disproportionately increasing numbers of African Americans populating one of our blossoming industries—the prison industry. Again I ask "Where's the horse for a kid that's black?"

# Chapter Ten

## Reinventing Love

How does one establish a workable educational system which gives credit to the notion that we as humans are always in a state of becoming and not just being? Further under what condition or conditions can we mesh fixed settled roles with the notion of being and becoming? Perhaps Shakespeare was correct when Cassius said to Brutus: "The fault, dear Brutus, is not in our stars, but in ourselves, that we are underlings." (Julius Caesar, Act 1, Scene 1). [1] More precisely stated is the African proverb taught to me by my mother: "Do not fear the Lion for he is us and we are all in Daniel's den." [2]

I am convinced as was Hugh Scott in a paper entitled "Black Consciousness and Professionalism" that effective leadership is the key to effective schools: "The effectiveness of any organization, regardless of its size and complexity, is dependent on its quality of leadership. Leadership is that which causes individuals and groups to perform in a manner that maximizes their contributions to the achievement of the objectives of an organization. Leadership is that quality which enables an individual within a given setting to motivate and inspire others to adopt, achieve and maintain organizational and individual goals. It is the leader who is given authority to take action, to require and receive performance of actions from others, and direct and give decisions to others." [3] Effective leadership, however, works best when it takes into account the multiplicity of inherited and environmental factors that impact us all—family, poverty, school climate, socio-economic factors, psychological factors and an understanding of cultural expectations. Many years ago Curtis Mayfield attacked notions of self image, leadership and some of the inherited and environmental factors in his song, *"We the People Who Are Darker Than Blue."* The lyrics read:

> We the people who are darker than blue
> Are we gonna stand around this town
> And let what others say come true?
> We're just good for nothing they all figure,
> A boyish grown up shiftless jigger.
> Now we can't hardly stand for that
> Or is that really where it's at?
> We the people who are darker than blue
> This ain't no time for segregating

# Resurrection

I'm talking 'bout brown and yellow too.
High yellow girl can't you tell?
You're just the surface of our dark, deep well.
If your mind could really see
You'd know your colour same as me.
Pardon me brother as you stand in your glory,
I know you won't mind if I tell the whole story.
Get yourself together, learn to know your sign.
Shall we commit our genocide before we check out our mind?
I know we've all got problems, that's why I'm here to say
Keep peace with me and I with you, let me love in my own way.
Now I know we have respect for the sister
And mother it's even better yet,
But there's the joker in the street
Loving one brother and killing the other.
When the time comes and we are really free,
There'll be no brothers left you see.
We people who are darker than blue
Don't let us hang around this town
And let what others say come true.
We're just good for nothing they all figure,
A boyish grown up shiftless jigger.
Now we can't hardly stand for that
Or is that really where it's at?
Pardon me brother, I know we've come a long way.
Let us stop being so satisfied,
For tomorrow can even be a brighter day. [4]

Mr. Mayfield succinctly attacks the inner psychological, historical, social dynamics of a people caught up in living an unrealistic dream, without hope for a resurrection. As mentioned in an earlier chapter, when I visited our prison system, all of the prisoners at one time or another were products of our educational systems. Most have failed because no one has taken enough time to love them, to make them aware of their history, to show them the path to a new brighter tomorrow, to move them from a state of being to one of becoming. Recall for a moment a few years ago when Tina Turner's song "What's Love Got to Do with It?" was the number one hit of the nation. It was a time in the nation when Marion Edelman, President of the Washington based Children's Defense Fund, in a report entitled, "Black and White Children in America—Key Facts" stated: "Black children are three times more likely than whites to have an absent parent. 80% of white children live in two parent families compared to 40% black children living in two parent families. Nearly half of black children are poor, compared to 1/6 of all white children. Black babies are more than twice as likely as white babies to be underweight at birth—low birth weight infants are 20 times more likely to die in the first year of life than normal weight infants. Black public school children are twice as likely to be suspended from school and 50% more likely to be corporally punished." [5]

On another front, nowhere in this country has a

voice been heard that could unite the minority community into a single resounding voice since Dr. Martin Luther King, Jr. Jesse Jackson tried to unite us, but we were so politically sophisticated, and so historically divided and mistrustful that we failed to solidify enough votes to even make the actor in the White House readjust the saddle girths and stirrups on his favorite chestnut horse. However, registration increased and more voters were eligible to exercise their rights at the polls. Fortunately, we added Mayor Wilson Goode in Philadelphia, Ronald Blackwood in Mt. Vernon, New York, kept Johnnie Jones in Mississippi and Ken Gibson in Newark, New Jersey. A circuit courthouse was named honoring Clarence Mitchell in Baltimore, Maryland. The South Carolina general assembly elected Judge Ernest Finney to the State Supreme Court, and Reuben Anderson was appointed to the Supreme Court in Mississippi, but where was our national clout? Today we have Senator Barack Obama on the presidential slate for 2008 contending with an early request for secret service security, while quietly suppressing the idea that it is related to his eternal blackness. Meanwhile, Colin Powell and Condoleezza Rice are caught up in the political strategies of a president whose vision has been limited to spreading democracy under the guise of a war in Iraq and Iran to save a people from themselves. But "What's love got to do with it? What's love, but a sweet old fashioned notion?"

On the educational scene, major black

superintendents stepped down from their prestigious positions with no place to go. The then Superintendent Ruth Love lost her position in Chicago; Superintendent Fred Holliday committed suicide in Detroit, Michigan. Superintendent Columbus Salley was suspended in Newark, New Jersey, while Superintendent Ronald Lewis, formally of New Jersey, the Governor's choice for Education Commissioner, was forced into oblivion somewhere in Philadelphia, Pennsylvania. Each of these astute major black heroes got caught up in the hatred and mistrust of irrational politics, a cutting edge still unrealized in the research annals of our most astute sociologists. But, "What's love got to do with it?" We could prick our consciousness relative to the former controversy surrounding the administration of justice in the Goetz family and the Eleanor Bumpers case in New York,[6] or with the fact that college admissions criteria and fees are forcing declines in minority enrollments, or with the rise of a class society schooled in the utilization and ownership of high technological devices, or with the hidden increases in hunger in America, while we spend billions on war and allow our own to starve and go homeless. Witness if you will the many visible veterans begging on the streets surrounding the highways of central Florida.

What's love got to do with it? Love has everything to do with it. To change America, we must start at home with our individual families. It makes no difference whether the family boasts of a single parent home or a nuclear family. Whatever we call home, start there! Pass the torch of freedom to your children. Tell them about the good times and the bad. Give them a sense of their own history. There were very precise and profitable advantages to the "good ole days". Yesterday's person understood his culture. Compare for a moment the community culture of a few years ago, when I was just a young lad, to the community culture of today. I lived in a community at the edge of Philadelphia. The expectancy for learning and scholarship was: (1) that the classroom teacher was an adult authority, (2) that the teacher was always right, (3) that a spanking at school meant a spanking at home. The home provided direct reinforcement for the school. At home there were divided responsibilities or chores to complete. Homework was essential and had to be completed without excuse. There weren't any separate rooms for a family of eight, and everyone studied at the dining room table. The social milieu was that of Jack Armstrong, Superman, radio shows, 10 cent movie matinees on Saturday( on occasion), and church almost four days a week plus three times on Sunday. Leisure time was limited and if a neighbor "down the street" caught you misbehaving, he/she could punish you via a spanking and send you home for yet another. Mrs. Armstead, my Sunday school teacher, was famous for that, but under today's standards and expectations we witness a few drastic changes. Mrs. Armstead doesn't dare reprimand Mrs. Warner's boy verbally or physically. A spanking at school means jail the principal, sue the superintendent, fire the teacher and the persistent murmuring from parents, "My child is always correct". Well, America, we need to wise up, because your child like mine is not always correct, and unless you constantly set standards, give direction and love them, they will receive misinformation and misdirection from those of the streets who would use them in the pursuit of selfish purposes.

Jack Armstrong and Superman have been replaced by Young Buck, Musiq Soulchild, Gerald Levert, Akon, Lloyd, 8Ball&MJB, Mims, Redman and Beyonce.

Look at your children. Today's children are tired. Too many young people of all socioeconomic classes arrive at our classroom doors late, and too tired to make a difference. Many children are unable to remain seated for 40 classroom minutes. A part of this is conditioned by the phenomenal amount of time our youngsters waste in front of the television tube, sending email notifications on My Space, and involved in play station activities. The television industry is forever supported by advertisers and business commercials—better known as the commercial break. Schools don't have the luxury of commercial breaks. Students who constantly need commercial breaks tend to fail. Failing students act out in negative ways and eventually drop out of school. Throughout America the process remains the same.

# Resurrection

Many years ago my mother asked the question, "What do you do now that you have graduated from the university?" My response was, "I teach". Her reply was, "Then don't ever return home saying you're tired". What she meant was that compared to her daily life style of family hardships, cleaning the homes of the neauveau riche, taking in washing and ironing on Saturdays and Sundays, teaching was easy. During her time, women worked in an effort to supplement the income of husbands who couldn't find work at a time when the local power structure would hire our women, but constantly failed to hire our fathers, causing the man to feel inferior to his female counterpart, and, in fact, psychologically destroyed because he couldn't support his family. Taken from that point of view, I shall never complain of being tired.

Again I ask, what's love got to do with it? Well, much of the lack of motivation in youngsters revolves around self esteem, that is, how I feel about me. Love and education and the development of skills must be a womb to tomb experience. Remember, any student who can memorize television commercials or the lyrics of Prince and Beyonce has the potential to recite Shakespeare, to create poetry, to become a noted scientist, to take a grain of sand and construct modern pyramids, to create another Colossus at Rome, to know courage, to know pride, to know dignity, to know themselves, to be different, to be scholars, to accommodate and cope with the conflict of a life style that has its reward in competition and the ability to express ideas clearly. Yet, many parents ask, "How can I make Johnny study?" If you seriously have to ask that question, then it's almost too late. The love of learning is basic. Learning is fun, but it's also discipline and hard work. We must supervise our youngsters as they study, especially during the formative elementary years. Ask inquisitive questions, "What did you just read? Was it interesting?" Don't get trapped into a reward system that promises "if you earn an A, I'll purchase you a moped". Instead, give other types of acceptances, even if it's merely a hug or a smile.

As an educator, it's clear to me that students can't learn if they're roaming the halls, and not in the classroom. Also, no teacher, administrator, cafeteria worker, classroom aide or other adult in the school system can be the object of physical or verbal abuse from students. When parents receive a telephone call from school or a handwritten note indicating that Johnny or Jane has broken a school rule, parents must support the school and do something to improve the student's behavior. Remember, a large part of instilling proper discipline hinges on consistency on the part of home and school in teaching common courtesies, i.e. please, thank you. I've witnessed discipline conferences where students exclaim to their mothers, "You don't know what the hell you're talking about!" When students at an early age tell parents, administrators, teachers and parents "to get off" their backs, then you ought to get all over their back and if necessary their backsides. But that takes a parent who knows where he "started from", one who passed the touch of freedom. I do not advocate physical abuse, just precautionary behaviors that inhibit poor performance.

One of the serious problems associated with today's human being is the use and abuse of the English language. Earlier I used the quote, "Do not fear the Lion, for he is us, and we are all in Daniels's den". The Lion is representative of a strange duality. It is a magnificently beautiful animal, strong and courageous, but must be feared and respected for its potential destructive powers— a strange duality. One must maintain an ambivalent posture wavering between love and hate as one contemplates on the one hand the magnificence of so powerful a creature and on the other hand, its potential for evil. But then, much of life represents that strange duality. The issue of "Black" language, as viewed in hip hop, rap music and street language, is representative of that strange duality. On the one hand, street language historically reflects the beauty, strength and courage of a people whose destiny is conditioned and modified by its ability to conform and accommodate to the demands of those in control, whose dominant language is standard English, and whose every institution respects an individual for his ability to properly manipulate and control the language. Yet, I believe that one common way out of the throes of poverty is through the development of verbal and language skills adequate to communicate in speech and writing to those who control the purse strings of America, with employers, business men and women. Young people who are unable to communicate in a manner acceptable to the mainstream of America will not succeed. At least the majority will not. This simply means that sub standard English, "What you be doing?" no matter what the justification, will not be acceptable to employers, to college admission officers, or business merchants. It is also true that a black youngster to survive, must at times develop two patterns of speech, strange duality, and must effectively use those patterns of speech when the occasion demands. Therefore parents need to remember while on the beach this summer not to reprimand your child by stating: "If you don't pick up that (defecation), I'm going to beat your (donkey)." Your child will imitate speech patterns and bring to school substandard patterns of learned language development.

It is true that street language is acceptable to many members of our individual peer groups, however, it is equally true that to use the so called King's English on every occasion, one might find himself without friends. For example, I wouldn't dare visit my hometown and approach Tommy Jones at the local Veterans of Foreign Wars Club stating: "Good afternoon, Thomas, what precipitated this visit to our lovely establishment?" It's usually, "Hey, babe, what's happening?" To do otherwise would categorize me as "Too uppity"; therefore, to survive one must develop two patterns of speech—one which allows you to communicate with friends and another to utilize in institutions of higher education, in completing job applications and interviews, in introducing the number of students in the National honor Society . I haven't seen a single job application in this country that accepted "I be 18 years of age"; nor have I witnessed an interviewer who accepted "What you be doin'" or "I 'pose to" as acceptable responses to questions. The end result to this process is that not enough of our youngsters can be found listed on Dean's Academic listings or acceptable as scholarship recipients.

The lesson to be learned is that our ancestors knew how to survive, but young people today aren't taught survival skills. A few African Americans assume that because a number of persons have become upwardly economically mobile, that you don't have to be better than your competitors. As school superintendent in Willingboro and Red Bank, New Jersey, I would never socialize at the local drinking establishment with other superintendents, for I knew my presence at a local bar would cause community members to view me negatively. Many fail to understand that every person who smiles at you and hands you a packet of cocaine is not your friend, nor is every person who frowns at you and directs your destiny your enemy.

There are many occasions in educational circles

when we are condemned through association and not accepted for who we really are. I once heard a teacher say. "Iven has so many problems. His brother is in jail; his sister is expecting and his father is an alcoholic; therefore poor Iven will never learn." Don't for one moment believe that story, as each person is unique. In order to love Iven, we must provide a learning environment at home; give books instead of candy bars and flashy non-utilitarian clothing. If you have a large family, set aside time for studying in the kitchen or at the dining room table. Give directions and have chores for them to do. Teach the wisdom of saving money. Teach them to have dignity, courage and pride in themselves. We once carried our shoes to elementary school and put them on at the door, but we had pride and dignity. We once picked coal from the railroad tracks, but we had a sense of self worth. We once followed freight trains to trade off vegetables with the train conductor for large chunks of coal to be used in our stoves, but we had a sense of belonging. We once were left with newspaper in our outhouses instead of toilet tissue, but we weren't ashamed of our parents. All of the above represents a kind of life style that builds character, teaches the appreciation of others, builds ego and self image and transcends the false dichotomy of making life better for our sons and daughters, without having them share in the joys and sorrows of maturing as knowledgeable individuals.

But, what about our obligations to family? The

family unit is the most important institution in the world community today. For ages it has been the preserver of our culture. It is the place where the difference between right and wrong is learned, values, manners and socially acceptable behavior is taught. When they once said "You ain't got no home training", it meant that either your parents had forgotten to instruct you in proper behavior or you simply failed to act on what you were taught. Don't allow scholars to confuse you by saying single parent families are weak. One good active and involved woman in the home is worth three men anytime. As the saying goes: "God made the world and rested; God made man and rested; Then God made woman; since then neither God nor man has rested." Also, don't worry about family members ever getting lonely. An 80 year old woman remarked to one who complained of loneliness: "I am not alone. I have not one, two or three, but four men in my life. I awaken each morning with Charlie Horse. I eat breakfast with Arthur Ritus. I spend the day with Will Power, and I go to bed with Ben Gay."

There exists a serious challenge for today's men and women to leave an exciting, vibrant legacy to our children, but we must develop visible leadership. We can't forever live on the past accomplishments of the Martin Luther Kings, the Malcolm X's and others. We have to move beyond the rhetoric of laissez faire and do nothingism and stand and be counted. We must be seen and heard at school board meetings, at municipal government meetings, in our churches, mosques and synagogues. We must be everywhere in numbers asking questions and providing answers. No longer can we stand by idle, allowing others to decide our destinies. No longer can we compromise the lives of our women, our sons and daughters, for each time we fail to be heard at a school board meeting where men and women decide who is to be educated through the allocation of funds and the administration of policies, we compromise the lives of our children. Each time we fail to appear at a municipal government meeting where men and women make decisions about garbage collection, housing erection and police protection, we compromise the futures of our children. Each time we fail to appear at our religious organization's business meeting where the differences between right and wrong are decided, we compromise the lives of our children. Never compromise. You can't negotiate dignity. True men are fashioned in the likeness of a coiled cobra. We must counsel one another, and when the assassin's bullet destroys one of the chosen leadership, we must volunteer anther mighty warrior to go forth and conquer the souls of men and women who would render us incapable of deciding our destinies.

Tina turner expressed love in her way, yet Tennyson in his poetic song to Ulysses, the Greek hero, expressed love in still another way:

*" ...Come my friends,*

Tis not too late to seek a newer world.
 Push off,...sail beyond the sunset,...
It may be that the gulfs will wash us down;
It may be we shall touch the Happy Isles,...
Though much is taken, much abides; and though
We are not that strength which in the old days
Moved earth and heaven,
That which we are, we are-
One equal temper of heroic hearts,
Made weak by time and fate, but strong in will
To strive, to seek, to find, and not to yield." [7]

Finally, our grandparents, the old freedom fighters, the builders and seekers of a new tomorrow expressed their love song stating:

" I don't feel no ways tired.
I come too far from where I started from.
Nobody told me the road would be easy.
I don't believe He brought me this far, just to leave me."

## The New Colossus

Even though the above mentioned love song of our forefathers alludes to aspects of love, hope, faith, endurance and not feeling tired, admittedly I have grown tired of the failure of educators to properly educate our children. However, in the midst of failure there is hope. There is light at the end of the tunnel and that light can best be viewed through Brookdale Community College, Lincroft, New Jersey. They are "The New Colossus" of the 21st Century. I am encouraged by Emma Lazaras' poem inscribed on the *Statue of Liberty* which reads:

"Not like the brazen giant of Greek fame,
With conquering limbs astride from land to land;
Here at our sea-washed, sunset gates shall stand
A mighty woman with a torch, whose flame
Is the imprisoned lightning, and her name
Mother of Exiles. From her beacon-hand
Glows world wide welcome; her mild eyes command
The air-bridged harbor that twin cities frame.
"Keep, ancient lands, your storied pomp!" cries she
With silent lips. "Give me your tired, your poor
Your huddled masses yearning to breathe free,
The wretched refuse of your teeming shore.
Send these, the homeless, tempest-tossed to me.
I lift my lamp beside the golden door!" [8]

Brookdale Community college is the "Mother of Exiles" among colleges and universities in New Jersey and the nation. Like many community colleges Brookdale embraces a vision that is more inclusive than exclusive in giving educational opportunity to all without regard to race, color, creed or ethnicity; however, its uniqueness rests in the college's ability to reach out into the full community embracing all and inviting their participation in the greatest educational institution in existence. To that end several higher educational centers have been established in local communities beyond the main campus; however, the direction of the college though spiraling upward had never reached the pinnacle of excellence it is today. The major critical issues of today vary little from the critical issues of community colleges forty years ago. As mentioned in an earlier chapter to achieve excellence in schools, the main focus must center on leadership and its impact upon students, staff, and community. Leadership, in turn, must not only be visionary, but must incorporate within the vision cooperative networks designed to activate and implement goal oriented strategic planning with measurable outcomes. Very few persons can fulfill the requirement listed above. In my short nineteen year tenure as voluntary participant and eventual Board Chair of the Board of Trustees at the college, I had the pleasure to interact with and observe five college presidents and every conceivable administrative style imaginable. Two of the former presidents, Mr. Tom Auch and Mr. Gershom Tomlinson gallantly served the college as Interim Presidents while search committees made efforts to locate a permanent leader for the college.

Meanwhile Dr. Bob Barringer and Dr. Joshua Smith served as President prior to the advent of Dr. Peter F. Burnham, our current and most prestigious of all the former presidents. Prestigious not because he exemplifies wealth, or has his name prominently displayed on permanent statuary, but prestigious because he brings to the college those elements of leadership that are designed to touch and enhance the hidden qualities in each person who embraces the life giving instructional activities of the college that eventually mesmerizes and changes the individual into an improved, mature living organism.

Interestingly, as I write to personally document a few of the accomplishments of the college over the past 20 years, Brookdale Community College is instituting a special 40th Anniversary President's Colloquium featuring several distinguished panelists inclusive of representatives from the American Association of Community Colleges (Dr. George Boggs), New Jersey Commission of Higher Education (Ms. Jane Oates), the Middle States Association on Higher Education (Dr. Elisabeth Sibolski) and former presidents, past interim presidents of the college. However, from an insiders point of view, I would expect the following accomplishments to be mentioned under the leadership and direction of Dr. Peter F. Burnham, who assumed the presidency June 5, 1991: (1) the establishment of a High Technology High School

(2) a new community Higher Education Learning Center initiated in Asbury Park, (3) reinvention of the Children's Learning Center, main campus (4) student enrollment increase to 11,931, the highest in Brookdale's history, (5) Alpha Pi Theta, academic honor society awarded 5 star status at the Pi Theta Kappa Middle States Regional Convention, (6) privatization of custodial services,(7) newly expanded police services headquarters' building completed, (8) initiated Leadership Shore, a cooperative leadership training program sponsored by Brookdale and the Monmouth Ocean Development Council,(9) established four year university based college credit transfer program with Kean University and others, (10) the Western Monmouth Higher Education Center established in Freehold, N.J. (11) received the highest ranking of " unqualified reaccreditation" from the Middle States Association of Colleges, (12)established new Culinary Education Center as a joint educational venture with the Monmouth Vocational School District, (13) dedicated new classroom building, Larrison Hall, (14) initiated first Brookdale parent orientation program, (15) the first New Jersey Coastal Communiversity classes held at Brookdale, (16)Brookdale Community College initiated continuous television broadcasting, (17) joint offering of information technology training and certificate program with Collegis (Deltak),(18) recipient of 28 acres of land from former U.S. Camp Evans to establish the Wall Higher Education

Center,(19) hosts first Health care Expo and Job Fair, (20) expands College Degree Transfer Program to include Rutgers University, Georgian Court and Montclair State College.

None of the few highlights mentioned above capture the man, Peter Burnham, or the intensity at which he pursues the dream for a better tomorrow. There is an eternal beating in his heart that is captivated by all the nuances of leadership woes surrounding governance and administration, student, staff, personnel services, finances, components of career , compensatory and community education as he responds to the ever changing needs of the collegiate function; yet deep within himself Peter Burnham is both poet and dreamer. John Keats once exclaimed, "The poet and the dreamer are distinct, diverse, sheer opposites, antipodes, the one pours out a balm upon the world, the other vexes it." [9] How strange Mr. Keats that Peter Burnham's success rests not in the division of opposites, but in his ability as leader to vex his charges while at the same time pour out balm upon their worlds; thus in what might appear to be a confusion of opposites is instead a melding of forces utilized to provide positive results in an atmosphere of trust and change in a caring educational environment. Thus, Peter Burnham's viable theme of "One Brookdale" resonates in the local, state and national community. Peter Burnham and Brookdale Community College have lifted their lamp beside the golden doors of educational opportunity, welcoming all who would embrace new beginnings and higher horizons. In stating the crux of the problem in excerpts taken from his white paper entitled: "Brookdale Community College: Leadership Planning for the Next Decade, An Essay on History and Change", Dr. Peter F. Burnham wrote:

"Without substantial redefinition of the functional leadership roles and the addition of an expanded team of second level leaders at Brookdale Community College over the next eighteen to twenty four months, the college will have significant difficulty implementing its vision and development of a multi campus, public comprehensive community college. The need for transformational leadership, working in close concert with the President and the Board of Trustees, will be essential to the success of the aspirations of Brookdale through the balance of this decade and beyond.

Further, the necessity for and the immediacy of the need for successors to the critical, functional leadership roles of the organization is fundamental to the long-term health of the institution. And, although the impact of individuals and unique personalities on leadership is a valid and appropriate hypothesis in this environment,

Brookdale Community College has become too 'person centric' in its leadership structure and needs to define functional lines of responsibility, authority and responsibility that can be easily and readily identified by all constituencies internal and external to the organization, with balanced and equitable allocations of these responsibilities and accountabilities clearly and unambiguously defined.

Finally, for the President to function effectively as the leader of this institution, and to actively participate in the roles of leadership defined by the Board of Trustees for the President, specifically advocacy in the public and political arena, fund raising and visioning and strategic positioning, it is necessary to support the president's role with a strong, functional leadership team whose authority and delegated responsibilities are clearly designated."

The Statement of the Problem listed above is but one small example what viable leadership looks like and how it functions. If all of our youngsters at the primary and secondary levels could have leadership with the vision, forethought, acumen and planning of a Dr, Peter Burnham, then the Asbury Park's, the Newark's, the Jersey Cities would fade into the dust of a thousand tomorrows and all would be right with the world of education. The full document identified above, too lengthy for our purposes, is over nine pages, and testifies to areas of reorganization, history and review, negotiators vs. leaders, former Presidential leaders, millennium planning, and responding to the need for change, with a view that transition is positive and "it can be done".

Many years ago Louis Gerstein, the Chief Executive Officer of Nabisco, in espousing his views about industry, technology and economics stated there should be "no more prizes for predicting rain, only prizes for building arks." This was termed the "Noah Principal". Gerstein was inferring that ark builders are individuals who possess vision, and are able to find workable solutions even when they are mocked by the crowd. We, in turn, must remember that life is a pilgrimage, a journey in which we experience many ups and downs; however, persistence to the very end is crucial. In life we find a continuous series of problems all requiring decisions and all having consequences. Topics range from chemical control of the aging process, direct recording of information on the brain, gene manipulation, human cloning, frozen body storage and emerging third world systems. The consequences of the decisions we make can be positive or negative depending upon our ability to persist to the very end.

Nikki Giovanni, poet and professor, has said that "a circle is a sunbeam that saw itself and fell in love"; therefore, as we form our organizational circles plotting who we are and who we shall become, we must fall in love with ourselves. We must become ark builders and not mere predictors of rain. We must know who we are, and that will determine who we can become. We must be brave in our endeavors, and have the courage to fight for what we believe to be right. If necessary, stand alone and be counted, but stand. Actually the more I investigate the predictions for the future, the more humble I become. The issues involve areas that mix ethics, morals, sex, government regulations, human rights and religion all thrown into one basket. Think about some of the consequences and decisions the following topics introduce: (1) chemical control of the aging process, (2) breeding humans to serve as organ transplant banks, (3)selective breeding, (4) frozen body storage to permit a form of time travel (5) drug usage to raise levels of intelligence (6) controlling behavior via radio wave stimulation, (7) knowledge explosion. The idea of cloning the unemployable to perform low level robotic skills may not be a far fetched idea. In the future the so called three "r's" of reading writing and arithmetic may give way to the four "i's" of ideas, inventions, innovation, and imitation.

During the year 1969, the number 1 one song on the *Billboard Charts* written by Richard Evans predicting the future was:

## In the Year 2525

In the year 2525
If man is still alive
If woman can survive
They may find….


In the year 3535
Ain't gonna need to tell the truth, tell no lies
Everything you think, do, or say
Is in the pill you took today


In the year 4545
Ain't gonna need your teeth, won't need your eyes
You won't find a thing to chew
Nobody's gonna look at you


In the year 5555
Your arms are hanging limp at your side
Your legs got nothing to do
Some machine, doing that for you………

# Chapter Eleven
## The Potter and the Clay

Thinking back to the time when Mozelle, my mother, insisted on our church attendance on almost a daily basis, I recall vividly Mrs. Dorothy Armstead, my Sunday School teacher, reciting James Weldon Johnson's version of the "Creation." [1] I can see Dorothy Armstead, on her knees dipping deeply into the earth, explaining how the omnipotent God fashioned humanity out of the dust and clay, fervently stating: "Then into it He blew the breath of life, and man became a living soul. Amen. Amen." This vision of God is deeply imbedded in my soul, as I imagined standing there at the beginning of creation with the potter and the breathing clay. We stood perfect before God, beautiful and sinless, free to roam across the multitudinous grandeur of the earth, free to drink from pure sparkling streams of the waters of delight, free to be me, free to be you. But then evil personified gazed out of the dark, damp, sinful, gritty hole and tempted the first Adam. Adam became a cracked pot. No longer stood he perfect before God, but imperfect, cracked, flawed, sinful, hoping against hope, and lost in the very world that God perfected for him.

In Isaiah 64 the prophets petitioned God to reveal his awesome might, to tear open the heavens, and come down to earth, make the mountains quake and the nations tremble in his presence. Come down Lord, so that we may remember your ways. Come down Lord for we are unclean and will "fade like a leaf" (Isaiah 64:6 KJV).[2] We are cracked pots. After all God, you are the potter and we are the clay. You formed us and shaped us in your image, and yet given first Adam's sin, we have become cracked pots. Some of us God when we first came to the mourners bench and declared ourselves saved through your grace, left the mourners bench filled with the joy of your goodness. But since that time, we have been drifting. We can't seem to find anything good in our lives. We complain about everybody and everything! No one is allowed to make a mistake, unless we find time to complain about how it used to be or how the new people aren't doing it the way we once did. And because it was done another way, that had to be the right way. We have lost our joy. We visit in the pews every Sunday, but God is not in us. Satan has taken over our hearts, and moved into our negative dispositions. We are cracked pots; we have lost our Holy victory dance. We have lost our willingness to pray.

Many of us are limited in our acceptance of others. We discriminate against those who differ from us. We proclaim belief in God and the commandment to love; yet, we are unable to love the young man on the corner with the do-rag or handkerchief on his head. We can't love the young boy with his baggy jeans, and his earrings that are almost as large as his head. We can't love his dip, sway, and swagger as he meanders past our churches on his way to the liquor store to purchase a six pack or a carton of cigarettes. We are so blind that we mistake the smoke of regular cigarettes for the stench of weed and marijuana. We are cracked pots!

Some of us have forgotten the teachings of our parents and have become "players". We establish tentative relationships with women who are lonely and forlorn. We visit with them once or twice a week, leave pieces of our clothing in their bedroom closets to mark out territory; but then when they're busy working in the church, we're out slipping and dipping, placing yet another piece of clothing in another person's closet. We're players; we're cracked pots! There is nothing solid in our lives. We need the potter to reform the clay, rework the wheel and cause us to mend our evil ways. Others of us, O God, are just plain ugly in our walk, ugly in our talk, ugly in our interactions with one another. We feel that if we didn't initiate it, it can't be done. We will serve on the Missionary Board as long as they visit the favorite person on "our" list. We will offer the membership rides to the church as long as it's not inconvenient and out of the way. We will sing on the choir as long as they sing "our" song. We will serve on the kitchen crew, as long as we don't have to wash the pots and pans. We will listen to the plans to carry out a new program, but as soon as we arrive home after the meeting, we dial brother James and Sister Sookie on the telephone in an effort to sabotage the mission of the organization. We are just plain ugly. We are cracked pots. God, have you any room in the kingdom for cracked pots? You are the potter and we are the clay.

There once was a water bearer who lived in China who carried two large pots, each hung on the ends of a pole which he carried across his neck. One of the pots had a crack in it, while the other pot was perfect and always delivered a full portion of water. At the end of the long walk from the stream to the house, the cracked pot arrived only half full. For a full two years this went on daily, with the water bearer delivering only one and a half pots of water to his house.

Of course the perfect pot was proud of its accomplishments, perfect for which it was made. But the poor cracked pot was ashamed of its imperfection, and miserable that it was only able to accomplish only half of what it had been made to do.

After two years of what it perceived to be bitter failure, the cracked pot spoke to the water bearer one day by the stream saying, "I am ashamed of myself, because this crack in my side causes water to leak out all the way to our house." The bearer said to the pot, "Did you not notice that there are flowers on your side of the path, but not on the other pot's side? That's because I have always known about your flaw, so I planted flowers on your side of the path, and every day while we walk back, you water them. For two years I have been able to pick these beautiful flowers to decorate the table. Without your being just the way you are, there would not be this beauty to grace the house."

God is saying to America today that He recognizes that each person has his/her own unique flaw, but it's the cracks and flaws each person has that make our lives together so interesting and rewarding. You must take individuals for what they are, and look for the good in them. We must come out of our comfort zones. Step out on faith, for God will cause you to stretch out into worlds never before realized. There should be no more business as usual. Each person, no matter what age or disposition, has a pioneering spirit. You are trailblazers. Each believer in God has an apostolic anointing. Remember God has given gifts and talents to each individual—some evangelists, some teachers, some preachers, some fathering spirits. 11Chronicles 7:14 reminds us that, "If my people who are called by my name, shall humble themselves and pray, and seek my face, and turn from their wicked ways; then will I hear from heaven, and will forgive their sin and will heal their land...for now have I chosen and sanctified this house, that my name may be there forever and mine eyes and my heart shall be there perpetually." [3]

God will make us a part of his Hawk ministry. The hawk is a symbol of the fathering ministry i.e. one who watches over, protects and cares for his family. The hawk, though similar to the eagle, is a warrior bird. It possesses keen eyesight and expert vision. It is a military and conquering bird. It flies high utilizing the currents to save energy and keep it aloft. Then when the hawk sights its prey, the hawk casts its wings to its sides, swoops down and captures its victims in its mighty claws. It has a conquering mind. If we are going to succeed in life, we need a warrior's mentality and a conquering mind. Like the Apostle Paul, we must turn over our full self to the Master. Half stepping and shuffling won't do. The reason it takes so long to get our prayers answered is because we haven't exercised our belief and faith, and turned over our problems and concerns to the Creator. Instead, we see ourselves as "know it alls", full of intelligence, but we are merely cracked pots. The things that you and I own or possess, we have, not because we're so great, but because God's grace has shone upon us. What do you really control? Where is your power? Why aren't you free? It is only through God that we are empowered and given our freedom. You must swoop down; pick up the broken pieces and use your hawk mentality. Declare to yourself, I'm ready to swoop down. I see my target; I see my mission; I understand my position in life. Even though I may be a crackpot, I know as David knew, "The Lord is my light and my salvation; whom shall I fear?" (Psalms 27:1 KJV) [4] In my sad ways and my dark days, God will shine the light from heaven and bless me with the grace of salvation. I need not be afraid, because God is my savior and my protector, my refuge and strength: "The lord is the strength of my life, of whom shall I be afraid?"(Psalms 27:1 KJV) [5] I'm a believer. I've been set aside for God's work; He will protect me. My pot may be cracked, but my heart is filled with love, thanksgiving, repentance and joy. In fact, "Now my head is lifted up above mine enemies round about me: therefore will I offer in his tabernacle sacrifices of joy.." (Psalms 27: 6 KJV) [6] In other words, I don't have to walk around saddened with my head bowed and buried in the ground. I can lift up my head; carry it high, proudly above my enemies. I don't have to attend the night club to offer cheers and sacrifices which are at the end headaches, heartache and pain. Instead I can offer shouts of joy in the sanctuary. Yes, I'm a crackpot, but I too can make beautiful flowers if I but: "Wait on the Lord, be of good courage, and He shall strengthen (my) heart..." (Psalms 27: 14 KJV) [7]

Who are you waiting for? Depending on the circumstance, they may show up and they may not! If you owe them something, or they need something from you, you may, I repeat, may see them. However the scriptures remind us to wait on a sure thing, a certain destiny, salvation and eternal life. Therefore, don't feel neglected, rejected, and unaffected. Be of good courage. God will heal your illness. God will mend your broken heart. O cracked pot be perfect in the Lord, God's son, empowered by the Holy Spirit.

Yes , the Creator scooped up the dust and breathed into us the breath of life and we became living beings, perfect before a Holy God until first Adam sinned.

As I look back over my blessed life, I am grateful for the guiding presence of the people from my hometown, Crestmont, who were allowed to reprimand me and spank me before sending me home to my parents for yet another spanking, many years before the Division of Youth and Family Services became a reality. Especially memorable are the guiding instructions from Mrs. Dorothy Armstead , Sunday School teacher, and Mrs. Mable Williams, both of whom encouraged me to reach far beyond what I perceived as my capabilities. Never to be forgotten are the many invisible faces of imbibers at the local beer garden (Crestmont Country Club), who left nickels, dimes, pennies and quarters in a coffee can for my use during four undergraduate years at Temple University.

Many persons encouraged me as an educator: Cecil Moore, attorney and Civil Rights Activist who paved the way for my first administrative position appointed without credentials; Golda Mier, Israel Prime Minister, who autographed her book at John Bartram High School and Vice President Hubert Humphrey, who dedicated our annex. Also, several outstanding teachers such as Hank Kopple and Julian Levy with whom I attended Anti-Viet Nam Protest marches in Washington, D.C., along with Albert Robbins, the Washington March, and the many teachers who demonstrated daily with me as we picketed Gerald College, Philadelphia back in the days when the school was designated for "white orphan boys" only. Audrey Jablonski, Ty Lewis, Rodney Sommerville, Sharon Portman, Joyce Diglio, Gwen Hewlett, Charles Askew, all deceased and many others have influenced my beliefs about equal education for all.

Beyond the development of leadership previously discussed, the most important aspect of any educational system is its curriculum. All students, regardless of income or birth circumstance, must be taught the great works of literature and be exposed to at least one foreign language. We can not expect our future generations to make appropriate decisions if they have not been exposed to great ideas, great art, great music and the nuances of languages. They must be taught the relationship between Shakespeare's *Hamlet* and the *Autobiography of Malcolm X*. They must know that Plato's "Allegory of the Cave" has implications for those who would rise up out of the throes of ignorance and reclaim a brighter tomorrow. One must be made to understand that the mathematical wonders associated with the great pyramids have associations with man's attempt to understand the ordering and structuring of the heavens and universe. There is a relationship between Piggy's attempt to survive in the *Lord of the Flies* and Topac Shakur's attempt to understand his destiny through gangster rap. There is a relationship between the nine concentric rings of hell found in Dante's *Inferno* and concepts found in J. Kelly's song "*I Believe I Can Fly*". A student who understands through literature and culture who he is and where he comes from will not likely resort to the use of guns and knives to determine a future which may never be.

My former students from Philadelphia and New Jersey are everywhere, employed as architects, doctors, engineers, teachers, health professionals, construction workers, etc. Unfortunately, some are incarcerated, witnessing to our failure as educators, family and community. In some areas I have failed. As Frank Sinatra sang," regrets I have a few". I failed, because I didn't teach them to hope. I failed, because I didn't teach them to love. I failed, because there wasn't enough of me to be a significant other to every student with whom I interacted, but how I tried. Nevertheless, I rejoice in our successes. We must continue to strive together until our jails can be turned into art museums, deteriorating urban buildings can be turned into computer factories, and houses of ill repute can be turned into houses of education and houses of worship. Yes, I tried to build an empire and legacy of love and hope. My passion is to love all individuals, to act upon that love and then to cherish the courage and wisdom garnered from my willingness to let free the inescapable spirit which hovers over us all. Its mystery is still untold and yet a heightened spirituality abides in us all. Life has no real meaning until one dies in faith and through faith is resurrected. Then and only then does the breath of life expand to greatness never before realized. Then and only then does one recognize the power which causes the white topped mountains to caress the pale blue sky, that causes the meandering streams to cascade downward forming deep blue seas and oceans of delight.

Now I must take time to witness the budding of the trees, the birds gathering twigs for their nests, squirrels meandering across the ground and flying atop trees, moths capturing the light and tiny insects in meaningless patterns of flight, a blade of grass erupting through the dark, black macadam, a firefly breaking the darkness with its luminous light. These are my champions. They lack perceivable intelligence, know nothing of goals, organizational skills, or strategic planning. They fail to display negative attitudes. Their desires are limited. Their hopes and aspirations are interrupted by a timeless fate; yet their destinies are as old as time itself and my God drives their futures. Each spring of my life

He resurrects them to a new beauty and a new grandeur. Inanimate though they may be, they are my heroes, my chevalier, my champions, my darlings of the night. They bask in the dew of my footsteps on a cold winter's night. They caress my shadow and understand the intermittent beatings of my heart. They know that though I've basked in the things of men, that now my soul, my bowels doth magnify the Lord God of my life.

Sister Pollard, an elderly woman from the Civil Rights Movement, once said to Rev. Dr. Martin Luther King Jr., "My feets is tired, but my soul is rested". [8] My personal destiny though controlled is at peace. My mother taught me the realities of life, but she allowed me to dream, and at the end of her days she taught me how to die with God at her side. An educated woman, she reminded me that Plato described God as the "Architectonic Good". Aristotle called him the "Unmoved Mover". Hegel called him the "Absolute Whole" and Paul Tillich called him "Being Itself". Mozelle reminded me that the psalmist David wrote:

"thou anointed my head with oil, my cup runneth over…" [9]

Whether you are Protestant, Catholic, Jew, Episcopal, Baptist, Methodist, Presbyterian, Muslim, slave or free, as long as you are a believer you are anointed, set aside, elect. You have been given the cup about which David wrote. For many of us the cup is only the size of a thimble, but its essence, its power lies in the fact that it is full and running over. Inside the cup is love. Inside the cup is joy. Inside the cup is compassion. Inside the cup is hope. Don't hold on to the cup. It "runneth over"; therefore, give it away to help somebody else. Together we can move from heart to heart; we can educate our children; we can feed the hungry; we can clothe the needy; we can love those who would despitefully use us; we can cure the illnesses of the sick. Together we have the strength, courage and power to change America to the point where each person in America one day will exclaim in the words of Henley's "*Invictus*":

"Out of the night that covers me,
Black as the pit from pole to pole,
I thank whatever gods may be
For my unconquerable soul.

In the fell clutch of circumstance,
I have not winched nor cried aloud.
Under the bludgeoning of chance
My head is bloody, but unbowed

Beyond this place of wrath and tears
Looms but the horror of the shade,
And yet the menace of the years
Finds, and shall find me, unafraid.

It matters not how strait the gate,

How charged with punishment the scrolls,
I am the master of my fate,
I am the captain of my soul. [10]

As I close this chapter of my life, I am reminded of a statement made by one of my role models at Brookdale Community College, Professor Geanna Merola, who stated: "There are many layers and many levels of understanding what we experience. No two of us will experience an object, a person or an event in exactly the same way. We bring to each moment our individual baggage of our personal history, our personal psychology and our previous conditioning. My process of working is about what I see, what I experience, and how I choose to make connections and explore ideas."

It was in the same year of her statement that I witnessed three major events. Earlier in the year, in the midst of 85,000 persons of like mind, I felt the warmth and charisma of Pope John Paul at Giants Stadium in New Jersey. This event was overshadowed by the intensity of a day's journey to Washington, D.C. to participate in the Million Man march with my two sons and my daughter, who is somewhat of a rebel with cause. And yet, in early November, this event was overshadowed when I was privileged to join hands with a small group of 350 people (National Park Ranger count) in Trenton, New Jersey. I had been invited to participate in the Kristallnacht Memorial Commemoration held at the state capital. As

Professor Merola had predicted, I experienced many layers and many levels of understanding. Internally, I wrestled subconsciously with Professor Merola's concepts of power and vulnerability.

As revealed in Neil Postman's book, *The End of Education*, [11] America must create a new narrative, one which incorporates the combined images of the Pope's visit, the Million Man March and the Kristallnacht Memorial. That narrative must be "the story of human beings as stewards of the earth, caretakers of a vulnerable space capsule. It is a relatively new narrative not fully developed and fraught with uncertainties and even contradictions…nonetheless, the story of Spaceship Earth has the power to bind people". All of us have a significant role to play in that narrative. Personally, I have thought much about that narrative, yet in the midst of our brilliance in thinking, there exists a wise Yiddish saying: "Man tracht un Got lacht" (Man thinks and God Laughs)[12]. Thus, we continue the ever evolving evolution of cracked pots in need of a resurrection!

# Notes

CHAPTER I

1. Sunday School Publishing Board, National Baptist Convention, USA, *Gospel Pearls* (Nashville: Music Committee, 1921) 110.

2. The song "Stout Hearted men" is credited to Sigmund Romberg and Oscar Hammerstein II. It has been associated with former U.S. Presidents and their involvement in Viet-Nam, the Green Berets, plus anti-women's issues.

3. "Swannee River (Old Folks at Home)" was authored by Stephen C. Foster, a musical story teller, in 1851. Foster is credited with authoring approximately 200 songs during his career. The state of Florida adopted "Swannee River" as its

official state song.

4. Edgar Allen Poe, "The Raven" and President Lincoln's "Gettysburg Address" were a part of the curriculum taught in Newport News, Virginia during Mozelle Warner's school years.

5. Arnold Adoff, ed., *The Poetry of Black America* (New York: Harper and Row, 1973) 10.

6. "C. C. Rider" is a blues standard first recorded by Ma Rainey in 1925, and sung by Chuck Willis in 1957 , Elvis Presley popularized the song under the title "See See Ryder".

CHAPTER III

1. Albert C. Baugh and George Wm. McClelland, eds., *English Literature: A Period Anthology* (New York: Appleton-Century Crofts, 1954) 1380.

2. J. Brantley Wilders and Art Peters, "Bartram Keg of Dynamite", *The Philadelphia Tribune,* October 22, 1966, p.1. This local newspaper has been in existence since 1884, and primarily targets informative articles and issues concerning the African American community.

3. "My Girl" was released in 1964. In 1965 it

was recorded by the singing "Temptations", featuring David Ruffin as lead singer. It was recorded as a part of the Gordy "Motown" label.

4. The Shook Ones, popularized as "The Shooks", is a band that describes itself as "just some dudes who play music". Its genre was generally classified as "hardcore and pop punk", but many lyrics border on typical "gangster rap".

5. Alfred Henry Bullen, *William Shakespeare: The Complete Works* (New York: Dorset Press, 1988) 584.

6. Nikki Giovanni, "The Lion in Daniel's Den", *The Women and the Men* (New York: William Morrow and Company, Inc., 1975) Chapter II. Other African expressions may be found in *African Proverbs* (New York: Peter Pauper Press, 1962).

7. Sunday School Publishing Board, 98.

CHAPTER IV

1. See "King David mourns for Absalom" (II Samuel 18: 33), *Holy Bible* (Iowa falls: World Bible Publishers, Inc., 1986).

2. To view a full body of research on Philadelphia based gangs, see Warner, Donald, *The Effects of Gang membership and Uncertainty*

*Absorption on the Interaction Patterns in Nuclear and Companionship Families* (Ann Arbor; University Microfilms Limited, 1972).

CHAPTER V

1. James M. Washington, ed., *A Testament of Hope* (San Francisco: Harper Collins, 1986) 494.

2.Ibid., pp.217-20.

3.Ibid., pp. 259-67.

4.Ibid., pp. 285.

5.Elijah Muhammad, *Message to the Black Man in America* (Chicago: Muhammad Mosque of Islam No. 2, 1965) 102.

CHAPTER VI

1.Bough and McClelland, 890.

2. Claude Lewis, "Signs of Progress in Willingboro", *Philadelphia Evening Bulletin,* September 22, 1971.

3. Oxford University Press Committee, *Dictionary of Quotations,2nd ed.,* (New York: Crescent Books, 1985) 201.

CHAPTER VII

1. Bough and McClelland, 890.

2. Address by Colin Powell, Former Chairman of the Joint Chiefs of Staff, "Sharing in the American Dream," April 28, 1997, National Volunteer Summit, Philadelphia, Pennsylvania.

3. Fran Lebowitz, "Fran Lebowitz on Race", *Vanity Fair,* October, 1997, 220.

4. William Barrett, *Irrational Man,* (New York: Doubleday and Company, 1958) 83.

5. Edmund Morris, *Beethoven, the Universal Composer* (New York: Harper Collins, 2005) 154-174.

6. Edmund Gibbons, *The Decline and Fall of the Roman Empire* (New York: Alfred A. Knolpf, Inc., 1993).

7. Ibid., 84, 85.

8. F. P. Lock, *Edmund Burke* United Kingdom: Clarendon Press, 2006).

9. Joseph Butler, *The Analogy of Religion* (New York: Cosimo, 2005).

10. Edith Hamilton, *Mythology* (New York: Penguin Group, 1940) 220-235.

11. Louis B. Wright and Virginia A. Lamar, *Hamlet* (New York: Washington Square Press,1975) 64.

12 Alex Haley, *The Autobiography of Malcolm X* (New York: Grove Press Inc., 1964).

13. Oscar Lewis, *La Vida* (New York: Vintage Press, 1968).

14. Beth S. Warner and Mark D. Weist, "Urban Youth as Witness to Violence: Beginning Assessment and Treatment Efforts" *Journal of Youth and Adolescence, Vol.25, Number 3, 1996, 361-77.*

15. Dr. Crystal Kuykendall is a former school teacher, attorney and human relations expert, who believes that "educating everyone takes everyone". See her recent book: Crystal Kunkendall, *From Rage to Hope: Strategies for Reclaiming Black and Hispanic Students* (Bloomington: National Educational Services, 2004) 1-18.

16. Lewis B. Wright and Virginia Lamar, 64.

17. B.B. King and David Ritz, *Blues All Around Me* (New York: Avon Books, 1996).

18. See *Holy Bible (KJV),* I Kings 18:1-44 and 20:35

19. Chanta L. Jackson, "Hands-on Educator Shapes Lives", *Asbury Park Press,* Community Profile, June 15, 1994, page G3.

20. Ibid, I Corinthians 13:1-13.

CHAPTER VIII

1.National Baptist Publishing Board,501.

2.Max Ehrmann, *The Desiderata of Love: A Collection of Poems for the* Beloved ( New York: Crown Publishers Inc., 1948) 11.

3. Eugene R. Fairweather, ed., *A Scholastic Miscellany: Anselm to Ockham* (Philadelphia: The Westminister Press, 1956) 102.

4. Bough and McClelland, 1036

5. See *Holy Bible, KJV* Philippians 4:13

6. Sherwin B. Nuland, *How We Die,* (New York: Vintage Books, 1995).

7. Eugene H. Peterson, *Living the Message,* (San Francisco: Harper Collins, 1996) 59

CHAPTER IX

1. Langston Hughes, *The Panther and the Lash* (New York: Alfred A. Knopf, 1980) 92.

2. Percy Bates and Ted Wilson, *Effective Schools: Critical Issues in the Education of Black Children* (Washington, D.C.: National Alliance of Black School Educators, 1989) 1-9.

CHAPTER X

1. Bullen, 584 (*Julius Caesar, Act I, Scene I*)

2. Nikki Giovanni, *The Women and the Men* ( New York: William Morrow and Company, 1975) See "The Lion in Daniel's den; for other African expressions, see *African Proverbs* ( New York: Peter Pauper Press, 1962).

3. Bates and Wilson, 1-9

4. Curtis Mayfield was a soul, funk rhythm and blues singer-songwriter and guitarist who utilized avant gaurde techniques in thematic musical lyrics found in recordings and albums featuring songs "Superfly" and "Got to Find a Way".

5. Marion Wright Edelman, founder and President of The Childrens Defense Fund, has presented many papers on "Strengthening,

Organizing and Saving Families". Dr. Edelman recently served as key note speaker at Essex County College, N.J., January 2006.

6. Eleanor Bumpers was a 300 pound African American woman who suffered from diabetes and arthritis in the borough of High Bridge, New York, and was assumed to be mentally ill; however, she was shot in the chest in her apartment by a N.Y. city police officer in 1984 after she reportedly lunged at him with a butcher knife. Today she is still thought of as a victim of police brutality.

7. Bough and McClelland, 1036.

8. Emma Lazarus wrote "The New Colossus" in 1883 for an art auction " In Aid of Bartholdi Pedestal Fund". The poem was engraved on the Statue of Liberty in 1903, sixteen years after her death.

9. Bough and McClelland, 906-22.

CHAPTER XI

1. Arnold Adoff, *The Poetry of Black America* (New York: Harper and Row, 1973) 3.

2. See *Holy Bible,* Isaiah 64: 6.

3. Ibid., IIChronicles 7: 14.

4. Ibid., Psalms 27:1

5. Ibid.

6. Ibid., Psalms 27:6.

7. Ibid., Psalms 27:14.

8. James M. Washington, *A Testament of Hope* (San Francisco: Harper Collins, 1986) 517.

9. See *Holy Bible,* Psalms 23:5.

10. Bough and McClelland, 1407

11. Neil Postman, *The End of Education,* (New York: Alfred A. Knoff, 1995) 64-67.

12. Over 100 Yiddish quotations may be found in: Kristine Swarner, *Yiddish Wisdom* (Hong Kong: LLC, 1996).

# ALSO BY Donald D. Warner

## Dark Destiny

Dark Destiny captures the experiences of all men and women who live within the diverse parameters of an America that promises great hope, but yields dark destinies for many of its inhabitants. African Americans in particular historically suffer in the midst of confusion experienced within the subtleties of covert and overt discrimination. Yet the miracle of truth exists. The intangible mystery of hope, strength and peace rests in the beauty of one shared moment. Our joy and our task is to grasp, hold and appreciate each moment as it embraces our hyphenated destinies. Explore the frailties of economic depravity after the great depression, the sixties, private thoughts, love and religion and affirm the longings of the immeasurable soul .

**Learn more at:**
**www.outskirtspress.com/darkdestiny**

Printed in the United States
100398LV00003B/76/P